FINAL
WARNING

FINAL
WARNING

AVERTING DISASTER IN THE NEW AGE OF TERRORISM

Robert Kupperman

Jeff Kamen

DOUBLEDAY

New York   London   Toronto   Sydney   Auckland

PUBLISHED BY DOUBLEDAY

a division of Bantam Doubleday Dell Publishing Group, Inc.
666 Fifth Avenue, New York, New York 10103

DOUBLEDAY and the portrayal of an anchor with a dolphin are trademarks of Doubleday, a
division of Bantam Doubleday Dell Publishing Group, Inc.

LIBRARY OF CONGRESS CATALOGING-IN-PUBLICATION DATA

Kupperman, Robert H., 1935–
    Final Warning : averting disaster in the new age of terrorism   /   Robert Kup-
perman and Jeff Kamen.—1st ed. in the United States of America.
        p.   cm.
    Includes index.
    1. Terrorism.   2. Terrorism—Prevention.   I. Kamen, Jeff.
    II. Title.
HV6431.K864   1989
363.3′2—dc20   89-30462
                                                                              CIP

ISBN 0-385-24584-X

For the 241 U.S. Marines blown up at their base in Beirut in 1983, for the 22 worshippers at the synagogue in Istanbul slaughtered while at prayer in 1986, for the 270 people killed by the bomb aboard Pan Am Flight 103 in 1988, for all the innocent victims of terrorism of all faiths and nations, past, present, and future—especially for those who perish because of the inaction or cowardice of governments that fail to act against terrorists and the nations that support and direct them.

For the heroic members of the counterterrorist police and military units who place their bodies in harm's way to rescue the innocent and punish the guilty, for the bomb defusers who tread where others flee, for the intelligence service bureaucrats who dare to tell the truth to political bosses who ignore the warning anyway, for the diplomats who expose themselves to attack because they must do their jobs, for the military men and women and their families who face needlessly high risk of attack because their government refuses to take seriously the terrorist threat and refuses to pay the bill for adequate security.

And finally, for those in our families who sustained us throughout the challenging and sometimes grueling process of writing—for Cynthia, for Helen, for Rose, and for Tammy, we dedicate this book.

ACKNOWLEDGMENTS

We are especially grateful to the courageous antiterrorists around the world who shared their fears and hopes about the future with us. While many asked to remain anonymous for political or security reasons, some did allow their names to be used despite the controversial nature of this book. Easily the most candid was Oliver L. "Buck" Revell, the Executive Assistant Director of the Federal Bureau of Investigation. He has been fighting an under-resourced war against terrorism for well over a decade, succeeding, in part, because foreign terrorists had not yet chosen to strike inside the United States. Revell has been trying to convince others in Government that relying on luck and wishful thinking is dangerous. Overseas, as well as at home, we often encountered a low priority attitude towards combatting terrorism amounting in some cases to arrogant nonfeasance. Innocent people will wind up paying with their lives for that.

It would not have been possible for us to bring you a depthful treatment of the relationship between terrorism and television without the participation of network anchormen who gave of their most precious commodity—time. Tom Brokaw of NBC, Peter Jennings of ABC, and Bernard Shaw of CNN knew that merely by permitting themselves to be quoted on the issue, they risked embroiling themselves in controversy. All agreed to be interviewed because they believe the issue must be confronted if the public is to be served.

During research in the Middle East and Europe, consulting clinical psychologist Dr. Cynthia Putchat interviewed social scientists who are working on terrorism-related issues. She obtained the informal candor and insight clinicians tend to share with one another. In Israel, Colonel Ya'acov Heichal, an innovative strategic and tactical thinker, was of invaluable assistance. Darrell Trent was a fine sounding board for several of the themes developed in the book.

Our publisher's faith in this effort and in us was crucial as was the wise counsel of Patrick Filley. Every author treading on the high-visibility turf of national security affairs should have so knowledgeable and caring an editor.

Dr. Franco Ferracuti at the University of Rome, a principal strategist of the defeat of the Red Brigades terrorists, 1978–81, offered inspiration and challenging ideas. We hope this work helps to encourage the kind of discussion Dr. Ferracuti finds lacking at this crucial time in the evolution of terrorism. We also drew on the work of a number of other scholars who have studied various terrorist movements and groups. The thinking of Dr. Marius Deeb, Dr. Mary Jane Deeb, and Dr. Martin Kramer is among the most illuminating on the role of the Shiite clergy. Dr. Simon Dinitz gave insight into the likely evolution of political and religious violence.

We are grateful to the many military, intelligence, and criminal justice experts who were interviewed and to those in and out of the antiterrorism field who read chapters and offered thoughtful criticism, analytical commentary, and editorial guidance, including: Dr. Laurence Birns, the Deebs, Dr. Andrew Goldberg, Judge Sharon Nelson, Dr. Barry Sherman, and Debra van Opstal.

We are indebted to Jay LaMonica Productions, KCET-TV, and the Center for Strategic and International Studies for their permission to present in condensed form the terrorism "war game" designed by Robert Kupperman and "played" by currently serving and former senior government officials.

To John Corporon and Carl Gottlieb of Independent Network News, we express appreciation for their encouragement.

To Elizabeth McGee, who typed and retyped these pages, offering good suggestions along the way, while ignoring the sometimes maddening traits of word processing systems and authors, we express our profound gratitude.

PREFACE

The United States, its allies, and the Soviet Union face more violent, more disruptive terrorist attacks than have ever before been seen. Ordinary citizens are more likely to become victims, even if they do not place themselves in high-risk areas such as international airports. In recent years, Americans and their interests have come under increasingly innovative terrorist assaults at home and abroad.

Some of these were "firsts," significant beyond their immediate impact; they dramatically revealed the shocking incapacity of government to protect its citizens, even when it was advised that specific terrorist action may be imminent. Government often behaved as though it were powerless just as a new age of domestic and international terrorism appeared to be on the horizon.

In March 1989, at the waterfront in Philadelphia, inspectors of the U.S. Food and Drug Administration acted on anonymous warnings phoned to the American embassy in Santiago; they examined crates of grapes arriving from Chile and discovered two cyanide-laced grapes, evidence that Chilean fruit had been poisoned, as the telephone callers had warned. While nobody in the United States reported eating any tainted grapes, the entire nation fibrillated. The same reaction was under way in Canada, Japan, and Western Europe. Chilean fruit was temporarily banned, triggering economic and political turmoil. All that was needed to induce near-hysteria was the FDA inspectors' finding a pair of poisoned grapes; never mind that eaten together, there was not enough cyanide in them to make anyone seriously ill. This bizarre incident demonstrated how vulnerable the food chain is to terrorism and, by implication, it showed the openness to attack of commerce, communications, and energy flow.

The week before, in San Diego, California, the family van of a U.S. Navy officer burst into flames after a pipe bomb exploded in the back of the vehicle. Only the amateurish placement of the device allowed the driver, the wife of the officer, to escape. Had an international terrorist attack finally been staged inside the United States? The incident was even more alarming because the officer in question is the American captain who made the decision to shoot down what was thought to be an attacking Iranian war plane over the Persian Gulf in July 1988. The missile Captain Will Rogers III fired destroyed the target, which turned out to be an Iranian civilian airliner carrying 290 passengers. It was known that the Iranians would likely seek revenge but the U.S. Navy failed to mount what should be a standard counter-surveillance operation to make sure Rogers was not being stalked. As a result, the Navy failed to protect the captain, his wife, their home, and their van. Members of congressional committees with national security responsibilities were stunned that the Defense Department had blundered so.

At the same time, it was revealed that the Immigration and Naturalization Service, the nation's barrier against unwanted, dangerous foreigners entering the United States, had been fooled by several dozen Iranian Revolutionary Guard Corps members. These highly trained terrorists claimed to be "students" and were permitted to enter the United States. The FBI made the discovery and brought the bad news to an open hearing of a Senate Foreign Relations subcommittee. It was the Bureau's way of both informing the Senate and the public of the threat and of making it quite clear that this screwup was not their doing, even though they may have to clean up the mess.

In early April of 1989, the Bush administration ordered high-tech airport bomb detection systems, which won't be ready for months or years, but failed to impose low-tech, ready-now methods of detecting the same explosives, including specially trained dogs and hand searches of the bags of suspicious passengers. A few weeks earlier, it was revealed that airline and government security officers in London and Frankfurt had received several warnings weeks in advance of the bombing of Pan Am Flight 103. Those warnings advised that terrorists could be expected to try to smuggle aboard an aircraft a bomb hidden in a Toshiba radio-cassette player, the identical device which brought the jumbo jet down in pieces over Lockerbie, Scotland, four days before Christmas 1988. One month before Pan Am Flight 103 was blown out of the sky, killing all 259 people on the plane and 11 others on the ground, security experts from Britain and West Germany, as well as experts from the ten other European Community countries, were shown a radio-cassette player bomb at a meeting in

Wiesbaden and instructed in how to detect the explosives and the fuse. But it was all for naught. They knew what to search for, but somehow nobody looked into one of the bags boarded on December 21 into the forward cargo compartment of the 747 bound for New York's John F. Kennedy International Airport. This disclosure, along with the Bush administration's avoidance of available approaches to bomb detection, brought home the fact that airtravel security is still not handled as a systems problem but as a series of incidents. That is a prescription for continuing failure and tragedy.

To break out of that pattern of defeat, it is essential to understand that terrorism and other forms of nonconventional warfare are becoming the *norms* in conflict around the world. Unfortunately, the United States, its allies and the Soviet Union are not adequately prepared or oriented to fight effectively against terrorism and other aspects of low-intensity conflict. As a first step, the United States and other great nations must realize their antiterrorism systems are so flawed that they must be reviewed from top to bottom. New equipment, procedures, and personnel have to be brought on line and policies refashioned so as to give people a better chance of surviving in an increasingly dangerous world. It will be no easy task.

The very idea of writing a book on terrorism that is predictive and prescriptive as opposed to historical is obviously controversial, wide open to criticism. Nevertheless, the failure of policymakers in government to go much beyond the *rhetoric* of antiterrorism demands that a public warning be sounded before unimpeded terrorists spread a new wave of fear, suffering, and death at home and abroad.

When the Ayatollah Khomeini died in June 1989, Khomeini-ism —the zeal of his most devoted followers, the Revolutionary Guards and their supporters in Hizballah—did not disappear with him. There is every reason to believe that the power struggle which broke out behind the scenes in Iran will continue, and both internal and external terrorism can be expected.

Terrorism has become a routine part of Iran's foreign policy. It may continue despite promises of moderation. The Islamic Revolution may claim many more lives. The innocent will suffer as opposing factions vie for power, the same people who lashed their children together with ropes and sent them marching ahead of tanks into minefields. They did that during the war with Iraq because, as one Iranian officer said, "We have so many children and so few tanks."

Let us never forget the Ayatollah's will. To America and the rest of
the West, Khomeini's wish was, "May the curse of God be upon
them." Even if only a tiny fraction of the fanatical mobs which
swarmed around his casket have the desire to be the instruments of
that implacable old man, the United States and its friends may face
formidable terrorism.

The murder of thousands of pro-democracy demonstrators in Bei-
jing and the vicious Stalinist purge which followed set the stage for
further violence. A grass-roots terrorism may emerge against the Communist regime and the foreign businesses which invested heavily in
China's economic future in the belief that a stable political environment was being created. While there can be no certainty about this,
history is replete with examples of repression and humiliation giving
rise to terrorism: from the French Revolution to the anarchists of
czarist Russia to the Jews of the Palestinian Mandate to the Palestinians of the Israeli-occupied territories.

In the case of China in 1989, terrorism may be chosen by tiny,
secret groups whose only wish might be to demonstrate to the rest of
the world that while the Deng regime can suppress and kill, it nevertheless cannot control fully the land of a billion human beings—half
of them under thirty years old.

Recent violence in Uzbekistan supports the thesis that the
U.S.S.R. will be the main target of terrorism over the next decade.
Age-old ethnic hatreds brought gunfire to yet another Soviet "republic" in the spring of 1989, just as did tensions involving other national
groups in Tblisi, Georgia, where Soviet troops did the unthinkable—
fired poison gas at the demonstrators, killing and wounding dozens.
Clearly the potential for terrorism against Soviet authority is growing
at an alarming rate, threatening the viability of the state.

These events are not isolated; they buttress the assessment that as
the globe becomes more complex and interdependent, terrorism and
violent expressions of national ethnicity have the most profound
ramifications.

CONTENTS

FINAL
WARNING

CHAPTER ONE

EMERGING TERRORISM

The White House
Office of the National Security Advisor
SENSITIVE

Ice storms riding powerful winds rip into London, shutting down all surface transportation.

In Paris, the relentless weather freezes the city.

In Rome, the same savage storm kills dozens of homeless people near the Coliseum.

En route to New York City, Air Force One is forced by sudden intensifying winds to turn back to Washington. There, an unusual warm spell gives way to violent winter weather on the American East Coast. The Midwest is already gripped by a relentless blizzard and frigid winds. The forecast calls for at least four more days of the same.

A tiny Shiite Moslem terrorist cell, the thirty-two members of the Islamic Peoples'

1

Action Directorate, has been waiting patiently for months, watching the long-range weather forecasts for a window of opportunity to stage its attack.

Shortly after 3 A.M., Washington time, a telephone call from the Secret Service wakes the President. On the phone's second line, his National Security Advisor runs down the message that is being given.

Top officials of the other NATO governments are being given similar messages. In the middle of the night, explosions have destroyed a dozen key elements of natural gas pipelines in the United States and Western Europe. The surprise assault on the essentially unprotected pipelines apparently has been accomplished by a dozen two-man terrorist teams striking at exactly midnight, Washington time. The average temperature on the streets of the American capital is currently fifteen degrees Fahrenheit, absent the windchill. The gas pipelines are empty and impossible to repair quickly because they were hit at critical choke points.

Oil-heated buildings, which became unfashionable in 1970s out of fear of another crippling oil boycott by Arab countries, are suddenly very desirable and scarce.

Most hospitals and other institutions, such as hotels and universities, rely on gas heat. They are quickly becoming refrigerators.

The previously unknown terrorist organization has in a matter of hours put millions of lives and the image of the U.S. Government, as well as that of its allies, in jeopardy. The Islamic Peoples' Action Directorate has phoned newsrooms in every major capital, claiming responsibility for "this blow against the enemies of Islam." A videocassette showing one of their units

firing a rocket into a gas pipeline compressor at a river crossing in Louisiana is
delivered to a news agency by a commercial
courier service. The tape proves the au-
thenticity of the terrorists' claim of responsibility. It is played over and over
again on local and network television newscasts. The Islamic Peoples' Action Directorate is suddenly big news.

As an increasingly alarmed public waits
for a sign of leadership from government
officials, emergency Cabinet meetings are
underway in London, Paris, Rome, and Washington, D.C., as well as in countries that
have not been victimized.

By the afternoon of the same day, all the
available electric space heaters have been
purchased and, as night falls on Boston,
New York, and Miami, Islamic Peoples' Action Directorate teams attempt to take out
their next targets in the United States.
But some local police have anticipated
their moves and four terrorists are shot to
death by SWAT units that had taken up positions at key electrical power stations in
Pennsylvania and North Carolina. But the
federal government provided no coordination. Six two-person commando units fired
small, easily concealed, rocket-propelled
grenades into a dozen power transformers,
blacking out almost the entire East Coast.
They are lynchpins of the huge and complex
power network, custom-built and literally
one-of-a-kind, for which there can be no
rapid replacement, since neither industry
nor government has bothered to purchase
backup units.

It will take weeks or months to get the power back on.
Bitter, deadly cold. Sudden darkness. Fear. Panic.
Possible? Unfortunately. Probable? Unknown. But a study com-

missioned jointly by the FBI and the CIA reached the following conclusion at the end of a detailed (and expensive) field assessment: "The infrastructure of the United States, like that of its allies, is essentially open to terrorist attack; we continue to live as though we dwelled in the post-World War II environment in which the United States is the undisputed master of all before it, a time in which no one would even dream of striking a major blow at our very core.

"Clearly, those conditions no longer pertain. It is not the 1950s; despite the approaching condominium of interest in stability with the Soviets, there are still many state and nonstate actors who would do us great harm. The wherewithal to inflict such damage is easily obtainable. Not to plan against a major attack on the infrastructure would be to invite disaster, humiliation, and potentially unacceptable political damage."

While the preceding scenario is fiction, the facts and observations contained within it are genuine. Today, the governments of the NATO alliance know with clarity that their societies are easy prey to such attacks, but they haven't taken the steps necessary to prevent that scenario from becoming reality. Their shield against taking responsible action is a combination of wishful thinking and refusing to deal honestly within an extremely difficult set of realities. If they were problem drinkers attending their first Alcoholics Anonymous meeting, these governments would be told that they are "in denial" and would be instructed that until they ended their denial of the true nature of their problem they would have no chance to find a way out of their life-threatening dilemma.

In the infrastructure scenario of the "memo," hundreds, if not thousands, especially the frail, the elderly, and the very young, would face unnecessary suffering and even death. Innocents would be menaced not only because of the actions of the terrorists, but also because the elected leaders of the West permitted key soft spots to go unprotected, despite having knowledge of their existence. The words "negligence" and "incompetence" should haunt policymakers who have been informed of the high state of risk and who persist in taking no significant action. The potential political costs of persisting on the current path are enormous. Excuses for inaction based on budgetary restraints are thin stuff—an indictment of the quality of thinking and leadership at the top.

Overview of the Final Warning

Massive civilian casualties, disruption of normal life, loss of confidence in governments, and global instability, leading even to the possible outbreak of war, are the risks inherent in the current United States and allied response to terrorism.

The governments of the civilized world must reevaluate and take effective countermeasures against the threat to human life, national security, and world peace posed by increasingly smarter, better-armed, and less predictable terrorist organizations. The number of groups that use the tactics of terror is growing. Some of them, virtually unknown at this time, may yet pose a serious threat to Americans and their friends at home and abroad.

This work is a hard look into the future of terrorism inside the United States and overseas, an analysis of how terrorism is changing, where and in what form it is likely to menace the lives of ordinary citizens as well as political leaders and institutions. This study confronts the vulnerability of America and its allies to super-violence and techno-terrorism, and offers some insights and possible solutions.

At this time, there are virtually no safeguards to prevent terrorists from acquiring biological, chemical, or radiological weapons components—many of which are readily available under the guise of legitimate academic or industrial uses. Applying controls will be difficult and imperfect but mandatory, to reduce the availability of these elements of the mechanisms of super-violence. Despite the obvious nature of the threat, there is virtually no preventive action being taken to block or soften the crippling effects of possible terrorist attacks on domestic infrastructure targets; prevention in this arena requires extensive analysis of choke points of maximum vulnerability and the commitment of significant financial resources to harden those nodes before a single low-tech attack upon a few of them does incalculable damage. Easy terrorist pickings include electric power distribution, natural gas pipelines, computer-based communications, banking and financial networks—the ligaments of modern society.

The failure of governments to deal realistically with those vulnerabilities in the face of the expanding terrorist threat is the motivation behind the issuance of this final warning.

If terrorism takes the turns the authors expect, there will be little or no time to invent policies or train people to react after an attack employing poison gas, virus, or radioactive materials. There may be no time to ponder the way out of crises triggered by the sabotaging of the infrastructure. The thinking, planning, allocation of resources, training of emergency personnel, and public education need to be done before society is hit by a new wave of terrorism. Helping to avert or at least blunt the coming terrorist assaults is the goal of this book.

Since the end of World War II, no foreign power had dared send its agents into the United States itself to murder Americans. When international terrorists were visibly busy around the world, they were not in evidence in the United States. For more than two decades, terrorist organizations kept their commandos away from the fifty states and satisfied their anti-American hatred by attacking U.S. citizens, facilities, and symbols elsewhere. Spilling blood on U.S. soil was probably perceived not only as problematic logistically but also too risky in terms of provoking a devastating reaction. But events would gradually discourage that caution and lead terrorists to consider strikes directly into the heart of America.

By the late 1980s, it was clear that the world's most powerful nation is paralyzed when it comes to punishing terrorists. Brazen gunmen can commit atrocities against Americans while seizing the world stage through media coverage of their crimes and get away with it all. The threat of Ronald Reagan to mete out "swift and effective retribution" to terrorists was made shortly after he assumed the presidency in January 1981. In most cases, it proved to be empty—a virtual invitation to terrorists to keep calling America's bluff.

Simultaneously with the beginning of the Reagan era, the United States was just starting to recover from the post–Vietnam War syndrome, the national aversion to even thinking about committing young American lives to possible combat, no matter how compelling the cause. It was no time for the American people to be dragged into the seething caldron of civil war in Lebanon. But poor analysis and decision-making would put U.S. forces in harm's way, for the second time in twenty years, bringing down disaster once again.

Ultimately, in an eerie replay of the most telling U.S. strategic blunder in Vietnam, the United States would fail to correctly define the real enemy and fail to take appropriate action against it. In Vietnam, the enemy which had to be defeated was not the Viet Cong; it was North Vietnam. In Lebanon, the collection of Shiite terrorists was only the hand of the enemy—his identities were Ayatollah Khomeini of Iran and Hafez al-Assad of Syria. The fundamental error of not seeing accurately which actors were the stars and which the bit players threw the United States into policy confusion and as a result two hundred and fifty young men were killed.

America turned tail and fled from state-sponsored terrorism in Lebanon. In that act of defeat and incompetence, the Reagan administration forfeited its opportunity to build peace in the Middle East and sent a clear signal to terrorists that they hold the whip hand. The whole grim scenario might as well have been written in Tehran by Hosein Sheikholislam, the principal architect of Iranian terrorism, but as much responsibility for this continuing debacle must be assigned to ignorant American leaders as to venal Iranian mass murderers.

Three-Time Loser

On April 18, 1983, a delivery van filled with explosives was driven to the front of the U.S. embassy in Beirut. When it detonated, it flattened most of the building, killing seventeen Americans and forty-six others. The American ambassador narrowly escaped what was intended to be his murder as well as the humiliation of the United States. The Reagan administration learned that Syria had been involved but Iran had ordered the attack, hired five men to carry it out, including a Palestinian employee of the embassy, and paid for the bombing with twenty-five thousand dollars especially authorized for the mission.[1] A Syrian intelligence officer wired the two thousand pounds of explosives to make sure it would go off with maximum effect. Although this information came to the attention of policymakers, the President took no action against either Iran or Syria, thereby sending a message that "The Great Satan," as Ayatollah Khomeini slandered the United States, could be attacked with no serious risk of retaliation.

Less than six months later, Iran sent another truck bomb against Americans. This time it was the biggest of the more than one hundred car and truck bombs used by Hizballah in its struggle for control of Beirut during 1983. It was October 23, and the yellow Mercedes truck driven by a smiling young Shiite roared right passed a lone U.S. Marine guard and into the center of the building that housed most of the Marine Battalion Landing Team near Beirut International Airport. In one blinding flash, the suiciding Shiite had taken the lives of 241 of America's finest young men. It was the worst single surprise attack on U.S. forces since Pearl Harbor, December 7, 1941. Japan paid for that with more than a million of its people dead. In Lebanon, nobody paid. Although the President was told that, once again, there was strong evidence tying both Iran and Syria to the mass murder of the Marines, Mr. Reagan took no action against the governments of the Ayatollah Khomeini or President Hafez al-Assad of Syria.

Only seven weeks after the massacre of the Marines, kamikaze Shiites drove car and truck bombs into six targets in Kuwait, a moderate Arab emirate on the Persian Gulf. Unbelievably, the U.S. Government's security people had learned absolutely nothing from the previous outrages. Not so much as a single parked car was placed in the path of motorists approaching the American embassy in Kuwait. It was thirteen days before Christmas, December 12, 1983. Five people were killed, another eighty-six wounded. For a third time in eight months, Iranian- and Syrian-supported terrorists savaged American symbols and people. The suiciding drivers were members of two Iranian movements, Hizballah (Party of God), based near Beirut, and Al-Dawa, with headquarters in Tehran. For a third consecutive time in less than a year, the telegenic President who talked tough failed to keep his promise of "swift and effective retribution." Mr. Reagan's defenders counter by saying, "We had no solid confirmation that it was Iran or Syria." But Beirut was not a court of law. Once more, the intelligence pointed powerfully to Tehran and Damascus. Ronald Reagan's refusal to strike back encouraged other terrorists to target the Americans since they won't fight back. That spirit, or lack of it, apparently became contagious.

Two years later, in 1985, when the U.S. Joint Chiefs of Staff were presented with a unique opportunity to kill the high command of

Iran's terrorist organization in Lebanon with a single strike at Hizballah headquarters in Baalbek, America's military leaders rejected the plan as too barbaric. Not that Reagan would necessarily have approved the proposal, but the JCS rejection was just another declaration of how utterly and dangerously out of touch with the reality of terrorism the Pentagon remains.[2]

At the same time, meek political leaders, turf-protecting bureaucrats, and logistical nightmares, mixed with problems of diplomacy, kept America's highly trained counterterrorist units, Delta Force and SEAL Team Six, out of action. Despite their deployment on security missions, like guarding the Pope on some of his travels and American ambassadors in high-risk areas, they have never had a chance to hit international terrorists who have kidnapped, tortured, and murdered U.S. citizens. They have never been given the opportunity to fulfill the mission for which their units were created—they have never been allowed to rescue Americans held hostage. They were ordered to liberate the captives aboard the Italian cruise ship *Achille Lauro*, seized by Palestinians in 1985, but the low priority assigned their mission by the U.S. Air Force meant they were delayed more than half a day when the aircraft given to them broke down.

Even a high-tech corps of virtual supermen has little credibility when it can't get to the scene of the action. Equally important, America's elite counterterrorists have never conducted a single act of retribution that might have been understood with clarity by those who seek to coerce the United States through terror.

Terrorists and their state sponsors have seen all that and learned from it. Unlike the Israeli Mossad, which penetrated Tunisia in the spring of 1988 to execute the PLO's master terrorist Abu Jihad, America's counterterrorist force is not feared by international terrorists, because it has not been allowed to earn a reputation in combat. The appearance, at least, is that the United States has no stomach for genuine antiterrorism, other than an occasional air strike against Libya and Muammar al-Qaddafi, its dictator and narcissistic supporter of terror.

So, in the late 1980s, some terrorist organizations and states began breaking out of the unwritten constraint, attempting operations inside the United States.

In two cases, foreign terrorists were stopped from hitting their targets in the United States by ordinary police officers whose primary function is routine patrol, not antiterrorism. The lawmen involved in the two incidents were not only cool and quick-witted, they were also very lucky, as was the nation. If either of those attempts had not been discovered and prevented, America could have suffered its worst terrorist incident on U.S. soil. Significantly, in the aftermath of each averted attack, the President took no action against the known sponsors. That failure also amounted to an invitation to keep trying. How frighteningly close these terrorists got to carrying out their missions is instructive and may be predictive of what the United States now faces.

The small Vermont town of Richford, population 1,500, is located a short distance from the Canadian border. On October 23, 1987, Police Chief Richard Jewett was following his standard pattern of patrol. At about 10 P.M., he noticed a van with two Middle Eastern men in the front seat parked in a no-parking zone. Jewett leaned out of his cruiser and told them to move to a legal spot a short distance away. Moments later, he spotted a backpacker walking along the railroad tracks. At first, the walker did not respond to Jewett's request for identification, but then he handed over papers identifying him as Walid Kabbani. He claimed to be hitchhiking back to Montreal from a shopping trip in Burlington.[3]

Jewett offered to drive Kabbani to the border and there handed him over to the U.S. Immigration Service. Something about the van and the hitchhiker made Jewett suspicious. After checking on the van and following it to a local motel, he returned to the area where he had picked up Kabbani. There he found the backpack the hiker had been carrying, which he took back to the border.

He and the Immigration Service officers opened the pack to find the components for a bomb, which experts later found would have been powerful enough to blow up a small building.

The men in the van were arrested at their motel and identified as Georges Younan and Walid Mourad. The two men, locally respected merchants, were convicted in federal court of conspiring to bring explosives into the United States. Later, investigation by the FBI revealed that all three men are actually members of the Syrian Socialist National Party, the same terrorist organization that was responsible for the 1982 assassination of Lebanon's President-elect Bashir Gemayel. That act plunged Lebanon even more deeply into chaos and led to the massacre of hundreds of Palestinian refugees in Beirut at the hands of enraged Gemayel supporters. In turn, that slaughter fueled terrorist actions by Palestinians against the United States.

In mid-April of 1988, a Japanese man attracted the attention of State Trooper Robert Cieplensky at a rest stop along the New Jersey turnpike. Functioning more on intuition than anything else, Cieplensky asked the traveler for his driver's license and decided to take a look in his car. On the backseat, the highway patrolman discovered three bombs hidden in the casings of fire extinguishers. The driver turned out to be Yu Kikumura, a known member of the Japanese Red Army, a very small global terror gang that usually is in the employ of North Korea, Libya, or the Popular Front for the Liberation of Palestine (a powerful terrorist organization). In 1986 Kikumura was arrested at Schipol Airport in Amsterdam with a bomb concealed in a can of breakfast food in his luggage. The detonators were so carefully disguised as parts of his portable radio that the X-ray machine operator could not detect anything except ordinary wiring for the radio. But it was all there: 2.2 pounds of powerful explosives and the trigger to make it detonate.

A Dutch judge decided to apply the same standard of probable cause for search and seizure in this case as in a routine burglary. The search of Kikumura's luggage was ruled illegal, and the case against him was kicked out of court. Instead of being prosecuted, convicted, and imprisoned in Holland, he was deported to Japan, where he quickly obtained his freedom. Almost two years later in New Jersey, the astonished state police officer arrested the same man with the bombs in his car and turned him over to a shocked FBI.

For years, the bureau and allied-intelligence agencies around the world believed the Japanese Red Army was dormant, no longer in strategy. Yet, two days after his arrest on the highway, several of Kikumura's comrades blew up the USO service club in Naples, Italy, killing a U.S. Navy enlisted woman and four other innocent victims.

In a nonjury trial, Kikumura did not deny that he was guilty of transporting explosives with intent to kill. But the thirty-seven-year-old declined to be helpful; he refused to reveal the identity or location of his targets. Nevertheless, in a confidential presentencing memorandum to the judge in February 1989, the U.S. Attorney said Kikumura's goal was "mass slaughter" of Americans in retaliation for the American air raid on Libya in 1986. During the sentencing, the judge admitted into evidence an affidavit by the FBI agent who heads up the government's investigation of the Japanese Red Army. Special Agent Michael Hartment said in the affidavit that he had interviewed another terrorist, a member of ASALA (the Armenian Secret Army for the Liberation of Armenia) who claims that he observed Kikumura training at a terrorist camp in 1986 and 1987 in Lebanon's Bekaa Valley.

When he was caught in April 1988, Kikumura was apparently on assignment for Colonel Muammar al-Qaddafi inside the United States, just as his friends were in Naples. A map discovered in Kikumura's car had three pinholes in it, all of them in Manhattan: the teeming Garment District, a busy Navy recruiting office, and the United Nations. U.S. District Court Judge Alfred J. Lechner looked the defiant Kikumura in the eye, sentenced him to thirty years behind bars, and said, "But for the alert and professional conduct of the state trooper, you would have succeeded in killing and maiming scores of innocent people for no other reason than that they were Americans." Noting that each of the bombs was made up of three pounds of explosives and three pounds of lead pellets, Judge Lechner said they "were intended for flesh and blood, not brick and mortar."

In a reminder of Kikumura's eluding justice in Holland in 1986, his New Jersey lawyers vowed to appeal his conviction—based on the alleged illegality of the search of his car, the seizure of his three bombs, and his subsequent arrest. Clearly, America's immunity from foreign terrorists bearing bombs on its soil is over. As demonstrated by the Vermont and New Jersey cases, foreign terrorists can arrive in the United States individually or in groups in flights from overseas, drive in separately as tourists from Canada or Mexico, or they could be here already, simply waiting for coded orders from their controllers in the United States or overseas to go into action against a broad spectrum of target persons or institutions.

Not only do terrorists have the capability of inflicting large numbers of casualties, but they can count on the news media coverage of their attacks to amplify the effects of their actions. This has proven to make terrorists' perceived power and the government's perceived impotence to cope with the terrorists all the greater.

The role of the news media in the new age of terrorism will be extremely controversial and perhaps crucial. It will be shown in a later chapter how evolving television technology runs the high risk of making journalism an even more helpful partner of terrorists than ever before. News program producers will have to understand that they already are key players in the complex game of terror and counterterror. Their burden of responsibility is about to get much heavier, as terrorists move toward the use of the weapons of super-violence and high-tech television.

Some groups, including Iranian-backed Shiite Moslems and radical Palestinians, have the political, ideological, and personality traits that make them most likely to break out of the machine gun, hand grenade, and car bomb tactics that have long been their trademarks. What these determined enemies of the West have in common is implacable rage mixed with a need to feel that their actions and sacrifices are effective—that they produce change. With Americans and others in the West taking less note of "routine" acts of terrorism, the incentive is at hand for the most committed of terrorists to ratchet up the intensity, the lethality of their tactics, in hopes of obtaining more dramatic response.

It should be noted that many antiterrorism officials say they do not believe terrorists will resort to instruments of mass slaughter because they have succeeded in capturing media attention with their current tactics. That view misses the fact that the news media of the world have become more sophisticated, less "capturable" by "ordinary" terrorist "theater." They are virtually jaded on past images of suffering offered up to the television lens by terrorists. These murderers know that when they go into action they are competitors in the marketplace of sensationalized images. To assume that terrorists will not innovate and up the ante in pursuit of an audience share is to engage in wishful thinking.

It is understandable but not helpful for public officials charged with antiterrorism to deny the evolving nature of the threat. One way to diminish the potential impact of future terrorist attacks is to educate the public by using the mass media before there is an incident. To do so would not be easy or without its own risks, but it would help to expose the truly criminal nature of terrorist organizations and explain their role in destabilizing of international relations. Such a proactive use of media could also enlist the public's help in locating and capturing known terrorists who have already attacked Americans. That kind of public-relations offensive could do more than undercut the dramatic, even romantic images some people have of terrorists. It could even help set the domestic and international political agendas on confronting terrorism. Every American administration has had to learn that bold policy initiatives that have broad public support have a much greater likelihood of success, while those which do not enjoy genuine consensus almost always fail. Even though many tactical tools have been developed for combating terrorism, few strategic concepts have arisen. The strategic use of the media in combating terrorism is now treated simplistically as an adversarial relationship between the media and governments. Media will only react, unless government seizes the initiative.

But no media campaign, no matter how well conceived and executed, can be a substitute for clear, open-minded analysis, excellent intelligence, and the allocation of sufficient funds to operate defenses against terrorist attack at the same time that an aggressive worldwide effort is under way to locate, isolate, arrest, and/or eliminate these killers before they strike. Any lesser strategy should be unacceptable.

The Enemies List—Short Form

Long spared any catastrophic assaults by terrorist organizations, the United States appears to be on the verge of suffering the first major terrorist attack on American soil. Those who are most likely to strike at American interests at home and abroad are a spectrum of violent individuals and organizations, including surrogates of terrorist states such as Iran, Syria, Libya, and Iraq. They are the terrorist groups that have their own agendas as well as that of their patrons, including the Palestinian radical Abu Nidal and the Hizballah of the Lebanese Shiites, both of which act independently as well as on orders from their state sponsors. They are narcotics traffickers, seeking to intimidate the criminal justice system. They are also Americans driven by political rage: fanatical anti-Castro Cuban-Americans trained by the CIA to overthrow the dictator three decades ago and now infuriated by the movement to normalize relations between Washington and Havana. They are radicalized and frustrated Americans of various single-interest movements who believe the only way to gain attention for their cause is to commit terrorist acts inside their own country, like the animal rights fanatics who plant fire bombs at the companies that test surgical materials on animals. They are self-styled violent revolutionaries and common hoodlums with no regard for the value of human life, willing to kill or place bombs for whomever pays their price.

Today, there are hundreds of ethnic, nationalist, and religious as well as political organizations that resort to terrorism, but the U.S. Defense Department lists only fifty-one as being of major concern. At least half a dozen could, with short notice, stage an attack inside the United States. In addition, so-called amateur, first-time terrorists who intend only a small, splashy action could lose control of an attack and accidentally unleash a devastating incident.

Ironically, profound and mostly desirable changes in the relationship between Moscow and Washington have triggered a new global instability that makes international terrorism less predictable—and more likely. In this new world, a realignment of forces that boggles the mind is under way. Yasir Arafat claimed in late 1988 that he was swearing off terrorism in all its forms and, much to the shock of Israel's Prime Minister Yitzhak Shamir, himself a former terrorist, the Chief of Staff of Israel's army publicly reported a month later that Arafat's own eleven-thousand-man guerrilla force, Al Fatah, had not been involved in a single act of terror. Shamir was stunned again when Defense Minister Rabin reported that Arafat's fighters inside Lebanon had "ceased all terrorist planning" for operations against Israel. If any entity could be expected to exaggerate the PLO threat to Israel, it would be the Israeli military. But that institution has a reverence for facts, and the facts on the ground appear to be supporting Arafat's claim of no more terrorism by units under his control and recognition of Israel's right to exist within secure borders.

In this age of the unexpected, what could be stranger than a turnabout by the original teachers of terrorist tactics in the modern age? That is exactly what seems to be under way as *glasnost* and *perestroika* collide with the status quo anti-Gorbachev. Uneasy KGB officers, whose elders taught Asian, African, Arab, and alienated Western European youths the arts of terror in the 1950s and 1960s, are now assigned the task of making the world more stable. That means trying to quiet at least some of the terrorists whose training is to create chaos and fear—exactly the wrong environment for Mikhail Gorbachev's attempt at restructuring his country's society and its interactions with the outside world.

Over the past quarter of a century, thousands of the brightest and angriest students from Europe, Asia, Africa, and the Middle East were given scholarships in the Soviet Union. At institutes for higher learning such as Patrice Lumumba University in Moscow, from which the legendary Venezuelan terrorist known as "Carlos" or "The Jackal" graduated, they were indoctrinated in the ways of Marxism and Leninism—first with the brutal Stalinist twist and later with the ideological spins promulgated by Khrushchev and Brezhnev. Despite the serious differences among all three schools, the common thread was support for the overthrow of colonial governments through campaigns of unrelenting terrorism which the Kremlin preferred to call "Wars of National Liberation." In Russia and elsewhere within the Soviet Empire, guerrilla warfare academies taught by Soviet military and intelligence officers educated Palestinian and other foreign cadres. The payback for Moscow came in the form of some influence over terrorist targeting and timing as well as the loyalty of its graduates to the interests of the U.S.S.R. But that is now a thing of the past.

In early 1989, Gorbachev began to implement what appeared to be a serious antiterrorism policy, reversing yet another historic policy. At the same time, groups over which the Kremlin used to have some influence moved away from Soviet control, as did several nations whose leaders had previously been highly responsive to the will of the men who rule in Moscow. As they set a more independent course, Middle Eastern nations that receive military equipment and training from the U.S.S.R. continued or increased their sponsorship of terrorist organizations, even though that runs contrary to Moscow's newly defined interests. Syria and Libya, for example, know full well that Gorbachev is seeking influence through peacemaking in the Middle East, but neither Assad nor Qaddafi has any interest in peace. Still, both countries buy their hundreds of millions of dollars of Soviet weaponry with hard cash that the Soviet Union eagerly accepts. The disconcerting announcement by Moscow in the spring of 1989 that it planned to sell long-range fighter bombers to both countries seemed to be further evidence of the Kremlin's addiction to Arab oil money and the persistence of some of the old ways of impressing Arab leaders that the Kremlin can be counted on. Those arms deals injected confusion about Gorbachev's commitment to stabilizing the volatile region, but some defense analysts believe the new Soviet planes will not make a significant change in the balance of forces in the Middle East. The most optimistic view is that by continuing to meet the armament demands of these client states, Moscow will be able, in the future, to influence them to reduce or abandon their support of terrorism. For now, these radical Arab regimes are continuing their own sponsor-client relations with terrorists. Moscow is either unwilling or unable to force them to stop.

That is part of the new world order of ungrateful and unreliable client states. They believe—and the Kremlin has not convinced them otherwise—that their worth to their sponsor is greater than the problems they create by helping terrorists. So they continue on their own high-risk course, with Moscow seemingly unwilling or unable to force a correction.

At the same time, some terrorist organizations developed improved working relationships among themselves, allowing for the sharing of information about targets and their defenses.[4] Both American and foreign intelligence officers believe this new communication among terrorists has already led to joint operations. The more ambitious of those collective actions have also drawn assistance from the espionage services of Arab governments hostile to the interests of the United States and its allies. The help obtained from state intelligence agencies has come in the forms of false passports, travel documents, safe houses, surveillance of targets, including wiretapping and overall guidance on where and when to strike and how to escape, as well as use of diplomatic facilities.

Terrorists are often supplied with guns and explosives that are brought into victim nations under the eyes of customs officers, who are forbidden by international law to open any shipment that arrives under the protection of diplomatic seal. The "diplomatic pouch," as it is known, is one of the most critical pieces of terrorist infrastructure. Without that assistance, many terrorist attacks could not be mounted.

For Syria, Libya, North Korea, South Yemen, Iraq, and Iran, terrorist groups are surrogate armies, whose acts are cost-effective and, when things go wrong, deniable.

Deadly Definitions

"Terrorism is premeditated, politically motivated violence perpetrated against noncombatant targets by subnational groups or clandestine state agents, usually to influence an audience. International terrorism is terrorism involving citizens or territory of more than one country."

—U.S. Department of Defense

The question of definition is not merely academic; it goes to the delicate business of extradition of terrorists from one country to another, to the surprisingly sensitive issue of what, exactly, constitutes a terrorist act versus a legitimate act of political opposition. This is such a politically sensitive issue that it winds up being central to bitter arguments between allies over the handling of captured terrorists, and can contribute to the souring of relations between otherwise friendly governments. How governments will respond to the more powerful terrorist attacks in the future will depend on a combination of policies, preparations, and personalities of those officials in charge of national security.

In early 1989, some hope arrived that a terrorist crisis out of control might not draw the superpowers into unintended nuclear collision. A Soviet literary institution invited American, British, and Soviet experts on terrorism, including Robert Kupperman, to meet in Moscow. The group agreed on the definitions of the most crucial aspects of terrorism and concurred on a joint statement of principles. It calls on the United States and the U.S.S.R. to take the difficult diplomatic steps necessary to making sure that terrorism by a third party never plunges the two superpowers into nuclear or conventional war. Obviously unthinkable only a year or two earlier, the week-long conference was only a first step. It would be a mistake to become euphoric about Soviet policies, plans, and intentions. Moscow's performance is what counts.

The antiterrorism conference was motivated at least in part by growing fear of terrorism from within. The Soviets' most immediate concerns focus on the ring of predominantly Moslem republics that became increasingly restive in 1988 and portend real trouble in the near future.

Nevertheless, the meeting in Moscow came at a crucial time. Middle Eastern terrorist states were alarming intelligent people by producing banned chemical weapons, while terrorist organizations were crossing historic thresholds of violence with the help of increasingly sophisticated technology.

A new age of terrorism is arriving, heralded by an act of breathtaking horror.

In a single moment, 189 American civilians were murdered at thirty-one thousand feet, over Lockerbie, Scotland, just before Christmas 1988. Their killers calculated the slaughter and its impact on the most powerful nation on earth and then placed the bomb aboard Pan Am Flight 103. The timing of the carnage in the air was highly suspicious; only six days previously, Palestine Liberation Organization Chairman Arafat pledged that the people loyal to him would cease all their terrorist operations.

But putting a bomb aboard a jumbo jet usually requires considerable planning and deployment of a coordinated team. Six days would "absolutely not be enough time to mount such an operation," Arafat aide Hassan Rahman insisted during an interview in Washington in January 1989.[5] It appears Rahman was correct. In May, the West German magazine *Quick* reported Iran had paid $1.3 million to the Palestinian terrorist Ahmad Jibril to destroy an American airliner. *Quick* said it based its report on the minutes of a meeting in July 1988 in Iran, attended by the Ayatollah Khomeini. According to *Quick*, the meeting was called to plot revenge for the destruction of an Iran Air flight by a U.S. Navy missile over the Persian Gulf earlier that month. The accidental shootdown took the lives of 290 Iranians. The United States said the missile was launched out of the mistaken belief that its radar image was that of an attacking Iranian fighter plane.

On May 11, 1989, the *Washington Post* reported that technologically sophisticated terrorists of Jibril's Popular Front for the Liberation of Palestine–General Command had been "hired" by Iran to bomb the plane, according to a CIA assessment. The *Post*'s David Ottaway wrote that the CIA was "confident" of its assessment but that the

FBI didn't have sufficient evidence to seek an indictment—not enough information "to satisfy everyone in the administration."

That may offer policymakers an excuse for not taking any risky action against Iran, but the revelation of the CIA's confidence in its conclusion that Iran was behind the attack was certain to bring pressure for retaliation from relatives and friends of the people killed aboard Flight 103.

Bitter Lessons

The destruction of Flight 103 exposed the U.S. aviation security "system" as a collection of often uncoordinated bits and pieces which are utterly inadequate.

Sheila Hershow, an investigator who initially led the Congressional probe of the government's role in the disaster, was astounded by what she did *not* discover: "I kept asking myself, 'Did the system break down?' And I kept finding the system that I had thought existed, in fact, does not exist."[6]

Through her interviews with intelligence and security officers at a variety of federal agencies, she determined that there is an alarming lack of coordination among the elements of the national security apparatus that are responsible for providing advance warning of terrorist attacks. There is, she was informed by officials of the major American intelligence services, no uniform system for flagging a particular terrorist threat as a top priority, no method for making sure that all airline and security personnel who must be informed of an imminent attack actually do get the word.

What emerged from Hershow's intensive probing of the air security "system" is a portrait of the CIA dutifully picking up terrorist-related intelligence, the National Security Agency listening in on terrorists' telephone conversations, and the State and Defense departments also collecting important information, all of which should be funneled into a centralized terrorist threat-assessment unit—but which is not. There simply isn't one. Battles over budgetary and status turf, as well as historic distrust of other services within the same government, play their roles in all this.

"There are some terrorist attacks which no one can ward off," Hershow said, "but we have a 'system' that makes it easy for terrorists to succeed. Just look at what was *not* done to protect Pan Am 103. After the FAA told Pan Am to be on the lookout for a plastic explosive device armed by a barometric pressure trigger, the airline sent out a security task-force wire. That message ordered Pan Am people to check carry-on baggage with X-ray equipment. Now, why would they check carry-on baggage when a bomb like this is plainly intended to go in the belly [checked luggage compartment] of the plane? And why would they use X-ray detection when this bomb was specifically designed to evade conventional X-ray detection? The FAA told Pan Am the bomb would be designed to evade X rays."

Without high-tech machines (only recently available and very difficult to manufacture) or enough specially trained dogs that can sniff out most plastic explosives, airlines can rely only on the skill of their employees, cooperation among governments, and timely intelligence well distributed throughout that segment of the aviation community believed to be at risk. Moreover, it was hardly the first time Pan Am had been confronted by terrorists, only to fail catastrophically.

Although the Federal Aviation Administration was aware of huge gaps in Pan Am's security operation, the FAA undertook no review of its own, as it is empowered to do under its regulatory function. It simply took Pan Am's word that the airline had cleaned up its security act.

In May of 1986, after terrorists killed some fifty Pan Am passengers or employees in several incidents, the chairman of the board of the airline personally hired an Israeli consulting company to conduct a global review of Pan Am's antiterrorism program.

As detailed in a congressional document, Ray Salazar, FAA's director of civil aviation security, was personally advised of the findings shortly after completion of the review by KPI, Inc. The consulting firm prepared two reports that were presented to Pan Am in September and November 1986. They were based on assessments of Pan Am security at nine locations, including Frankfurt and London. The report concludes that: "Pan Am is highly vulnerable to most forms of terrorist attack. The fact that no major disaster has occurred to date is merely providential."[7]

Was anyone paying attention? Within days of the delivery of that dire prophecy, 18 Pan Am passengers and crew were killed in a September 6, 1986, shooting in Karachi, Pakistan. Two years later, an additional 270 lives were lost following the bombing of Pan Am Flight 103 over Scotland on December 21, 1988. Based on Hershow's investigation, it is clear that many of the gaps in Pan Am's security system identified in the 1986 KPI reports were not corrected. If they had been, it is possible that those lives could have been saved.

Although the full text of the KPI reports has been sealed by a court, pending massive liability litigation over the failure of security for Flight 103 and the resultant deaths, some of the specific findings contained in the documents have been made available through an unnamed source. What is remarkable, in addition to their content, is how much of what was found deficient should have been obvious to any thoughtful person, let alone the executives of the airline that claims in its advertising: "You can't beat the experience." The authors of the KPI report were formerly in charge of Israel's aviation security system. Their experience and unannounced on-site evaluations, brought them to these observations of Pan Am's operations in areas likely to be targeted by terrorists:

- "At most European stations there is a misconception that citizenship is a classifier for security. As a rule, American citizens and citizens of the host country are considered 'safer' as regards their belly baggage, which is not checked in any way . . .
  "It might be pointed out that the question of citizenship is irrelevant to the terrorist threat. Most terrorist organizations find it easier to operate in their home countries. Most international terrorist organizations carry out proxy operations for each other, and false passports are widely used."
- "Local security officers have no sufficient contacts with local security services or intelligence sources."
- "A misguided security concept . . . [including] an overreliance on technical appliances [X-ray machines], which, inherently, cannot serve today as instrumental aids, and inadequate efforts to mark out suspects."
- "An organizational setup, which suffers, among other things,

from a lack of authority in various functions . . . and an alarmingly low level of training/instruction."

• "Hardly a control or testing procedure for the security system."

Those findings amount to an indictment—not only of America's biggest overseas airline, but also of the FAA, which has the statutory responsibility of making sure the commercial air carriers are safeguarding the public.

Investigator Hershow said both the FAA and Pan Am resisted her requests for documents. Those memos and directives reveal the steps that were taken—and those which were not—to protect Flight 103. But it goes well beyond the loss of the 270 lives and the aircraft. Hershow said it goes to the government's overall approach to antiterrorism for airports and planes. "We have an aviation security system that was almost entirely designed to ward off hijackings when, for at least the past five years, the threat has come from bombings . . . and this happened at a time in which the current President of the United States was Vice President, and in charge of fighting terrorism. This has to be an embarrassment to the Administration."

In the same way, the results of KPI's examination of Pan Am, as cited by Representative Cardiss Collins in a letter to the FAA, must be an embarrassment to the airline, especially since some of the findings appear to bear direct relevance to the bombing of Pan Am 103. They included the following:

• "Security-conscious handling of 'Lost and Found' baggage is very rare, opening an easy way of letting a baggage item with barometrically present explosive charges to be sent ownerless to a supposed destination."

• "At various stations, such as London and Hamburg, it is possible to put on the conveyor belt a baggage item with an attached Pan Am baggage tag. This item will reach the Pan Am loading area in the baggage area in the baggage room and be loaded in the plane even though no one is registered as the traveling passenger."

• "No effort was found at most airports to mark out a passenger or suspect according to profile criteria, and accordingly to subject him to special questioning or searching.

"In cases where baggage is checked by X-raying . . . even an experienced and watchful security officer cannot see and identify a weapon or an explosive charge, and the right course of action is to open the baggage and search it manually. Yet, from the many baggage items we saw being X-rayed, almost none were opened and hand-searched . . .

"Moreover, even when belly baggage is occasionally opened and searched by hand . . . the search is inefficient. On the whole, the presently employed search techniques stand a low chance of discovering concealed explosive charges, if at all."

- "Out of the prescribed six departure questions," [part of the behavioral profile used to determine which traveler may be high-risk, requiring closer examination] "passengers are usually asked few, if any. From the way the questions are put, it is clear that the questioners do not understand the importance of the questions, nor do the passengers. Thus, remarkably, at most stations, there had not been for weeks even one passenger who was delivering a gift. Our experience is that by asking the questions in a proper way, one gets completely different and much better responses.

"In conclusion, there are no adequate safeguards under the presently operating security system that would prevent a passenger from boarding a plane with explosives on his person or in his baggage, whether or not he is aware of the fact."

- "Cases are on records [sic] where early warnings were received at some level in the station, but were not passed on to all members of the local [Pan Am] security staff, who remained ignorant of them even at a later date. Examples: At Frankfurt and Paris airports, warnings had been received about two women of Middle East origin, planning to place explosives aboard a plane. This warning did not reach all members of the staff. JFK and Miami airports were alerted early in June on the possibility of explosives being smuggled in a doll. Most of the security officers still had not received the warning by mid-July."

- "There is virtually no training program for the security staff, not even at senior office level. The few hours of training which they do get do not afford the elementary expertise required for detecting explosive charges. At some stations there are staff members who have not had any training whatsoever. Most security officers have never seen explosive devices, whether real or dummy, nor have they handled explosives. It is doubtful whether they would recognize such articles if they came across them."

Although Pan Am insists that the security breaches identified in the KPI reports have been addressed, the Karachi attack and the bombing of Pan Am 103 test that assertion, as does other information obtained by congressional investigators from a variety of sources. Unfortunately, there is every reason to believe that most other international air carriers are little better at securing their passengers and planes than Pan Am.

El Al, the Israeli airline, is the best model of security. It is reflective of a nation which would not exist if it did not maintain a constant security alert. But that does not mean only airlines based in countries on the brink of war can have good security. It does mean that any nation which insists on having a secure airline can have one. As with so much of the complex issue of counterterrorism, the most fundamental requirement is for clear, determined, political will to accomplish the mission. Without that component, all efforts at safeguarding airlines or any other sector of society are likely to fail.

The Bush administration demonstrated in April of 1989 that it either had not learned the most important lessons of the Pan Am Flight 103 bombing or that it wished to pretend that everything really is all right. In its role as supervisor of the FAA, the U.S. Transportation Department declared that it had decided to require the installation of state-of-the-art plastic explosives detectors, costing roughly a million dollars apiece, at over one hundred "high-risk airports" over the next several years. That is clearly good news for travelers in the distant future, but the government failed to take steps that would quickly, sharply reduce the risk of such bombs getting aboard.

The Israelis have caught several of those high-explosive devices at passenger check-in by using interviewing techniques that lead trained security people to examine certain baggage with extra care. The best-known successful use of the technique prevented the loss of a packed

747 jumbo jet set to take off from London to Tel Aviv. An El Al security man, following standard interrogation practices, determined that a young woman and her bag looked suspicious. Upon examination, it was discovered that her lover, later to be revealed as a Syrian terrorist, had placed a bomb in her checked valise. More than four hundred lives were spared by that single piece of low-tech antiterrorism at Heathrow Airport in the spring of 1986.

The new measures announced by Transportation Secretary Samuel Skinner did not include mandating the use of such interviewing techniques, called behavioral profiles. They did not include improving the recruitment, screening, training, and management of baggage handlers and carry-on luggage examiners, as well as other security personnel. And those steps *not* taken are exactly the ones that could provide significant improvement at once in the safety of the flying public. The only rational explanation for the failure to impose those substantive measures is the government's desire not to take over the security end of air travel. In the post-deregulation, post-Reagan laissez-faire environment, the Bush administration apparently is intimidated by, does not wish to offend, or actually believes the airline industry when it says it can do the security job better than the government. Any of those three options is the stuff of future tragedies. There is no systems approach to airplane and airport security; until there is, passengers will pay with their lives for the intransigent incompetence of government and industry. Skinner repeatedly affirmed that "Money will not stand in the way" of providing good security to the American people. But a poverty of comprehension and absence of truly responsive action continue to block the path to security.

There is available right now an array of low-tech approaches to aviation antiterrorism, which, taken together, amount to a workable, credible system. They include simple changes in the way airports are run, like restricting nonpassengers from most of the airport, having a single security operation for all the airlines with centralized intelligence and communication, widespread use of behavioral profiles, meticulous screening and training of security personnel, and the deployment of canine explosive detectors. While their effectiveness against all forms of plastic explosives has not been established, bomb dogs can sniff out many of the explosives favored by terrorists around the world. Unlike the new machines, they do not take a year to build. The canines can be trained in a matter of weeks. The true dilemma is that government policymakers persist in acting as though they themselves are inadequately trained to think through the security problem, which already is of crisis proportions.

Noel Koch, the former chief of counterterrorism at the U.S. Defense Department, advised, "Let the airlines do what they do best, which is move people from place to place, and let the government take charge of security . . . [but] if you're going to let airlines fight wars, and make no mistake about it, terrorism is war, then you better let passengers know they are cannon fodder in those wars."[8]

Asked directly about putting the government in charge of security, Transportation Secretary Skinner brushed aside that concept and said having the Federal Aviation Administration work in partnership with the airlines "is the best way." That statement during a news conference followed a conversation between Skinner and the heads of the major airlines. But less than two weeks later, the chief of security for Pan Am said he favored putting the government in charge.[9]

The timing of Skinner's announcement about improving bomb detection and other antiterrorism efforts at airports fueled cynicism about the role of politics in security. His news conference was held the same day that dozens of relatives of the Americans killed on Pan Am Flight 103 visited the White House and Congress to lobby for better security and for an investigation of how government agencies responded to warnings that a bomb would be put aboard an American plane leaving from Frankfurt. While Skinner's words about better security measures won praise from the grieving relatives, his opposition to an independent probe angered the family members. There is no question that such an investigation could prove politically embarrassing, since it would reveal in detail the patchwork nonsystems on which the government depends for passenger security.

The absence of a systems approach is not only problematic overseas but at home as well. Most Americans have no idea that checked baggage on domestic flights is not even X-rayed, let alone hand-examined for plastic explosives. Sounding like a public relations spokesman for the airlines, who don't want to be bothered with more pre-takeoff procedures, the FAA is on record saying there is no need for such expensive, time-consuming security. But it is important to have a good memory; the FAA also said there was no need to order airline employees to pass through metal detectors like everyone else. They changed that rule only after an angry, fired airline employee used his company badge to carry a pistol past security and take it aboard a plane carrying his former boss. Once airborne, the man with the gun forced his way into the cockpit and shot the man who had fired him; the shooting also caused the crash of the PSA flight and the death of forty-three people on the plane.

Too often, things change only after people die unnecessarily. Unless the U.S., British, and West German Governments make serious changes in aviation security, the 270 victims of Pan Am Flight 103 will have perished in vain.

No matter who was responsible for the bombing of Flight 103, it was a watershed event, a statement in blood that there is no high ground anywhere—not even for American civilians, who had never before been targeted in such large numbers.

Only once before had a jumbo jet been destroyed in the air by terrorists, and the circumstances were markedly different. Americans and their government were not the intended targets. The Air India bombing was a direct attack on the government of India—an extension of a religion-based civil war in which radical members of the Sikh minority are fighting to make the Indian state of Punjab their own independent nation. While there was not enough wreckage recovered from the ocean to determine the level of technology of the device that killed the Air India passengers, other evidence, obtained at the site of a second bomb, which went off at the same time at an airport in Japan, suggests a powerful but more rudimentary explosive device. The Pan Am jet was struck down by a bomb of intricate design—an example of the increasing technological sophistication of America's terrorist enemies.

Along with the targeting of Flight 103, another measure of the new lengths to which perpetrators of terror will go was seen in the repeated use of poison gas by Iraq in its successful war against Iran. Other than suffering a relatively ineffective counterattack by Iran and a few impotent verbal expressions of outrage by the United States, Britain, and some of their allies, Iraq paid no tangible price for its breaching of the wall of international law that kept chemical weapons out of World War II and other international conflicts since then. Iraq continues to be a covert sponsor of terrorist groups and, like Syria and Libya, has the capability of arming its surrogates with chemical and— most worrisome—biological weapons, if it so chooses.

During 1989, greedy corporations in the West—especially in the Federal Republic of Germany, Japan, Italy, France, and the United States—were caught making huge profits selling chemical-weapons-manufacturing facilities and precursor chemical ingredients to terrorist states. Some governments, most notably that of Chancellor Helmut Kohl in West Germany, engaged in an apparent cover-up of the role some of their country's corporations were playing in providing poison-gas-making technology and supplies to fanatical and corrupt regimes. The exposure of all this, led by the U.S. State Department, slowed down the rapid expansion of chemical-weapons-making capacity in the Middle East, but there already was a stockpile of the tools of mass killing available for possible use by terrorists.

New Threat New Think

In the aftermath of the Iraqi use of poison gas and the bombing of Flight 103, Western intelligence officials have grudgingly come to believe that it is only a matter of time before the United States and, indeed, the rest of the West and perhaps the Soviet bloc as well are hit by chemical, biological, radiological, and infrastructure terrorist attacks. Long regarded as unlikely, unreasonable, and so difficult to deal with as to be "unthinkable," these scenarios were largely ignored at the highest levels of government.

Now, the new thinking must rise up the chain of command from analysts, who tend to be better-educated, into the minds of policymakers, including presidents, prime ministers, Cabinet secretaries, and politburo members, as well as the chairmen of the national security committees in Congress, Parliament, and the other legislative bodies of the world.

Even a nation that is able to prevent or deter some terrorist attacks must still be prepared to control the damage created by an assault that defies detection and defense. That includes a wide range of actions and policies, including—unfortunately—very expensive civil defense planning, purchasing, and training. A high-tech terrorist hit inside the United States could easily leave millions of people in confusion, fear, and danger. There just will not be any time for thinking through the kinds of decisions that must be taken to help civilians, physically and emotionally, if a massive and shocking terrorist emergency strikes. The resources for coping with the possible consequences of a major terrorist assault—including detailed response plans—must be in place in advance.

Whether terrorists wipe out hundreds of people at a shopping center with poisonous aerosols, blow up a natural gas pipeline compressor at a river crossing, or cripple one-of-a-kind electrical transformers with gunfire or explosives, the demands on the government by a justifiably scared public will be for actions that demonstrate genuine mastery of a new kind of calculated chaos.

At least one democracy is already preparing. Shocked into action by the Iraqi government's deployment of poison gas against unarmed civilian populations during its war with Iran, Israel quickly organized and funded civil defense training against chemical weapons for its citizens. Israeli Air Force facilities, among other key defense installations, had long been designed to resist chemical weapons attacks. Living under the notion that they would not face such threats, other allied countries did not exercise the same caution in their construction. By 1989, Israel was the only Western nation known to have gone public with its citizens on the risk of chemical weapons attacks.

At this point, America's resources for dealing with such threats are not remotely adequate.

Some intelligence analysts, whose reputations have been marked by calm and understatement, now go so far as to suggest privately that hybrid terrorist groups might soon emerge, made up of the usual gunmen, as well as some highly educated women and men who have the knowledge necessary to building and using advanced weaponry. These groups might try to steal a small, portable nuclear weapon, or actually make a crude bomb. But the danger of a shocking, massively effective nonnuclear attack drawing on chemicals, biologicals, or radiologicals (distinct from a nuclear explosive, artillery shell, or land mine) is actually greater because the materials for such an enterprise are far easier to obtain than those required for a nuclear device.

With the apparent easing of superpower tensions and the promise of increasingly successful arms control, the great terror—fear of thermonuclear war—has been largely removed from the emotional lives of most people. The motivation for that sense of dread was easy to grasp intellectually. Nevertheless, it is very difficult to get decision makers to grasp that high-tech terrorism is currently more likely to take large numbers of innocent civilian lives than nuclear weapons.

One of the most difficult concepts that confronts antiterrorists and their policy-making bosses is the fact that fewer than a dozen guerrillas could kill hundreds or thousands of children, women, and men in a single forty-eight-hour period. The open nature of democracy makes the United States and its allies easier and increasingly more likely targets.

Europe is expected to become even more difficult to secure against terrorist assaults beginning in 1992, when barriers to trade and travel are scheduled to be dropped as part of the European Economic Community's transition into an open and free market for its member states. While political and economic leaders prepare for that day, the security officers of each nation are becoming more concerned over the implications for transnational crimes and terrorism. Long before the European Community decision was made, most of Europe was virtually free of rigorous border security. Anyone not obviously carrying a weapon could board a train in Paris and travel throughout the Continent without being subjected once to a personal or luggage search. A single terrorist could leave a lethal trail of time-delayed bombs in public luggage rooms or in secluded areas of train stations or in the towns and cities along the rail lines. There are heavily armed police on patrol at some terminals, but they seem to be there mostly for show— as a deterrent to anyone who might impulsively attempt disruptive acts. They are also on the lookout for the handful of known terrorists being sought for previous attacks. However, there is no "systems" approach in most of Europe, either. Bomb-detecting dogs are not routinely brought aboard trains or walked through baggage-holding offices to sniff for explosives. Without a specific cause for alert, antiterrorism on Western Europe's vital rail lines is almost nonexistent.

There are also serious intelligence-gathering problems emerging in the United States. Until recently, the FBI was able to preempt some sixty terrorist events over a five-year period—events that would definitely have caused massive casualties, including:

- Indian Sikhs were attempting to put another bomb aboard another jumbo jet—this time at Kennedy Airport in New York

- a pro-Khomeini group of Iranians in America plotted to incinerate five hundred anti-Khomeini people at a political rally in a Seattle theater
- in Chicago, a street-gang-turned-terrorist group bought a shoulder-fired missile to destroy an airliner taking off from O'Hare International Airport
- assassination plots against visiting foreign leaders, among them: Daniel Ortega of Nicaragua and Rajiv Gandhi of India[10]

The FBI's renowned system of foreign counterintelligence, composed of undercover agents and their sources, decoys, confidence "sting" operations, and high-technology surveillance prevented every one of those plots from succeeding.

Unfortunately, a single mishandled surveillance operation against a group of American citizens sympathetic to the cause of leftists in El Salvador brought down a great deal of political heat on the Bureau.

In 1987, the FBI was charged in a civil action in federal court with conducting a "political" investigation of CISPES, the Committee in Solidarity with the People of El Salvador. CISPES, a group of American citizens—some of them church-affiliated—accused the FBI of violating the constitutional rights of members of the organization by wiretapping their telephones, opening their mail, and infiltrating their organization. All of those charges were shown to be false, but the handling of the investigation of CISPES, which triggered the lawsuit, was so bad that the FBI case agent was fired. The bureau's most senior investigator, Executive Assistant Director Oliver L. "Buck" Revell, was furious when he learned of the way the probe was managed. Not only did he dismiss the agent but also recommended that he be prosecuted.

Law enforcement critics used the case to tear into the FBI. The bureau's own director, former Federal Judge William Sessions, testified at an open congressional hearing, where he sounded like a boss admitting his organization had been out of control and ended up promising that there would be no repeat of the offensive actions. The entire investigation into CISPES was discredited. It began when the bureau received intelligence that alleged that CISPES was in direct

contact with the most violent terrorist element of El Salvador's Marx-
ists. The information turned out to be unsubstantiated.

However, Revell, the top antiterrorist with responsibility for protecting the United States, admits that "given the same facts and
circumstances today, we'd have no choice but to institute such an
investigation [of an American group said to have ties to a foreign
terrorist organization which has already killed Americans overseas].
But now, because of the bad handling of CISPES and the resulting
criticism, it would be difficult for us to penetrate that type of organization again."[11]

The net effect is the partial impairment of the FBI's antiterrorist
capabilities just as the threat to the United States posed by international and home-grown terrorism expands and intensifies. What is not
understood by a surprising number of people who should know and
need to know is that, in order to have the kinds of successes at pre-
empting terrorist acts the FBI previously achieved, intelligence must
be collected. That intelligence-gathering effort will probably go nowhere if it is confined to people who have already committed criminal
acts. The collection of information about American citizens is not, per
se, a violation of their constitutional rights.

Frustrated and profoundly worried, Revell said, "The FBI does
not interfere with anyone's rights. What we are doing is collecting
information to analyze, to see within those groups which elements,
based on prior intelligence, are likely to either directly support or be
able to participate in terrorist acts. Frankly, we have not reached that
level of sophistication in the knowledge of the requirements of effective antiterrorism in our Congress and even in our director. Judge
Sessions doesn't understand it yet, and I told him this direct, so I'm
not telling you anything I haven't told him. His testimony in the
CISPES case gives us great problems."

The bottom line is that by holding the FBI to the very same
standards in antiterrorism as in routine criminal conspiracy cases,
there is the very high risk of crippling the frontline force in the war
against terrorism inside the United States.

"You simply cannot do the job if you are held to that standard,"
said Revell. "We are stating that you cannot protect the United States
from terrorism if you cannot collect intelligence. The collection of
that intelligence should always be done in the least intrusive manner
and it should always be lawful. . . . We should not be doing any-

thing that is not articulated within standards set by our political leadership. But once those rules are established, we've got to be given the flexibility to operate within them in order to carry out our mission."

Nobody, least of all Revell, is asking that the bureau be given unlimited authority. But if the government fails to provide clarity and direction in its antiterrorism posture and policies, terrorists will find America a pleasant place to work.

As things stand now, the United States is poorly prepared to prevent or limit the damage of the new kinds of terrorist attacks that are most likely in the near future. Although some of the groups have been infiltrated by agents in the employ of Israel or the United States, others, especially Hizballah, seem to defy intelligence penetration. The result is that nations that have been targeted often receive no warning, or nothing so specific that a focused effort can be mounted in time to block the attack.

There are methods of gaining much higher-quality intelligence on terrorist groups, but they are considered repugnant by many national leaders, who find them morally repelling or just too dangerous politically.

"If the United States seriously wants to avert another calamity like the downing of Pan Am Flight 103," warns former deputy to the director of the CIA Dr. George Carver, "it will have to allow its assets [intelligence agents] to join, participate in and even commit acts of violence for terrorist organizations to gain necessary credibility and be regarded as a trusted member of the cell. And understand well: that will probably mean American-paid agents doing anything from armed robbery to kidnapping to assassinations.

"Unless our assets are permitted to commit such crimes, they will never be admitted to the councils of terrorist groups where decisions like the one to destroy Flight 103 were made. Had we had a man or a woman inside, we probably could have blocked the attack, captured or killed the terrorists, exposed the sponsoring intelligence service, and gotten our agent out. But that asset would probably had to have been a member of the terrorist organization for years prior to the decision to hit the Pan Am jumbo." Dr. Carver maintains that America's ability to combat foreign terrorist organizations has never recovered from the gutting of the CIA's most experienced operations staff during the Carter administration. Under the orders of CIA Director Admiral Stansfield Turner, satellite- and sensor-gathered information took precedence over human source material from 1977 through 1981.[12]

Turner took over the agency on the heels of the disastrous public hearings into CIA excesses by the U.S. Senate in 1976. Many individuals and governments on whom the CIA relied saw how secrets that they provided were turned into public scandal; some became convinced that, ultimately, the CIA did not have the power to guarantee that shared secrets would always remain secret. The implication was that sensitive sources and methods used by U.S. allies could be put at risk, placing intelligence officers, their bosses, and contract employees, including undercover spies in the field, in jeopardy of exposure. From 1981 until his death from a brain tumor in 1987, Ronald Reagan's Director of Central Intelligence, William Casey, spent billions trying to rebuild the agency's "humint" (human-gathered intelligence) capability and its credibility with its allies.

The sharing of time-urgent intelligence among the United States, NATO, and Israel on most imminent or actually under way terrorist actions was widely regarded as very good,[13] until the Flight 103 disaster. For weeks, security experts knew what kind of bomb to look for, but it slipped aboard the plane anyway.[14] Well before the Pan Am flight was blown up, there was deep worry over the validity of longer-range analysis and forecasts. Predicting which terrorist groups are planning escalations of violence and changes in tactics with any degree of certainty requires an array of resources—everything from high-tech surveillance equipment to a large number of agents and informants who are members of or associated with the terrorists. Some experts in Germany, Italy, and Israel privately expressed their unhappiness with this part of the mutual effort against terror. In this area, the West is weak and therefore vulnerable to switches in tactics and targets by groups whose previous behavior had been deemed relatively predictable.

Less and less inhibited by the boundaries of geographic distance and traditional defenses, international terrorist organizations pose a much greater threat to public safety, commerce, diplomacy, and democratic institutions than governments choose to acknowledge. At their current level of readiness and planning, the United States and its allies are all but inviting disaster, despite aggressive and creative work by some intelligence and law enforcement agencies. There simply are not enough highly trained and reliable antiterrorists deployed in critical areas with sufficient resources to do the job. Making matters much worse, there is no established multilateral crisis management machinery for coping with an international or domestic terrorist incident that goes wrong and leaves serious consequences in its aftermath. That is a reflection of a still much larger reality—the low level of priority placed on counterterrorism by policymakers.

At least part of the reason for the failure of national leaders to accurately perceive the dimensions of the terrorist threat is the simple fact that it has not yet manifested its full power and therefore seems not quite so problematic—merely episodic in its nature and, despite the inherent drama, not a major contender for attention or resources. Underlying that is the assumption that past patterns will persist, that there will be no profound change.

If that is not correct, however, whole nations will be menaced. At the same time, some senior intelligence officers are afraid that the Bush administration will follow the lead of the Reagan administration and neither take seriously, nor be prepared to defend against, the range of terrorist attacks. CIA analysts believe America is currently helpless on the homefront to defend against any serious, organized terrorist campaign against the complex, interwoven infrastructure.

What that means is Colonel Muammar al-Qaddafi of Libya, the Ayatollahs of Iran, Hafez al-Assad of Syria, the Abu Nidal gang, and other international terrorist groups have, to some degree, already secretly set up shop within America's borders, and if those elements receive orders to strike, the federal government probably won't be able to stop all of them before they hit their targets.

Terrorists are bound to indirectly endanger civil liberties as they pose a direct threat to institutions of government, places of employment, transportation facilities, public utilities, schools, homes, and human life.

If senior government officials fail to take the appropriate steps quickly, they will find themselves forced to act under the guns of crisis. It will be under those panicked circumstances that there will be the greatest temptation to resort to extreme measures. Political overreaction is what most terrorists work to achieve. It is a victory they can be denied only if political leaders take decisions that go well beyond the public-relations hype that has passed for counterterrorism for many years. There will have to be planning, allocation of resources, and a great deal of hard work, as well as some courage.

Up until recently, most terrorists had been technological incompetents. There were, of course, some important exceptions. Most notable was the 1983 truck bomb that killed 241 U.S. Marines in Beirut. Cold-eyed munitions experts considered it a small marvel of engineering, the equivalent of twelve thousand pounds of TNT. When it exploded, it lifted the whole concrete building off the ground, then brought it down atop the sleeping Marines. Palestinian terrorists who specialize in bombing civilian aircraft, including Abu Ibrahim, Ahmad Jibril, and Abdallah Abd al-Hamid Labib (better known as Colonel Hawari), have also demonstrated impressive technological know-how. But the hijackers of a Kuwait Airlines jumbo jet to Algiers in April 1988 were easily the most sophisticated. One of the terrorists was actually capable of flying the aircraft. The team of hijackers wired all possible entry points with explosives, making any hostage rescue operation highly unlikely if not impossible. They took other precautions in their handling of the passengers and the press which made it appear they had studied their mission with the thoroughness and scholarship of naval aviators, not wild-eyed fanatics.[15] Unfortunately, since then evidence has mounted that confirms that many terrorists are now embracing technology, thanks to their increasingly close relationships with state sponsors. The motivation of those foreign intelligence agencies is their hope that the terrorists will do what they are told when they are told to do it. On its face, that is chilling, when one considers the agendas of the sponsoring states. But add to that the growing independence of terrorist groups—even those which accept state sponsors—and you have the situation that truly alarms anyone with experience in diplomacy and defense: an environment of decreasing predictability and increasing risk of sudden, massive violence with no definable entity to hold accountable.

Victory Is Possible

Marshalling the unmatched resources of American society to head off terrorist assaults has proved much more difficult than intelligent people might have expected. In fact, there are times when calm analy-

CHAPTER TWO

THE EXPANDING THREAT

The end of the war between Iran and Iraq, the PLO's recognition of Israel and rejection of terrorism, along with other dramatic changes in the international struggle for power, are contributing to the expanding threat of terrorism. In the aftermath of its defeat in battle, Iran is using terror as a cost-effective method of force projection to create crises and divert attention from the collapse of the Ayatollah Khomeini's Islamic revolution on the homefront. On the other hand, a victorious Iraq is in position to challenge other Arab nations for primacy and should be expected to resume terrorist operations, directly through its intelligence service or via radical Palestinian surrogates, to intimidate other governments.

Yasir Arafat's new course for the PLO mainstream is a direct affront to all rejectionist Arab states and groups, and began triggering terrorist acts by his rivals almost from the moment of his declaration of no more terror.[1] Anti-Arafat forces, including Libyan-backed terrorists as well as Iranian units and other anti-Western groups, pose an increasing danger to the United States, its allies, and strategic interests.

In a parallel development of historic proportions, the Soviet Union is bracing for an outbreak of international and *domestic* terror, the first since the Bolshevik revolution. That profound concern is moving Moscow into a tentative antiterrorism partnership with other nations, including the United States.[2] The Kremlin's fear of terrorism is well founded, and Mikhail Gorbachev's government is correct in assessing the urgency of the situation. Similar candor and openness to "new thinking" on terror in the West would be welcome, as would seriousness of antiterrorist action, which has rarely been seen. Much is at stake.

Unless major improvements are made in antiterrorism around the world, the next five years will see a sharp rise in the number of innocent people killed or wounded by terrorists, even though the number of such attacks may be significantly reduced. The anticipated reduction of incidents is tied to the withdrawal from this kind of combat by Soviet surrogates, especially the Afghan State Security Service. Its assaults inside Pakistan killed scores of noncombatants and distorted the numerical picture of global terrorism in the late 1980s.[3] The increase in fatalities is linked to possible qualitative changes in terrorists' tactics and strategy.

Shootings and bombings will persist as the standard terrorist methodologies, but tactical breakouts, including attacks on the infrastructure and the use of super-violence—biological, chemical, and radiological weapons—may recast the terrorist threat. A single successful assault employing such sophisticated methods could kill more than all those lost in every incident of modern terror's worst year. In 1987, more than six hundred people were murdered and over two thousand wounded in eight hundred thirty-two attacks against the citizens and property of eighty-four nations.[4] Only imaginative improvements in counterterrorism can prevent or, failing that, soften the blows of this "new" terrorism.

In the face of the expanding threat, there seems to be some very good news—cooperation where before there had been only antagonism and menace: the United States and its allies may be joined by the Soviet Union in fighting terrorism.

One immediate implication of this dramatic change is that other nations that support terrorist organizations will work even harder at *appearing* to have clean hands. At the same time, the governments of Libya, Syria, and Iran, as well as some others, may not only maintain but expand their links to such groups. Meanwhile, because some counterterrorism efforts are making life more difficult for terrorists, even the most independent of these violent people are being forced into dependent relationships with state intelligence services.[5] Indeed, these agencies can give early warning of attempts by governments to apprehend or eliminate terrorists. They also provide official passports that defy detection at border crossings. Terrorists simply cannot continue to travel and elude detection if they do not have the resources to stay one step ahead of the United States, Israel, Japan, Britain, the Federal Republic of Germany, and other nations that have undertaken expensive efforts to track and capture them. While those counterterrorism programs are of widely varying quality, their very existence is a starting point for building multitiered defenses against a devastating brand of terrorist attacks, such as the destruction of Pan Am Flight 103. As it spreads, escalated terror will emanate from new players as well as from some of the old ones, whose current style is still a reflection of the original Palestinian terrorist role model of the early 1970s. Even then, there was only small hesitation about blowing up planes or committing assassinations. A major difference between then and now is the large number of terrorists prepared to commit acts of political violence *outside* the Middle East. Another dissimilarity is the increased availability of sophisticated man-portable rockets, chemical warfare agents, and the knowledge necessary to use them.

The terrorists who pose the most obvious threat of resorting to super-violence and infrastructure attacks have already established an array of support networks; command, control, and communications systems; and steady funding from one or more governments around the world. Along with the Iranians and some other Shiites, Syrians, Libyans, and Sikhs, radical Palestinians and their ideological comrades must be viewed as most likely to innovate, and least likely to be inhibited culturally or politically from carrying out what would be widely viewed as atrocities. Added to this list are narcotics traffickers who may choose the most shocking forms of terrorism to blackmail governments into leaving them alone.[6]

Role Models

Palestinians evicted from their ancestral homes by a series of conflicts culminating in the 1967 Middle East War gave rebirth to international terrorism in 1968, more than half a century after World War I ended the previous outbreak of terror.

Capturing global attention for their cause, young Palestinians became the role models for tens of thousands of other angry, often fanatical young men and women from diverse cultures who would take up the gun and the bomb as their means of trying to tear down the old order to establish a new one.

The Palestine Liberation Organization was the pioneer in terrorist innovations through two decades:

- the first airplane hijacking, an El Al (Israel) flight in 1968
- the first multiple hijacking and destruction of three jet airliners in 1970
- the first midair bombing of a jet, killing all forty-seven aboard a Swissair flight in 1970
- the first attack on the Olympics, the kidnapping and, later, the murder of eleven Israeli athletes at the Munich Games in 1972
- the first modern seizure of an embassy, Israel's diplomatic mission in Bangkok in 1972
- the first massacre of passengers at an airport, Ben-Gurion in Israel, where twenty-six people were murdered and seventy-six were wounded in 1972 by friends of the PLO, the Japanese Red Army
- the first massacre at an Israeli farm collective, twenty-seven dead, one hundred thirty-four wounded, at Ma'alot in 1974[7]

After initially targeting Israelis, the various PLO factions broadened their field of fire, selecting non-Jewish victims as well. Furious with Saudi Arabia over its low and slow payment of "fraternal support" (blackmail), the PLO invaded the Saudi embassy in Khartoum, Sudan, during a party for Western diplomats in 1973. The hit team murdered the U.S. and Belgian ambassadors. In 1975, the legendary Venezuelan-born, Moscow-educated Middle Eastern terrorist Illych Ramirez Sanchez, better known as "Carlos" or "The Jackal," engineered and led the attack on the OPEC ministers' conference in Vienna. In one of the greatest media spectaculars up to that time, Carlos took hostage the oil ministers of the world, thereby serving notice that rich Arab nations had better line up on the side of the Palestinians or pay a price in blood. As far back as 1971, the PLO demonstrated its capacity to commit political murder by assassinating the Prime Minister of Jordan, Wasfi al-Tal, while he was attending the Arab Defense Ministers' Conference in Cairo.[8]

While Arafat finally publicly disavowed terrorism in late 1988, other Palestinian leaders—some who support him, others who have called for his death—pursued their war against Israel and its friends. It is from this collection of unrelenting killers that Americans and their allies must expect more and perhaps different forms of attack.

None is as feared as Sabri al-Banna, whose *nom de guerre* is Abu Nidal. ANO, the Abu Nidal Organization (formally, Fatah—the Revolutionary Council), has been committing a wide range of atrocities since 1974, murdering more than three hundred people, wounding another six hundred fifty in more than twenty countries.[9] Its operatives assassinated three prominent PLO officials in 1978 and then went on a worldwide rampage against Palestinians who dared to seek a peaceful settlement of the Arab-Israeli conflict. Abu Nidal has either struck at or threatened to attack every moderate Arab nation: Egypt, Jordan, Kuwait, Saudi Arabia, and the Gulf emirates.

Estimated at five hundred trained terrorist members based in Libya and twenty-two hundred militiamen in Lebanon, ANO defines the Middle East struggle only in terms of warfare, not diplomacy. The spoken words and writings of Abu Nidal make clear his conviction that before Israel can be defeated, there must be a pan-Arab revolution uniting the many factions and nations to achieve "total destruction of the Zionist entity."[10]

Abu Nidal broke from Yasir Arafat and the PLO after the 1973 Middle East war because of Arafat's promise to confine his terrorist attacks to Israel and the occupied territories of the West Bank of the Jordan River and the Gaza Strip. An incensed Nidal plotted the assassination of Arafat, but fled when his plan was discovered. He took his supporters to Iraq, where he won the backing of the country's intelligence service, for whom Nidal's killers carried out terrorist actions that also complemented his agenda, including the assassination of many PLO officials in Europe and the Middle East and two attempts to kill Syria's foreign minister. But by 1983 Iraq wanted to shed its terrorist image in hopes of securing assistance from the West for the war with Iran. The Iraqi intelligence agency ordered Abu Nidal to get out of Iraq. In a remarkable shift of loyalties, Abu Nidal moved his headquarters to the capital of Iraq's bitter rival, Syria, and began hitting the targets on President Hafez al-Assad's enemies list. It was from this base in Damascus that Abu Nidal carried out many of his most outrageous missions:

- the assassination of the United Arab Emirates ambassador to Paris, France, in 1984
- the bombing of the Frankfurt Airport, three dead, seventy-four wounded, in 1985
- the coordinated bomb attacks on two Kuwaiti outdoor cafes, eight dead, eighty-nine wounded, in 1985
- the grenade attack in Rome at the Café de Paris, thirty-eight tourists wounded, in 1985
- the hijacking to Malta of an Egyptair jet, eighty dead or wounded, in 1985
- the coordinated attacks at airports in Rome and Vienna, fourteen dead, one hundred eleven wounded, in 1985 (Syrian supported operation with passports provided by Libyan intelligence)
- the seizure of a Pan Am 747 in Pakistan, twenty-one dead, more than a hundred wounded, in 1986
- the mass murder of twenty-two worshippers at a Jewish temple in Turkey in 1986[11]

In 1986 British authorities caught Syria in the midst of plotting major terrorist incidents in London, including the attempted midair bombing of a jumbo jet. Under tremendous pressure to appear to abandon terrorism, in June of 1987, Syrian intelligence told Abu Nidal to remove his office from downtown Damascus and leave the country. But, in a revealing piece of Middle Eastern duplicity, Nidal's gunmen were allowed to remain in Lebanon's Bekaa Valley, which is controlled by Syria. The next headquarters of the most efficient and best-financed terrorist organization in the Middle East was Libya, under the protective wing of ANO's longtime sponsor, Muammar al-Qaddafi. After months of moving into new facilities and establishing communications, command, and control systems, ANO[12] went back to work with Qaddafi's enthusiastic support for a wide range of strikes, including the simultaneous attacks at the Sudan Club and Acropole

Hotel, eight dead, twenty-one wounded, in Khartoum, Sudan, in May 1988, and the grenade and machine gun assault on a Greek ferry, nine dead, ninety-eight wounded, in July of 1988.[13]

If Abu Nidal were to be supplied with weapons of mass destruction, there is no question that this tightly disciplined, well-organized mercenary/terrorist organization would be capable of delivering the weapons on target. Moving up from dozens to hundreds or even thousands of victims would represent no shock to Nidal or his primary backers.

In 1982 President Assad of Syria responded to a challenge to his leadership inside Syria by ordering the mass murder of an entire city, Hamma, population twelve thousand. Because it was home to the movement known as the Moslem Brotherhood, Assad sent his elite army units to crush all resistance, and then gave the command to level the town and plow it under.[14] His elegant Savile Row suits and smiling countenance notwithstanding, Mr. Assad has a demonstrated taste for human slaughter. Similarly, Libya's grandiose leader Qaddafi has shown during his military forays into neighboring African states that he has absolutely no compunction about wiping out hundreds of innocent people who happen to be in his way. Qaddafi has also deployed chemical weapons during these armed adventures.

If any established group should be expected to innovate and escalate its violence, it is ANO, which has the distinction of being regarded by the U.S. Department of Defense as "the most dangerous terrorist organization in existence." In 1987 the FBI arrested an Abu Nidal Organization member in New York on an Israeli warrant, charging him with participating in an attack on a bus carrying civilians in the Israeli-occupied West Bank in 1986. The accused terrorist, Mahmoud Atta, is an American citizen who had been operating out of Venezuela for ANO, according to the Justice Department.

The FBI's antiterrorist unit has discovered that ANO has established "infrastructure here" in the United States that could assist the group if it chose to attack Americans at home, although its greatest threat is still perceived by the State Department as an overseas one.[15]

In the Name of God?

There is much larger support apparatus in the United States for Iranian terrorism. While only a few hundred of the more than thirty thousand Iranian students currently living in the United States are believed by the FBI to be members of Iran's intelligence services or willing to commit terrorist acts if so ordered, that still makes the Iranian network the single most dangerous foreign threat inside the United States.[16]

The ability of a small number of hard-core, professionally trained covert agents who are highly motivated to organize and exploit the openness of a democracy like the United States, to select targets, procure materials, form strike teams, and initiate action should be of major concern.[17] Yet, sloppy work by the U.S. Immigration and Naturalization Service allowed several dozen members of Iran's Revolutionary Guards Corps to slip into the United States as "students" in early 1989, according to congressional testimony by the FBI's most senior investigator, Oliver L. "Buck" Revell.

His former FBI colleague in fighting terrorism, L. Carter Cornick, now a consultant on counterterrorism, worries that "just a few of the dedicated, fanatical followers of Iran's Ayatollah Khomeini who reside in the United States may be spiritually motivated" to commit acts of violence out of belief that such actions would be of service to their God. The firebombings of bookstores selling Salman Rushdie's *The Satanic Verses* were a hint of things to come.

It is not widely understood in the Western world that in the Shiite faith of Iran, the Imam, as Khomeini was called, is much more highly revered than any Pope, the most powerful single figure in Western religion. Indeed, the Imam is regarded by some of his followers as superior even to the Prophet Muhammad, because they believe Khomeini had direct, personal access to Allah. It is in that very special context that the potential for Iranian terrorism must be evaluated.[18] Unlike the Rushdie affair, other acts of Shiite terror need not originate with a Holy Writ or *Fatwah;* they could be generated strictly out of the inner conviction of the devotee that he or she is functioning within the context of a legitimate jihad, or religious war.

From 1979, when the Islamic revolution overthrew the Shah of Iran and placed Khomeini on the throne of the theocracy, until 1989, there were only two known incidents of Iranian terrorism in the United States. One was an assassination; the other, the attempted incineration of hundreds of innocent people. In each case, the targets were anti-Khomeini Iranians.[19]

The first incident, which took place in July of 1980, has even greater significance in the light of the 1989 murder contract put out by Khomeini on Rushdie, whose book offended many Moslems. On July 22, 1980, an outspoken critic of Iran's Islamic revolution, Ali Akbar Tabatabai, was assassinated at his home in Bethesda, Maryland, a Washington, D.C., suburb. The killer, identified by the FBI as David Belfield, an American who converted to Shiite Islam and adopted the name Daoud Salahuddin, waited in ambush until his victim walked out of his house and then opened fire with a 9 mm semiautomatic pistol. The investigation of this homicide revealed the existence in the United States of a terrorist organization that called itself the Islamic Guerrillas of America. Two of its members were convicted in 1981 of aiding and abetting the flight from prosecution of the murderer. Mr. Belfield (Salahuddin) was last seen by American intelligence sources in Iran at a training academy for Iranian Revolutionary Guards, where he is an instructor in hand-to-hand combat and assassination techniques. He is an honored member of the international Shiite terrorist community that is headquartered in Tehran.

The second of the Iranian terrorist incidents in the United States is of even greater concern, even though it is a tale of successful and even brilliant preemption. There is a large community of anti-Khomeini Iranian expatriates in the Seattle, Washington, area. In December of 1983, a rally of anti-Khomeini Iranians was scheduled in a rented theater in Seattle. It was widely known that the event would take place. Pro-Khomeini students, some of them secret members of the Hizballah terrorist organization, learned of it and decided to seize the opportunity to demonstrate that those who oppose the Imam and his Islamic revolution have no hiding place. An estimated five hundred men, women, and children were expected to attend. The "students" purchased gasoline to ignite inside the theater. According to their plan, once the flames began to burn, the pro-Khomeini plotters were set to block all exits, transforming the theater into an oven. If they had had their way, all five hundred would have been burned and trampled to death, making Seattle the scene of the single most brutal act of terrorism in the modern age—worse than the bombing of Pan Am Flight 103, because the death toll would have surpassed the jumbo jet disaster by more than two hundred.

But one of the plotters boasted about their horrific plans to an undercover agent of the FBI. The "students" were totally surprised when, on the eve of the show, teams of federal agents and Seattle police officers descended on them. They warned the followers of the Imam that if they attempted to carry out their conspiracy at any time in the future, they could look forward to spending the rest of their lives in prison with very unsympathetic roommates.[20] Unfortunately, police could not arrest and charge them with conspiracy, because proving the case in court would have forced the identification of the FBI undercover. Nevertheless, the slaughter was prevented, the would-be terrorists identified and placed under continuing surveillance. (Under American law, there was then, and still is today, no way to deport the plotters absent a trial and conviction. Most other democracies grant nonjudicial powers to their police to kick out such would-be terrorists, and the FBI wants the same authority.)[21]

Other than these two incidents, Iran's terrorist commanders avoided a direct clash with America at home, satisfied with hitting easier-to-reach overseas Americans and American interests.

Through its slavishly loyal Lebanese arm, Hizballah, Iran repeatedly used car and truck bombers with great success against the United States in Beirut and Kuwait. Born in late 1982 out of the union of two radical organizations in Lebanon—Islamic Amal and the Da'Wa Party, Hizballah (literally, Party of God) is a messianic religious/political force of remarkable influence and reach. It is the indirect servant of the Ayatollah Khomeini in Lebanon; it is the recruiter and trainer of fanatical terrorists numbering in excess of five hundred. In addition, Hizballah has a militia, which competes through urban guerrilla warfare with other factions for control of blocks, neighborhoods, and whole chunks of the country. Intelligence estimates of the militia's strength put it at more than five thousand.[22]

The number of Hizballah sympathizers in the United States now is not known but, since 1983, the FBI has assigned undisclosed but significant resources to discover, track, and penetrate the terrorist support cells in the United States that are loyal to Khomeini-ism. Revell believes Iran could not order an attack within the fifty states without the FBI hearing about it in time to block it. But, as Revell admits, "You can't know what you don't know," and the existence of one or more Iranian cells capable of supporting, directing, or carrying out terrorist activity inside the United States could escape his dragnet.[23] If that were the case, the FBI would have to rely on the CIA's obtaining information on Iranian intentions from Israel's Mossad or other non-American intelligence sources. The United States is still trying to rebuild its own intelligence collection capabilities in the Middle East. The Agency's seven best area experts, who had developed networks of assets over many years to provide timely warning of planned attacks, were killed by Hizballah with Syrian-supplied bombs at U.S. embassy facilities in Beirut in 1983.

In the event that Iran's Revolutionary Guards Corps were to order a hit in the United States by Hizballah terrorists, informants paid by the United States might get wind of the plan. But Iran's master terrorists are not stupid—indeed, they are among the quickest minds in Teheran, including the most senior officials of the regime. They would probably compartmentalize the knowledge of any imminent strike on the United States. Penetrating that secrecy would require extremely good fortune, including the National Security Agency's sifting out crucial Iranian telephone conversations and quickly translating those that would be the specific orders for an attack in Washington or elsewhere. Hizballah poses a substantial threat and must not be underestimated.

In cooperation with Iran's Revolutionary Guards Corps and armed by Syria, which, like Iran, wants all Western influence out of Lebanon, the Party of God targets the enemies of Khomeini. Through its intelligence unit, Islamic Jihad, Hizballah carries out unrelenting holy war against those who have offended the Ayatollah; kidnappings and car bombings, as well as small-unit paramilitary assaults, are their standard tactics. Hizballah's immediate spiritual guide is a gentle-looking Islamic scholar, Shaykh Muhammad Husayn Fadlallah. Behind his kindly clerical mask is a leader of unrelenting brutality. His highly controversial interpretation of the Holy Koran has laid the foundation for a new wave of terrorism that is carried out by young Shiite Moslems whose imaginations have been inspired by Fadlallah's vision of a pure Islamic Lebanon, free of all Western non-Islamic influence. He has taught them that only their obedient, single-minded dedication can liberate their land and cleanse it for the creation of a holy and wonderful realm in which Islam reigns supreme.[24]

But Fadlallah does not preach a universal Islam, which, if it reflected the majority Sunni branch, would be gentler and intellectually more open. Instead, his is a very doctrinaire, absolutist theocracy built on the Iranian model, with no room for any other faith or faction in Lebanon. That is one reason competing militias are often engaged in ferocious battles with Hizballah for control of pieces of Beirut and its suburbs. If Hizballah were to become truly dominant in Lebanon, it would portend a major conflict with Israel and could lead to the outbreak of the next full-scale Middle East war. However, Hizballah's official spokesman, Sayyid Ibrahim al-Amin, said in 1985 that Hizballah was already at war with America.[25] The year before, his people had kidnapped and tortured William Buckley, the CIA's station chief in Beirut and, more importantly, the top American antiterrorist in all of the Middle East. The information they squeezed out of Buckley before he died cost the lives of an undisclosed number of U.S. sources. Operating under fundamental principles of espionage services, the CIA assumed that Buckley would be brutally tortured and broken. For legitimate professional and personal reasons, the Reagan administration went all-out to retrieve him but failed. It was principally the desperation to free Buckley that led the Reagan administration into the Iran/Contra scandal (including swapping weapons for hostages with Iran), which almost brought down the President.

In the year before Buckley was snatched off a Beirut street, Hizballah "kamikaze" terrorists drove trucks loaded with explosives into the U.S. embassy in Beirut and the American Marines headquarters there, as well as into French and Israeli military bases in Lebanon. About five hundred allied soldiers were slaughtered in the four virtually identical attacks that dumbfounded analysts around the world, not only by their boldness but also because they were carried out by devout Moslems.

Committing suicide is taboo in Islam, just as it is in Judaism and Christianity. However, Fadlallah had reinterpreted the Koran to fit the needs of the terrorist operation he runs. More than a year later, Fadlallah explained to the outside world that "there is no difference between dying with a gun in your hand or exploding yourself."[26]

Psychologists in the West had declared his suicide bombers must have been brainwashed into believing they would enter paradise by their action. But Fadlallah ridiculed these detached analyses, indicting the doctors for being out of touch with the passions inspired by oppression. The bombers who were observed smiling by startled sentries as they drove to their deaths and the resulting doom of Western policy in Lebanon were not filled with visions of paradise, Fadlallah insisted. They were grinning, he told his followers, because they realized they were about to advance their political cause a single step. He also affirmed in an interview that "those who carried out suicide operations against the enemy are in paradise."[27] The Shaykh had become a very dangerous man, inimical to America's interests. He was shielded from U.S. assassination by the same presidential order signed by all presidents starting with Gerald Ford. The executive order strictly forbids Americans from committing murder off the battlefield.

In 1985 CIA Director William Casey ordered Lebanese intelligence officers to hit Fadlallah. The operation spun out of control. The Lebanese used a car bomb, detonating it on the street where Fadlallah was believed to live. The attack killed eighty innocent people in the area of the blast, but the Shaykh wasn't home.[28]

Although the Reagan administration denied involvement, U.S. political fingerprints were all over the bombing. Having failed to eliminate Fadlallah, the bombing became a recruitment motivator for Hizballah, while making the Shaykh appear even more powerful. These people, whose faith focuses their passions in ways alien to the Western mind, remain at war with the United States. Their use of suicide-vehicle bombings dropped off temporarily because, Fadlallah said, such missions should be undertaken "only if they can bring about a military or political change in proportion to the passions that incite a person to make of his body an explosive bomb."[29]

Hizballah's eerie, almost invincible, image was earned by its mass murderers. But it had extra help from an unseen ally—the almost unbelievable incompetence and cultural arrogance of the United States, whose tactical blunders kept offering up ideal, unprotected targets for Fadlallah's human bombs.[30] Thus emboldened, Hizballah reached beyond the narrow confines of Lebanon itself in pursuit of its goal of acquiring the power necessary for imposing an Islamic state in Lebanon.

Fadlallah's disciples inflicted the second-worst humiliation on the Reagan administration after the Marines' bombing by hijacking TWA

Flight 847, torturing and shooting to death passenger Robert Stethem, a U.S. Navy enlisted man, holding thirty-nine other U.S. passengers hostage for seventeen days in Beirut, and temporarily paralyzing the mighty U.S. Government, which became obsessed with the hostage crisis in June of 1985.

The next month Hizballah simultaneously bombed a Jewish synagogue and a Northwest Orient Airlines office in Copenhagen, leaving one dead and twenty-six wounded. The Party of God was operating in Europe as well as in Lebanon. Over the next three years, Fadlallah's gunmen would become the most politically effective terrorists in the world, coercing major powers into paying ransom for their hostages (seized, by the way, in absolute violation of Islamic law, which Fadlallah would later condemn, but to no avail for the hostages), and intimidating Western nations into abandoning Lebanon. Hizballah, the identified perpetrator of these acts of terror, remained immune from punishment.

But on March 22, 1987, the terrorists lost a round and the world won an insight into the expanding nature of Iran's terrorist threat. In Paris, police captured a team of eight terrorists, including an Iranian, a Lebanese, and six Tunisians. All of them were tied to a West European Iranian-sponsored support network. Two months later, ten more terrorists—all of them North Africans and Lebanese—were seized by French security. The eighteen operatives were planning attacks inside France under the direction of officials at the Iranian embassy in Paris. As the French pressed their investigation, sixty Hizballah and Iranian bombers, gunmen, and support personnel were swept into prison. Many of them, it was later discovered, had been involved in planting the bombs that plagued Paris in 1986, murdering fifteen people and wounding more than a hundred and fifty others.[31] That campaign was designed to intimidate the government into stopping the resupply of Iraqi arms and releasing assassin George Ibrahim Abdallah, leader of the Marxist Christian Lebanese terrorist organization, Lebanese Armed Resistance Faction (LARF), which allied itself to radical Palestinians and Hizballah. Smashing this multinational terrorist conspiracy could not have been possible without the information obtained through the arrest of three Hizballah men in Milan and Frankfurt, whose bomb factory in Germany was also discovered. One of them, Mohammed Ali Hamadei, was the lead hijacker of TWA Flight 847 and the triggerman in the murder of Stethem.[32]

While the sixty-three arrests in West Germany and France (based on intelligence supplied by Israel's Mossad) slowed down some Hizballah operations, they did no more than that. Kidnappings of Westerners in Lebanon, including Americans, continued, as did assassinations and hijackings.

In April 1988 Hizballah operatives staged the most technologically sophisticated terrorist act to date. They seized Kuwait Airlines Flight 422 from Bangkok to Kuwait, diverting it first to Iran, where it refueled, on to Cyprus, and then to Algiers. It was there that the hijackers wired the entire aircraft with high explosives to prevent a successful hostage rescue, communicated by radio with their controllers on the ground, and demonstrated enough knowledge about the aircraft to fly it, or at least to make sure the crew followed their orders.[33]

As part of their obviously detailed and subtle training and planning, the terrorists also changed clothes from time to time, altering their appearance to confuse the hostages, who would later be asked by police to describe their tormentors. As significant as the escalated technical knowledge of the terrorists in this incident was, so was the clarity of the connection to Iran's government. When the hijackers ordered the crew to stop at a little-used airport in the Iranian town of Mashhad, one terrorist said to the pilot, "You don't have to tell [radio] the control tower. They know we're coming." On the ground, more gunmen got on board and the plane took off on the rest of its journey.[34]

Meanwhile, Hizballah's covert diplomats continued to widen their international connections with other anti-American, anti-Western terrorist groups, especially radical Palestinians, including the Popular Front for the Liberation of Palestine-General Command (PFLP-GC). Through that connection, the Iranian Revolutionary Guards contracted with the PFLP-GC to strike U.S. targets in Europe. Apparently in reprisal for the U.S. Navy's downing of a civilian Iran Air widebody, the Revolutionary Guards ordered attacks on trains carrying U.S. soldiers and the downing of at least one American-owned airliner.[35] The PFLP-GC is run by Ahmad Jibril, a master at making high-tech plastic bombs secreted in radio-cassette players that escape detection and kill planes.[36] One of his ingenious bombs is believed to have been the device that brought down Pan Am Flight 103, killing 270 people on the aircraft and on the ground in Lockerbie, Scotland. A similar, if not identical, weapon with altimeter/timer trigger was captured by West German antiterrorist police two months before the jumbo jet blew up.[37] The bomb materials were seized in raids that netted sixteen members of the PFLP-GC in Frankfurt, which was also the point of origination of Flight 103. But if the authorities arrested the plotters and grabbed their bomb, how did the crime happen anyway? Investigators now theorize that there were two teams of PFLP-GC bombers and either one was capable of the mission, which could have been many months in the planning. Following the logic of this theory, after one team of terrorists was captured, the second unit did the job on its own. It is strategic attack planning and must be factored into counterterrorist thinking in the future. Capturing one assault team may remove only one half or one third of the actual threat.

As terrorists rely more and more on state intelligence, they should be expected to reflect the sophistication of those espionage services, including multiple, perhaps compartmentalized, strikes with each attacking unit unknown to the others. These tactics would make the work of antiterrorists all the more difficult.

Because there was no history of such compartmentalized attacks, it did not occur to the West German intelligence service that there might have been a second PFLP-GC unit operating in Frankfurt. Antiterrorism, per se, is hobbled by surprisingly inflexible bureaucratic thinkers, whose fundamental approach was epitomized by an Israeli security officer who said, "We shall handle whatever new comes up just as we always have; there is no need for anything different."[38] Unfortunately, his mentality is typical. Call it a "We'll fix it after it fails" approach to antiterrorism.

The same mindset gets in the way of preparing to defend against —and failing that, coping with—the consequences of possible attacks on the infrastructure. Because the most ambitious assaults on utilities in the United States have been occasional gunfire attacks on electric power pylons, there is little constituency for protecting the vast networks of natural gas pipelines, electrical power nodes, and critical computer-controlled networks for the financial and communications industries. A similar political problem comes into play when the focus is on the possible escalation to the tactics of super-violence—the use of biological, chemical, and radiological weapons.

The most senior antiterrorism officials in the U.S. Government agreed in an open hearing at the U.S. Senate in May of 1988 that the next likely change in terrorism would be the use of chemical weapons

—possibly in the United States. Still, there is not even the beginning of a public education campaign. If the United States is hit by chemical weapons, there may be unnecessary panic because of the absence of cool, clear information. That is a statement about the potentially lethal effects of the disconnected relationship between policymakers and their finest experts.

At that hearing, Ambassador L. Paul Bremer, the State Department's chief of counterterrorism, told Senator Patrick Leahy, "The handling of the very first incident, especially if it's an incident of mass casualties, must be done very well. It must not be [perceived as] a terrorist success. It is the absolute view of everybody in intelligence and those of us who work on terrorism that if the first incident, whether it's chemical, biological, or a mass casualty of some kind, succeeds, we will see copycat terrorism right afterwards."

Bremer is correct. But his wisdom is not producing action to match. Government is simply not taking the necessary steps. One way to reduce the chances of success for that first attack is to have a coherent systems-based policy, including public education. The only education Americans received on chemical weapons came through the State Department. It exposed Libya's construction of the world's largest chemical weapons manufacturing plant and led a worldwide campaign to stop it from going into production. But that is only one aspect of what is needed to reduce the risk of chemical weapons terrorism. The awful fact is Qaddafi's factory is not necessary to the decision to deploy a few terrorists using chemicals. The materials necessary for mass murder by nerve agents, poisons, and even some biological agents are available for purchase in the United States and virtually everywhere else in the industrialized world.

The Frustration Factor

Whether it is Iran's global death warrant for author Salman Rushdie and anyone who protects him and his novel *The Satanic Verses* or the bombing of Flight 103, all terrorism is extortion. All terrorism is psychological warfare. All terrorism is played out on the international media stage. And all terrorists are the same in at least one way—they seek to capture their audience by fear and violence and then reshape their universe. In terms of their impact on the rest of humanity, it really does not matter much if their motivation is primarily religious or political: the pain they bring is the same. But beyond the suffering associated with their acts, terrorists have actually accomplished few of their goals. Frustration is their most commonly shared experience throughout the world. (A notable exception is Hizballah, which, with the help of Syria's dictator, was able to drive the United States and its allies out of Lebanon.)

Despite their best efforts, most terrorists are failing to trigger the political upheaval necessary to achieving the destabilization of the governments they are attacking. In fact, their traditional methods of assault are running into increasingly effective countermeasures, which deny them most of the victories they seek.

Airport security at some international terminals is finally being taken seriously, making aircraft more difficult to seize than they had been. Access to the most obvious symbolic targets—including major government buildings—has been restricted by physical barriers and stepped-up screening of visitors. Intelligence gathering on the whereabouts of known terrorists is improving. In many places, terrorists find themselves confronted by formidable obstructions. Thanks to coordinated efforts of police and security agencies, dozens of planned terrorist attacks are being intercepted.[39]

While all of this is positive, it also carries with it the chemistry of greater danger. That is not the paradox it seems. For, as nations become effective against some forms of terror, terrorists are not scared out of business; that is not their nature. For many of them, no other existence is imaginable. Their "righteous struggle" is what and who they have become, and frustration appears to be driving them, not out of their passionately chosen trade but into new thinking and tactics. Terrorists are after results, not just putting themselves in harm's way. They cannot help but notice that the response to their most shocking actions has been diminished. Countries that had previously been victimized have become numb to the shock. It just doesn't register with the impact of the same crimes committed only a year or two earlier. Increasingly, after terrorists stage an attack, the media, the public, and elected officials no longer panic so easily; more important, they don't pressure governments to "just do something."

That means those who want to manipulate nations and change their policies by political violence will probably adapt, choosing bloodier, more shocking forms of attack. The slaughter of 270 innocents by the bombers of Pan Am Flight 103 at the end of 1988 and the attempted murder of more than 50 sleeping British soldiers by Irish Republican Army bombers in central England in early 1989 were evidence that change is under way. This partial metamorphosis is not arriving in a vacuum. It is a clear and even predictable outgrowth of historical forces, some of which could have been diluted or even derailed if enough countries had been alert to what was taking shape and had possessed the courage and political will required for effective intervention.

The world will soon pay a high price for more than twenty years of collective cowardice and indecision by democracies that failed to take terrorism seriously, and for a concomitant period of callous, Machiavellian use of terror by hostile governments. Those hostile regimes correctly defined terror as a cost-effective and plausibly deniable method of waging war, which carried little, if any, risk to their homelands. Nations that have employed terrorist groups as surrogates, including Syria, Iran, and Libya, have only lately been called to account —and with insignificant consequences.

Very few countries have truly clean hands in all of this, and that complicates everything. The United States, which claims the moral high ground in the fight against terrorism, has problems with hypocrisy. During the Reagan administration's attempt to overthrow the leftist Sandinista regime in Nicaragua, the United States was actively advising Contra rebels to demoralize the Nicaraguan government and people by committing specific acts of terrorism. In an easily understood, comic-book-style manual, the CIA instructed America's proxies to assassinate Nicaraguan civilians—among them, judges and village administrators.[40] If a foreign power were discovered to have provided similar guidance to their surrogates inside the United States, that could easily be considered reason to go to war. Any nation that wishes to exercise moral authority must eschew supporting terrorists of every stripe—no matter how ideologically comfortable an administration may be with the declared goals of the terrorists. To choose any other course is to join those who have claimed throughout history that the ends justify the means—bad company for the righteously indignant.

Whether it's the United States and the Contras, or Libya and

Abu Nidal, or Iran and Hizballah, when state intelligence agencies are behind terrorist groups, the whole calculus of attack becomes much more sophisticated and potentially more dangerous. The growing reliance of terrorists on their sponsoring states adds to the depth and potential intensity of the threat.

Luck and Cost-Benefit

As the 1980s were ending, Americans who were paying close attention realized that their nation's antiterrorism system had been probed by foreign enemies on the homefront and been pronounced lucky if not effective. The implicit warning was clear to anyone who was willing to read it.

The interception of the Japanese Red Army terrorist, apparently on his way to commit mass murder in Manhattan, and of the three Syrian agents grabbed en route from Vermont to targets unknown suggested that U.S. defenses are in poor shape and that international terrorists can strike deep inside the nation if they choose. Only very good luck and a couple of suspicious lawmen spared the American people the pain packed in those terrorists' bombs and any plans they may have had for additional strikes. Taken together, those two incidents and the botched bombing of a Navy captain's family van in San Diego force the question: Where might the next foreign terrorist attack in the United States originate?

Based on previous performance, the list is daunting. At its head are surrogates of Iran, Libya, and Syria, with whom the four terrorists captured in Vermont and New Jersey had connections. None of these three nations would dare challenge the United States militarily or economically, but with terrorism, they bring the American colossus down to their size—or even smaller. With terrorism, their options are many, while those of the United States have apparently been few—or at least they have been perceived as such by succeeding American administrations. A great deal of that perception has to do with cost-benefit analyses which keep telling U.S. leaders that the costs of retaliation could be too high, including disruption of relations with countries whose cooperation in other areas is regarded as even more important than their role in terrorism.

Long-held American hopes that Syria's dictator Assad would join in the quest for peace in the Middle East have repeatedly gotten in the way of tough U.S. action against Syria for its documented support of terrorism. Official State Department publications declared that Assad has backed away from terrorism and that no terrorist acts were attributable to Syria in 1988. But Syria controls the territory that is home to Hizballah and most, if not all, other terrorists holding American hostages. That means Syria does have power over what these groups do. Even Abu Nidal owes fealty to Assad for being allowed to station his militia inside Lebanon, while he and his senior deputies are headquartered in Libya.

Assad is no fanatic. His employment of terrorism is always part of a larger stratagem. His loyalty is always and only to himself. He meticulously stretches and then tests the limits of atrocious behavior in which he can engage without bringing down America's rage. The conventional wisdom in Washington holds that Assad could not be removed without bringing on even more uncertainty in the Middle East. As a result, the United States persists in the mistaken belief that his indirect but substantial support of terrorism must be tolerated— save some occasional and most polite pressure. That thinking must change if Assad and his global intelligence network are not to further contribute to the expanding terrorist threat. This ruthless and resourceful master terrorist must not be allowed to exercise control over how and when America and her allies are attacked. It is a serious error to assume he will always exercise restraint.

Another important example of how U.S. inconsistency and lack of coherent policy feed the terrorist threat is evident in America's relationship with Greece, its most ambivalent ally. Increasingly anti-American and terrified of Turkey, its historic enemy but partner in NATO, Athens has long been both a friend to and victim of terrorists.[41]

Beginning with Richard M. Nixon, succeeding presidents have watched with paralyzed astonishment and anger as Greek leaders have cozied up to terrorists, hoping that by so doing they will curry favor in the Arab world and somehow exploit that against the interests and plans of Turkey.[42]

Because the United States has not wished to offend Greece, whose ports serve as important bases for the U.S. Navy's mission in the Mediterranean Sea, it has been regarded by Democratic and Republican presidents as politically unwise to put great pressure on Athens to change its behavior. There has been the additional strategic concern that Greece might walk away from NATO and become neutral, with leanings more toward Moscow than Washington.

Driven by those worries, American policymakers chose a path of avoiding confrontation, which seemed—on the surface, anyway—to be less risky to U.S. interests. Only the most egregious and embarrassing incidents smoked out American outrage. In 1985 the State Department told American travelers to stay away from the Athens airport because its poor security had played a major role in the hijacking of a TWA jet. The "Travel Advisory" was withdrawn in a matter of days after improved antiterrorism measures were implemented. But Greece had previously violated Western antiterrorism efforts time and time again and did so after the "Travel Advisory" was called off, and Washington remained silent for almost all of it and never took tough action to force major changes in Greek behavior.

The net effect of this fearful policy has been to encourage terrorists from the Middle East to use Greece as a common transit point en route to targets in Western Europe. Meanwhile, their homegrown ideological comrades have used Athens as a killing ground for American embassy military attachés and other military personnel.[43] Greece drives professional antiterrorists at the U.S. Departments of State and Defense into a fury. While they know it will do little good, these analysts and policymakers will, when sufficiently provoked, push the administration to temporarily put some heat on Greece, in hopes of limiting the extent to which terrorism is encouraged. Recent instances of Greek complicity with terrorism are highly instructive of the way in which pandering to terrorists serves only to further spread their activity, not limit it.

Washington officially objected in public when, shortly before Christmas in 1988, Athens rejected the Italian government's formal extradition request for Abdel Asama al-Zomar, an Abu Nidal terrorist. Mr. Zomar is charged with the 1982 hand grenade and machine gun attack on a Jewish temple in Rome. The unprovoked assault killed a two-year-old child and wounded thirty-seven other people. Instead of fulfilling its treaty obligation to hand over the accused murderer, the Justice Minister of Greece released Mr. Zomar and put him aboard a jet bound "for the country of his choice." No surprises here; next stop: Tripoli, Libya, headquarters of the Abu Nidal Organization.[44]

Justice Minister Vasilis Rotis declared his rationale for freeing the terrorist: "The actions for which he was being accused fall within the domain of the struggle to regain the independence of his homeland [Palestine] and thus suggest action for freedom."[45] One need not be a diplomat to realize that, with those words, the senior Greek official sanctioned any act of terror which the perpetrator may feel is "action for freedom," including murdering babies. Rotis cited the PLO's declaration of an independent Palestinian state and its disavowal of terrorism as additional authority for his decision to free the Abu Nidal hitman. Perhaps the Greek Government forgot that ANO has sworn to kill PLO Chairman Arafat and has already murdered several of Arafat's lieutenants, especially those who were attempting to initiate peace talks with Israelis.[46]

The Peace Killers

Radical Palestinian terrorist organizations are attempting to create a climate hostile to the Middle East peace process. The Popular Front for the Liberation of Palestine–General Command is among them. It is the organization that, the CIA believes, provided at least the technical expertise behind the bombing of Pan Am Flight 103 on orders from Iran. While the motivation for that bombing may have had more to do with the conflict between the United States and Iran, there is no question that the destruction of the Pan Am jumbo jet heated up the political environment.

Usually sponsored by Syria, its host, and Libya, the PFLP–GC has an estimated five hundred members and a reputation as an innovator in the tactics and technologies of terrorism. Shock is a part of all successful terrorist attacks, but the PFLP–GC has also achieved noteworthy status in this area. This is the same organization that was responsible for the massacre of 18 unarmed people at an apartment house in Qiryat Shemona, Israel, in 1974. The PFLP–GC surprised intelligence experts, who thought it was dormant, by capturing 3 Israeli soldiers in Lebanon in 1982 and trading them for 1,150 Palestinians captured by Israel. That disproportionate swap demonstrated how well the terrorist organization understands the psyche of its enemy, whose exploitable weakness is its high value on the life of each one of its citizens.

The PFLP–GC has access to a wide range of sophisticated armaments, including Soviet-manufactured shoulder-fired antiaircraft missiles. But it has not brought down any planes with missiles.

Ahmad Jibril, the technologically savvy leader of the Popular Front for the Liberation of Palestine–General Command, crafted the first terrorist-deployed altimeter-controlled bomb. It blew a Swissair jet out of the sky over Zurich on February 21, 1970, slaughtering 47 people, including 6 Americans and 12 Israelis. PFLP–GC Commander Jibril was only twenty-five years old when his sophisticated bomb, which was hidden in a checked luggage bag, dropped the airliner from fourteen thousand feet into a forest near the town of Wurenlingen only minutes after a normal takeoff. One of Jibril's spokesmen quickly claimed responsibility for the mass murder but after the civilized world recoiled in revulsion, the PFLP–GC denied it was their bomb. (A similar denial was issued after Flight 103 went down; although the group had not claimed responsibility, Israel had accused Jibril.)

Three months after the PFLP–GC detonated its bomb aboard Swissair Flight 330 in 1970, members of the gang sneaked from Lebanon into the Galilee. They crawled five hundred yards to cover along the side of a road, waited patiently until an Israeli school bus arrived on its regular schedule, and opened fire with bazooka rocket shells. Twelve Jewish children were killed, another twenty-two were wounded.

In November 1987, six Israeli soldiers were killed and seven others wounded by a single follower of Ahmad Jibril who escaped detection by flying into Israel from Lebanon on a powered *hang-glider*. The lone gunman's surprise assault on an Israeli Defense Forces camp cost him his life, but it also established the PFLP–GC as a Palestinian guerrilla unit unafraid of taking on Israeli troops as well as civilians. The hang-glider attack came as a small shock to Israel and as a signal to Palestinians that the Israelis are not invincible. Exactly two weeks later, the Intifada broke out in the occupied territories. Although the fuel for the revolt was obviously in place, this may have been a historic case in which an act of terrorism sparked the massive rebellion that cost Israel dearly—in the enormous drain on resources needed to contain the uprising, in the serious damage to its national image, and the fear of random violence it created—resulting in the short-term collapse of tourism with its vital flow of foreign currency.

Mr. Jibril and other terrorist leaders are intelligent people. They read the international press and assess carefully the impact of their acts. If the Intifada and the U.S.–PLO–Soviet–Israeli dialogues fail to produce an acceptable deal on Palestinian statehood, Jibril or another of his antipeace colleagues may come to see as their next step, an escalation of tactics and weaponry including instruments of super-violence. An alternative, perhaps even more depressing scenario, suggests they may choose that path if a settlement *is* at hand. Their business, after all, is murder; their ideology is so extreme that no negotiated deal with Israel is acceptable to them. They are emotionally stuck in 1948; their cry remains, "Drive the Jews into the sea." In the absence of Israeli surrender, the radical Palestinians must be counted on for more and possibly worse kinds of terrorism.

Terrorism is the tool that opponents of the Middle East peace process will continue to use to disrupt the fragile efforts to make peace between Israel and the Palestinians. While Palestine Liberation Organization Chairman Yasir Arafat attempted to maintain his compliance with the U.S. conditions for dialogue with the PLO, at least three Arab nations and nine radical Palestinian groups, as well as Iran, through Hizballah, tried to wreck the atmosphere for peace talks.

In the summer of 1988, Arafat's senior advisors were signaling that the chairman was about to recognize Israel's right to exist within secure borders and renounce terrorism so as to draw the United States back into the arena as an active participant. Without American involvement, Arafat knew, there was no hope of getting the Israelis to negotiate.

In the fall of 1988, several developments were on track simultaneously: the uprising in the occupied territories was successfully drawing Israeli soldiers into the role of brutal occupiers, and the Jewish State was suffering the condemnation of much of the world as a result; Arafat and some of his intimates were staking out increasingly conciliatory positions, setting the stage for a Palestine National Council meeting that promised a breakthrough; in Israel, the coalition government of Yitzhak Shamir's Likud bloc and the Labor Party, led by

Shimon Peres, was coming apart, with new elections in the offing. If Peres won, there would be a chance for both an international peace conference with Soviet participation and indirect talks with American mediation, perhaps leading toward meetings on the style of the Camp David talks that crafted the Egypt–Israel peace treaty. Most of all, Peres favored trading land for peace with the Palestinians; Shamir opposed it.

As the election campaign moved toward its climax, some of those who would kill the peace process staged an act of violent propaganda.

In the heavily guarded security zone that stretches across Israel's border with Lebanon, a lone motorist raced around a bend, aimed his car at a group of occupied Israeli vehicles, and put his foot down to the floor. The explosion that followed was so powerful that pieces of the killer's automobile became fused with the Israeli jeeps it hit. Seconds later, amid the shock, screaming, and confusion, it became apparent that eight young Israeli soldiers had literally been blown up. Only parts of their bodies would ever be recovered. In the days that followed, their comrades in the Israeli Air Force would rage across the sky of Lebanon, exacting a price in Shiite Moslem blood, and a communiqué from Hizballah would announce that the car bombing had been "a gift" to the Intifada.[47]

Was this "gift" really wanted by the Palestinians? Many of them had worked to keep a low profile in hopes of helping Peres win and giving peace a chance. So, instead of a "gift" to the Palestinians, the bombing seems to have been a calculated assault on their interests. Its political impact could not be directly determined, but there is no question that it contributed to the hardening of attitudes among Jews who had been undecided about supporting Peres and his peace plank and wound up voting for Shamir and his rejection of any land-for-peace negotiations.

That is how Iran meddled in Israeli politics to help defeat a peacemaker. Five years earlier, the Ayatollah used Hizballah terror to savage peace hopes for the Middle East by driving American Marines out of Lebanon. It wasn't until 1988 that the United States got back into the business of promoting peace in the region.

By mid-February of 1989, less than two months into its tentative conversations with the PLO, the U.S. State Department was putting heavy pressure on Arafat to do something about other Palestinian leaders who continued to launch terrorist attacks into Israel. In each case, the attackers were gunned down by the Israeli Army and the Lebanese Christian militia it supports. As in the case of that Shiite car bomber's suicide mission, the Israeli Air Force flew retaliatory air raids against the bases in Lebanon from which the missions began. Along with terrorists and their facilities, the bombs also killed or wounded innocent bystanders. Although there were no terrorist successes, the incidents were ammunition for those in Israel who claimed that Arafat could not be trusted. They accused the American government of naïveté and creating unreasonable expectations. The delicate dialogue between the United States and the PLO, the first such formal talks in fourteen years, was under acute stress and threatening to come undone.

Working to smash it completely from his headquarters in Damascus was Naif Hawatmeh, leader of the Marxist–Leninist terrorist organization called the Democratic Front for the Liberation of Palestine. Hawatmeh and Arafat have sharply different views on how to reach the same goal.

Hawatmeh holds that the nation of Palestine cannot come into being unless there is first a revolutionary change in the Arab world. The doctrine of his extremely independent terrorist organization calls for the overthrow of the conservative Arab monarchies (Jordan, Saudi Arabia, Morocco, Kuwait, Qatar, Dubai) as a necessary step on the way to Palestinian statehood.[48] The monarchies Hawatmeh wants to help overthrow, through a Bolshevik-style revolution, happen to be among Arafat's most important diplomatic and financial supporters.

That is the backdrop to Hawatmeh's attempt to throttle the peace process. During the first three months of the PLO–U.S. dialogue, he repeatedly sent small units of DFLP terrorists on infiltration missions, knowing that the odds against their military success were enormous. In fact, in each case, the terrorists were wiped out by aggressive Israeli and Christian militia patrols, assisted by the world's most sophisticated high-technology motion- and sound-sensing devices. The young Palestinians who perished in these incidents appear to have been duped by Hawatmeh. He knew that getting through the security zone was close to impossible. But the DFLP leader had another political agenda in mind. He was out to disconnect Arafat from the Bush administration.

Speaking from his office in the Syrian capital, where only President Assad's friends are welcome, Hawatmeh declared his organization (estimated strength: five hundred) will not be bound by Arafat's promise of no terrorism. The head of the Democratic Front for the Liberation of Palestine also insisted that he would brook no criticism from the United States.

Despite the fact that his military moves met with defeat, they were having the political effect for which they were apparently designed. After the third attack by Hawatmeh's men, the U.S. State Department publicly questioned Arafat's capacity to deliver on anything if he cannot stop dissident Palestinian factors from engaging in terrorism. "If the PLO cannot or will not exercise such control, it raises questions concerning the commitment undertaken in the name of the PLO—indeed, questions about the PLO's ability to carry out its commitments," warned Charles Redman, Assistant Secretary of State.

If Arafat wants to keep his dialogue with the United States alive, he might attempt to silence the guns of his political opponents within the diverse and often fratricidal Palestinian movement. To accomplish that, Arafat might have to resort to intra-Palestinian terror. But even if he had the will to conduct such operations, they would pose formidable, perhaps insurmountable, tactical challenges. Hated by Syria's President Hafez al-Assad, who is one reason Arafat must have elaborate personal security, the PLO has little or no infrastructure in Damascus. Getting a commando unit in and out of Hawatmeh's office or home might be impossible. Even on the off chance that Arafat's men were to succeed in killing the DFLP leader, Hawatmeh's principal deputy, Abed Rabbu, would probably pick up the same antipeace strategy.

The Bloody Guru

The Sikh Dashmesh Regiment was the first group to blow a jumbo jet out of the sky. That watershed in modern terrorism was reached June 23, 1985, when Air India Flight 182, a Boeing 747 carrying 329 passengers and crew from London to Montreal, suddenly disappeared from the air traffic controller's radar screen about 110 miles west of

Cork, Ireland, over the ocean. That same day, one hour earlier, at Tokyo's Narita International Airport, a suitcase being transferred from a Canadian airliner to another Air India flight exploded, killing 2 baggage handlers. It too was apparently supposed to go off over the ocean, leaving not a trace of another Air India jumbo jet. Both bombs were said by intelligence sources to be the work of Dashmesh, founded by the most charismatic and arguably most dangerous religious figure India has seen in many years.

Jarnail Singh Bhindranwale was born in 1947 to a family of poor farmers in the state of Punjab. Trained to lead a spiritual life of calm and meditation, he became a great firebrand of the rebellion by militant members of the Sikh religious community of India, which continues today. Hailed by his most devoted disciples as the first great guru in more than two centuries, he preached a message of fundamentalism and violence and lived as though he were destined for martyrdom.[49]

There will be "no deliverance without weapons," he warned his followers as they raised their voices and their guns in pursuit of carving their own nation out of the richest land in India. Guru Bhindranwale always travelled heavily armed. He once declared, "There is no greater sin for a Sikh than having weapons and not using them to protect his faith," which he felt to be under attack at all times by the Hindu majority. In his fanatical drive to force India to release the Punjab so Sikhs could establish their own nation, to be called Khalistan, the guru personally led a modern-day reign of terror in the early 1980s. By 1984, Prime Minister Indira Gandhi had become frustrated, since negotiations with Sikh leaders were going nowhere. She could no longer tolerate the civil disorder and loss of life triggered by Dashmesh and other Sikh terrorist units. After appealing to Bhindranwale to stop, she received reports of widening troubles. Mrs. Gandhi ordered the Indian Army to enter the holiest Sikh shrine, the Golden Temple, remove its stockpile of guns and break the terrifying grip Sikh extremists had on the Punjab. The action became a shootout; the Army won and, by most accounts, did it by killing everyone in sight, including Bhindranwale, martyring him to the cause and satisfying his previously declared intent: "When the struggle reaches the decisive phase, may I die fighting in its midst."[50]

Unlike the bloody guru, Prime Minister Gandhi sought no martyrdom, but she felt it was important for Indians to see she still trusted her Sikh bodyguards. So she entrusted her security to them. It was her

last mistake. They assassinated her, touching off a wave of anti-Sikh
rioting across India. Hundreds were killed, thousands injured, and
hundreds of millions were left fearing, afraid that their country's democracy was in serious danger of being swept aside in a flood of
religious violence.

Defeated militarily, Sikh extremists targeted Air India worldwide,
bringing down Flight 182. They failed to destroy the jumbo jet scheduled for takeoff from Tokyo, only because the bomb went off prema-
turely. Sikh terrorists include a number of highly educated people—
among them, retired Indian Army generals and scientists. Their intel-
lects, combined with their fanatical loathing of the Indian government and devotion to Bhindranwale's utopian dream of establishing a
nation where Sikhs can live a life of piety, make them extremely
dangerous.

Almost a year after they murdered the more than three hundred
people aboard the flight from London, Sikh terrorists based in Canada
were plotting to do it again. Intelligence information acquired by the
Royal Canadian Mounted Police set off alarms in Ottawa and Washington. Informants told the Mounties of a plan to blow up an Air
India facility or aircraft—either in Canada or at Kennedy International Airport in New York. The FBI and the RCMP pinpointed five
Canadian resident Sikhs and determined that they were in the process
of making a bomb to put aboard an Air India 747. All five were
arrested and convicted.[51]

There is little doubt that Sikh terrorists will persist in their revenge against India, and that anyone who happens to be in the wrong
place at the wrong time will be in mortal danger. As with other frustrated terrorist organizations, there is some reason to expect an escalation of tactics, since what they have done and been caught trying to
do has had no positive impact on their cause. Internal documents of
the World Sikh Organization headquartered in Ottawa indicate that
Sikhs who reside in the United States as well as in Canada have been
involved in secret military planning for the secession of Punjab (Khalistan).[52] It is clear that Sikhs in Canada and the United States have
the capacity to mount almost any kind of operation they choose to in
North America. That poses the need for careful, ongoing surveillance
by both the FBI and the Mounties' antiterrorism unit.

Making It Easy for Them

Sloppy, inconsistent, undertrained, overstressed, and poorly managed antiterrorism programs in the United States and Western Europe virtually conspire to make it easy for bright, patient terrorists to succeed. To better understand what the security people begin with as the real challenge, suffer for the moment the cliché excuse offered to inexperienced reporters by prison wardens embarrassed by a fresh jailbreak. "We've got only so many guards and they've got to watch all these inmates while, at the same time, they've got ordinary family problems on their minds, too. But inmates, they've got nothing but time, twenty-four hours a day, to figure out just one thing: how to break out of here. That's what we're up against."

While the warden's complaint is a fair one, it is no excuse for failing to think ahead of the determined convict. So it is with terrorists and antiterrorists. The antiterrorist knows the terrorist wants to strike. His mission is to make the task of successfully assaulting the target so difficult that the terrorist decides against attacking or is detected and defeated when he does. In the contemporary setting, that means putting imaginative security in place, then testing it and retesting it from different approaches and with no warning. Only then will the defending forces be able to maximize their effectiveness while reducing that of any would-be attacker.

After the loss to terrorist attack of Pan Am Flight 103, investigators determined that the high-tech barometric fused bomb was originally loaded aboard the plane in Frankfurt, West Germany. Following the short trip to London, the Frankfurt baggage was moved routinely to a jumbo jet for the trip from London across the Atlantic. If there had been a comprehensive security "system" in operation at Frankfurt Airport, that bomb probably would have been discovered before it got anywhere near a plane. But the "system" is not a unity—rather a collection of uncoordinated authorities, including the airlines.

Contrary to its reputation as one of the best antiterrorist airports in Western Europe, security at Frankfurt suffers from a fault that may have contributed to the attack on Pan Am Flight 103. Long identified as a key transit point for Middle Eastern terrorists, as well as for members of West Germany's homegrown Red Army Faction and Revolutionary Cells, Frankfurt International's antiterrorists are well armed, but their capacity to discern and act against terrorists who pass before them is unreliable. Despite requests for resources necessary to test and refresh the counterterrorist training of the airport police, the government has refused to provide the funds.[53]

The airport police are the first line of defense against terrorists— before they get to the security area, which is run by Pan Am and the other airlines. From the moment anyone enters the passenger terminal, he or she is supposed to come under the immediate and skilled scrutiny of police trained in antiterrorism at the Policy Academy in Hesse. That curriculum is taught by one of the most experienced experts in the field, Klaus Eberhard Theussen, director of the police psychology department. By 1989, Theussen had spent twenty years studying the evolving terrorist threat and had adapted the training of his men to meet it. But during an interview in his sparse office at the Policy Academy before the Flight 103 bombing, he complained that he had been denied the budget necessary to test the level of alertness of the airport police as well as their retention of the terrorist identification profile in which he schools each new cadet.

Theussen could not, in good conscience, be satisfied with the capacity of the airport police to detect and move against potential terrorists. He said, "This is one of our biggest problems. I have neither the money nor the manpower nor the time to run the tests needed to make sure our people are prepared to spot them; and, without this, I cannot say how well they will do [if terrorists walk into Frankfurt International Airport]. I have asked for the resources, but it is very difficult."

Sadly, this is the way it is almost everywhere in Western Europe, as well as in the United States. The hands-on experts generally know what is needed, ask repeatedly, but not so loudly as to get marked as troublemakers, not so aggressively as to risk promotion. Vindication for these analysts comes only when their grim predictions and warnings go unheeded long enough for opportunistic terrorists to strike.

"After there is an incident or attack," the West German police psychologist said, "then the government officials say, 'There must be something done'—*then* they give money. But it goes the wrong way.

It goes to the wrong place. The money goes to more helicopters and more water cannons, not to more effective training."

From perimeters to innermost areas, security at airports in the Western world is generally awful. All kinds of people routinely get around security systems without being checked. Among them are food and service suppliers, as well as duty-free shop personnel. Intelligence sources have asserted that some duty-free shop owners may be connected to terrorist organizations. If so, the duty-free shops, which hand over bags filled with purchases only at planeside, could provide weapons to terrorists as they board flights.[54]

Moreover, security people at airports often earn less than street sweepers. Their initially thin training is rarely refreshed; their tasks, though vital, are repetitive, boring, routine—the kind of work that can quickly produce a glazed-over consciousness. The men and women whose job it is to stare into those X-ray machines that scan carry-on bags should never be asked to perform this operation for more than half an hour without a break. At many airports, the X-ray machine operators work much longer periods and so invite error and disaster.[55]

Security consultant Noel Koch tells the story of the airline security chief who wanted to remove some of the physical stress from his X-ray machine operators. The security man asked that comfortable metal stools be purchased for the operators. Not only would that make his people more comfortable, he reasoned, but it would also make them more efficient. The request for stools was bucked all the way up the corporate ladder, because it would have meant an expense of hundreds of thousands of dollars worldwide. "No" was the answer from the airline's chairman of the board. Too expensive. What the chairman might as well have said is, "Let 'em stand, let 'em fidget, let 'em lose their concentration on that screen."[56] Though in itself seemingly trivial, this story is repeated in every aspect of security.

Not only have some airlines pumped up their profits by underfunding security, others have used their security "image" to help sell the public on flying with them.

Pan Am, the airline whose security measures failed catastrophically for the victims of Flight 103, used to advertise its antiterrorist measures, and even made its customers pay extra for the additional security. The company announced in June 1986 that it had formed what it termed "an elite, highly visible security force to protect passengers and crew." A five-dollar security surcharge was tacked onto

the ticket price of each Pan Am overseas passenger. It is unclear what
—if anything—the customers got for their money.

By the end of 1986, Pan Am's top corporate officers had received a
two-hundred-page report from a consulting team led by Isaac Yeffet.
The KPI Inc. study told the airline its security was broken and how to
fix it.

"Unfortunately," Yeffet said in an interview, "the man in charge
who ordered the study had been replaced, and the new [Pan Am]
chairman was much more interested in financial matters than security."

Yeffet insists that the price tag for implementing the recommendations would have been more like seven dollars and fifty cents per
occupied seat. Had those proposals been followed, Yeffet believes
three things would have happened:

- Pan Am's facilities worldwide would have become much more
  secure in less than a month
- Pan Am's insurance rates would have dropped because of the
  sharp improvement in security
- Flight 103 could not have been the victim of a bomb

Mr. Yeffet is all but certain to be called into court to say these
things and more, under oath, as liability litigation over the loss of
Flight 103 gets under way. Under the provisions of the international
civil aviation treaty called the Warsaw Convention, the air carrier's
liability is limited to seventy-five thousand dollars per passenger. However, that limitation does not apply if, in the language of the law,
"willful misconduct" can be proved on the part of the airline in question. In the event that a court finds Pan Am acted irresponsibly, the
sky will be the limit on how much the airline may be forced to pay the
survivors of the terrorist attack that killed 270 passengers, crew, and
innocent bystanders on the ground at Lockerbie.

While Pan Am may yell foul because terrorism is a global menace
aimed *at* governments *through* airlines, in democracies, concerns over
money seem to produce the quickest changes in policy and performance. Fear of massive dollar losses because of weak security might be
the only hope for encouraging the implementation of comprehensive
and aggressive antiterrorist measures. Most governments, unfortu-

nately, act as though they were powerless to require such safeguards. Without them in place, you are unnecessarily exposed to loss of life, limb, and freedom; without them, you are a much more likely candidate for becoming a victim of terrorism.

As the threat of terrorist attacks expands, little comfort can be taken from past performance by the Federal Aviation Administration. Based on an analysis of FAA security bulletins written from mid-November 1988 up until three days before Flight 103 detonated over Lockerbie, congressional investigators called the bulletins "sometimes untimely, sometimes dangerously inaccurate, and almost completely devoid of effective instructions for countering possible threats." Some bulletins recommended actions that were pointless or even absurd. Taken as a group, the FAA bulletins (which are issued to airlines and on which they must rely) failed to provide meaningful guidance to airlines faced with the risk of terrorist attack.

For example:

- *Bulletin 19,* describing a radio-cassette player containing a hard-to-detect bomb designed to blow up an aircraft, was written November 17, *three weeks* after the device was discovered when West German police arrested members of the Popular Front for the Liberation of Palestine–General Command.

- That bulletin mistakenly advised that the PFLP–GC "has not been known to undertake terrorist attacks in Europe." According to the Defense Department's recent study, *Terrorist Group Profiles,* the PFLP–GC had machine-gunned an airliner in Zurich, hijacked two other airliners bound for European cities, and, in 1986, warned that "there will be no safety for any traveler on . . . [a] U.S. airliner."

- *Bulletin 19* followed two earlier bulletins (17 and 18) describing the PFLP–GC arrests. *Bulletin 18,* written more than a week after the raids, does not mention the radio-cassette player bomb. Instead, it merely directed airline security personnel to set up a system to pass along specific threat information "extremely quickly." Although *Bulletin 18* noted the seizure of PFLP–GC "explosives," it focused entirely on the possibility that a U.S. airliner would be *hijacked.* Bombing was not mentioned as a possible or probable terrorist act.

- *Bulletin 20,* dated December 5, warned that "the use of IEDs [improvised explosive devices] or bombs remains a favored method of attack." But FAA did not recommend any action to airlines beyond requiring them to "rigorously" apply existing, and we now know inadequate, security measures.

- *Bulletin 21,* dated December 7, described "two incidents that may indicate attempts to test security procedures of a U.S. carrier operating from Frankfurt." One involved a man (who fraudulently claimed to be a law enforcement officer) questioning a TWA ticket clerk about procedures for transporting pistols, explosives, and a detonator. Apparently, no attempt was made to detain and question him. The FAA's sole response to this episode was to disseminate *Bulletin 21.*

- *Bulletin 22,* written on December 7 and describing the December 5 Helsinki embassy warning, was never updated nor rescinded, although numerous federal officials now claim the telephone call describing a planned bombing attack on a Pan Am flight from Frankfurt was a hoax and a coincidence.

- *Bulletin 25,* dated three days after the Pan Am bombing, listed thirteen individuals suspected of planning a hijacking. The FAA advised air carriers that, if a passenger with one of these names attempts to board an airliner, *"the individual should be subjected to intense scrutiny during the check-in process."* Inexplicably, the FAA did not recommend summoning law enforcement officials or denying boarding.

It is not just aviation security that fails to meet the challenges of terrorism. It is the underlying mentality of "Business as usual" in virtually all existing antiterrorist programs that makes so much so vulnerable.

Inside America

Tightly organized ultraright-wing, heavily armed fundamentalist Christian bigots constitute the single biggest domestic terrorist threat to the security of the United States.[57] They far outnumber and out-gun the remnants of leftist terrorists still hanging on since the end of the Vietnam War. Unlike the seminihilistic, Communist-supporting, white-elite-dominated terror groups such as the defunct Weather Underground, the right-wing organizations are growing, thanks to recruitment in prisons of young, mostly working-class skinheads, whose ideology is roughly made up of slogans such as "America for White People," as well as denunciations of blacks, Jews, gays, and lesbians. The old Ku Klux Klan is their true lineage. Their acts include bank and armored-car robberies and a demonstrated willingness to kill law enforcement officers.

Of all the right-wing groups that are active inside the United States, the most dangerous is the Aryan Nations, which declares itself to be a defender of white people and white values. Aryan Nations' policy calls for the elimination of Jews and blacks from American society. During the early 1980s, a covert unit of the Aryan Nations was created to act as its enforcer, bomber, and hitman. That special unit is called the Order of Bruders Schweign, "The Silent Brotherhood." Similar organizations worthy of special attention are The Covenant, The Sword, the Arm of the Lord, and The Sheriff's Posse Comitatus, which has nothing to do with any genuine sheriff. Besides voicing the same old Klan hatreds, these groups have opened fire on police and federal agents, resulting in the murder of two law enforcement officers. Ultraright-wing, white supremacist groups have been involved in other murders, including that of Denver radio talk show host Alan Berg, whom they had vowed to silence.

FBI agents did arrest the main leaders of these groups, but some will soon complete their prison sentences and find that their organizations are still there, waiting for them. The leaders, in many cases, are former military officers and ministers with an unusual, some say distorted, interpretation of the gospels. The Midwest, Far West, and Southwest are home base for these groups.

These fascist elements in American society are predominantly working-class, poorly educated, and angry. They seek a new insularity, a retreat from the incipient chaos and social flux that mark society. In their pursuit of this utopian environment, recruits will find themselves drawn into, or forced to participate in, terrorist acts in defense of their group, which casts the outside world as inherently hostile and evil. Their violence, unlike the message-is-for-the-media terrorism of the political left, is not designed for a mass audience. Robberies are done to finance the work of the movement; killings are assassinations of people who get in the way of the spreading of their message. Like so many other religion-based terrorist communities, they regard themselves as above the laws of the state, which they view as illegitimate at its core.[58]

"They have no compunction about using violence," said FBI Executive Assistant Director Revell, as he reviewed the recent past of the ultraright terrorist groups.

Would these organizations escalate their tactics to include chemical and other weapons of super-violence? One law enforcement raid on a neofascist group netted a drum of cyanide—enough to poison thousands of people.

An Army of Terrorists in the Philippines

The struggle between terrorism and democracy in the Philippines is a clear example of how large organizations can employ terrorist tactics because they are the most effective and efficient means of accomplishing their mission. The twenty-thousand-member New People's Army,[59] a growing Maoist guerrilla force, is dedicated to overthrowing the elected government. It is so powerful that its units occasionally set ambushes of police or military patrols. Through the use of assassinations, NPA terrorists have spread fear in many rural areas. Over a seven-year period, ending in 1985, they killed at least half a dozen mayors, several senior police commanders, and the son of the then-commanding general of the Philippines Army. The strategic interests of the United States are at stake in the struggle between the Communists and the democratically elected government. The largest American military bases outside the United States are in the Philippines—the Air Force's Clark Field and the Navy's base at Subic Bay. They are vital support elements for American forces in the Pacific and the Indian Ocean.

In 1974 three U.S. Navy men were murdered by the NPA; two others were killed by the terrorists in 1987, along with an American retiree. In both of these cases, the victims lost their lives because of what they symbolized to their killers: the United States Government.

On April 21, 1989, the terrorists targeted an American official—Colonel Nick Rowe, the U.S. military advisor to President Aquino's counterterrorism forces. A Vietnam War hero who refused to be broken by his North Vietnamese torturers during more than five years of captivity, Rowe's dramatic background and fame made him a target of especially important symbolic value. The NPA murder of the American colonel was powerful propaganda. It sent the message that no one in the Philippines is safe from the terror of the New People's Army. That is bound to further weaken the Aquino government and additionally empower the NPA and its political wing, the Communist Party of the Philippines. They are certain to draw strength from the symbolic defeat of American power embodied in the assassination of Nick Rowe.

Euro-Terror

Nihilistic, mostly leftist terrorist groups that dominated the headlines in France, Italy, West Germany, and Belgium for most of the 1970s and early 1980s have never recovered from their own failure to win popular support and the effective action taken against them by counterterrorist police and intelligence agencies.

While there were 150 international terrorist incidents in Western Europe in 1988, only 81 were conducted by Europeans against other Europeans. Unlike the situation a decade before, there was never the feeling in the air that terrorists might shatter democracy itself in Europe. In fact, at no point in 1988 was the orderly process of government disrupted. But that does not mean the terrorists still around did not try.

On April 16, terrorists assassinated a member of the Italian Senate, Roberto Ruffilli, in his home. On September 20, terrorists in West Germany failed in their plot to kill a senior Finance Ministry official who was involved in setting up a major banking conference in Berlin.

Almost half of all international terrorist incidents reported in

Western Europe are what State Department analysts label Middle East "spillovers." That major category includes the Abu Nidal assault on the Greek ferry and other, less spectacular attacks.[60] The incidents relating to the Arab–Israeli conflict and other Mideastern and African disputes merely used Europe as a battleground or staging area. They were not targeted on the European governments.

The great danger of terrorism in Western Europe committed by Europeans is that for so long there has been virtually nothing major to capture the imaginations of the public or the police. While that is good news, it creates a situation in which officials may become blasé and miss the next phase until it is up and running hard, out of control. Big-name groups like the Red Army Faction (West Germany), Direct Action (France), and Red Brigades (Italy) are mostly dormant. But some of them committed minor terrorist acts during 1988 and still deserve to be watched closely.

Meanwhile, U.S. military personnel and their families in Western Europe remain at high risk because they are such obvious and easy targets. Little or no security considerations go into the housing of these service people, which means anyone who wants to can take a couple of shots at, or plant a bomb close to, the family of an American soldier. Those U.S. dependents, like their military fathers and mothers, will be easy targets for European or visiting Middle Eastern terrorists looking for soft, undefended pieces of America to hit.[61]

PIRA

The Provisional Irish Republican Army has carried its high-casualty approach to terrorism into central Europe, gunning for off-duty, preferably drunk, or, better yet, sleeping members of the British military. In 1988 Irish terrorists opened fire on unsuspecting young Royal Air Force enlisted men as they walked out of a bar in Roermond, the Netherlands. On the same May day, in Holland, a PIRA car bomb tore apart a vehicle in which two other British military men were driving. In the two incidents, two people were killed, another wounded. In July of 1988, PIRA struck again—this time in West

Germany, blowing the roof off a British Army barracks and wounding nine men. The same tactics were employed against a pair of residential buildings at military bases in England, where the intent was clearly mass murder.

British security experts do not believe PIRA will go chemical or biological because the organization has a pro-environmentalism position.[62] That is pretty thin logic. PIRA is a violent Marxist terror gang that claims to be dedicated to driving the "Brits Out!"

Hopefully, the Crown's antiterrorists are correct in assuming that cultural and political inhibitors will proscribe any PIRA entry into the mass killing arena. Nevertheless, some officials do fear that the Provisional IRA's good friend and weapons supplier, Muammar al-Qaddafi, may choose to provide lethal chemicals to the Irish terrorists. For that and other reasons, British Intelligence tries to maintain a careful watch on the Libya–PIRA connection. In the past, however, that vigilance has failed to get in the way of several boatloads of conventional weapons believed to include shoulder-fired surface-to-air missiles manufactured in the Soviet Union and supplied by Moscow to Qaddafi over many years. Thus far, PIRA has not used any of the SAMs in its arsenal. But it has used plenty of Qaddafi's explosives. It has become expert in building bombs that can be set to explode in *days* rather than hours. The PIRA placed such a bomb in their 1985 attempt on Prime Minister Thatcher.

Libyan arms may have been used by the PIRA unit that attacked a receiving station for North Sea oil. The assault failed to do any serious harm, but it demonstrated that Irish terrorists have an appetite for striking at Britain's infrastructure in a way that—if successful—could damage the quality of life of millions of ordinary citizens and result in many deaths.

As a result of the FBI's increasing effectiveness against PIRA conspirators in the United States and cooperation with British police, there is concern at the Bureau for the safety of agents who become identified publicly with PIRA investigations. The feeling is that PIRA is not beyond attempting assassinations of FBI agents to punish the U.S. Government for joining in the effort to stop Irish terrorism.[63] The FBI should assume the worst from the Provisional Irish Republican Army and plan for it.

The ETA

In Spain, the one hundred to two hundred Basque separatists who belong to the gang called ETA (Basque Fatherland and Liberty) are continuing to bomb, kidnap, and assassinate Spanish Government officials; some French targets in Spain have also been hit in apparent revenge for French cooperation with Spanish National Police. There have been a few clandestine cross-border assaults by these killers inside French territory. American intelligence analysts call the ETA bombing attacks sophisticated, lethal, and increasingly indiscriminate. As allied cooperation mounts, ETA can be expected to target U.S. interests in Spain, especially around U.S. military bases. While this terrorist group has not really gone international, some of its members have received training in Libya, Nicaragua, and Lebanon. Along with sporadic attacks on U.S.–NATO fuel pipelines, this is one terrorist group that has shown an innovative approach to attacking the infrastructure: it assassinated two engineers who were responsible for the construction of a nuclear power plant. That was a bizarre attempt at seizing the popular "high ground" in the nuclear power debate in Spain.[64]

Latin America

Half a world away, a virulently anti-American, anti-Western terrorism organization called *Sendero Luminoso* (The Shining Path) has been conducting a campaign of political murder and infrastructure sabotage which has repeatedly blacked out whole sections of the nation, including the capital of Peru, Lima. While the rest of the Communist world, including China, has dropped Chairman Mao's teachings, the *guerrilleros* of the Shining Path cling to Mao's philosophy and practice of making revolution. Since Shining Path began its terror campaign, a staggering twelve thousand people have been killed by the terrorists and counterattacking government forces. Shining Path sabotage and murder have helped push Peru's fragile democracy close to disintegration and cost an estimated ten billion dollars in material losses. While the United States is not a primary target, several American facilities in and around Lima have been hit since the terrorists of this gang joined forces with cocaine traffickers in 1987.[65] More assaults on Americans and their properties should be anticipated, since the Senderos have twin motives: ideology—force the Yanquis out—and greed, now that they are on the payroll of the cocaine lords. Would these unusual Andean terrorists resort to weapons of mass killing? Their very strict adherence to Maoist thought suggests they would use whatever means came into their grasp to damage their enemies. According to the ideology revered by the terrorists of the Shining Path, the preachments of Mao: "I shall oppose what my enemy supports and support what my enemy opposes" and "Power flows from the barrel of a gun" or, perhaps, a chemical weapon, a biological agent, a radiological source.

In Colombia, local terrorists are already making good on the predictions by the CIA[66] that there will be a growing number of attacks against U.S. interests in the Third World. By the end of 1988, about half of all anti-U.S. terrorist actions worldwide had been carried out in Latin America, by groups like the National Liberation Army of Colombia, with membership estimated at under a thousand. Unlike most terrorist organizations in Europe, the Middle East, or the United States, ELN (its initials in Spanish) is big and diverse enough in its broad-based membership to function as a "full-service" institution, performing the whole gamut of coercive, ferocious acts usually associated with a collection of such organizations. This one concentrates its anti-American energies on blowing up pieces of infrastructure, specifically U.S.–Colombian-owned oil pipelines.[67] ELN terrorists also attack oil company encampments and set elaborate ambushes to mass-murder police officers and soldiers. They kidnap wealthy businessmen and ranchers and assassinate their opponents, be they military commanders, peasants, or labor leaders. The Bush administration claims all four major Colombian terrorist groups have received weapons and training from Cuba.

If Castro still has clout with them, that could turn out to be helpful in controlling Colombian terrorists. Castro, though acting as if he were his own man, is heavily dependent on Moscow; if Gorbachev asked him to cool down terrorists under his influence, he would probably comply. Unfortunately, these groups' access to cocaine money has made many of them financially quite independent and therefore less vulnerable to pressure from Fidel.

In neighboring Bolivia, terrorism was virtually unheard of in the 1980s until drug traffickers began flexing their muscles. In 1988 some members of the far left began conducting terrorist acts. The bombing of visiting U.S. Secretary of State George Shultz's motorcade—which narrowly missed its target—was a warning of things to come. But in Bolivia, the most significant terrorist danger probably comes from drug dealers protecting their business interests. Ambassador Paul Bremer was absolutely correct when he said, "The United States Government is at the top of the drug dealers' enemies list." The organization that planted the bomb could as easily have been a leftist group or a cocaine enterprise. Either way, the goal was the same—an assassination, or a dramatic warning.

Narco-Terror

A genuine escalation of the war on drugs, as promised by President Bush, is likely to trigger an expanding terrorist threat to the United States. While that does not mean the government should lay off the drug business, it does mean officials will have to think more carefully about their own security as they prosecute a real war and be prepared for more of a national security problem with drugs than they've seen so far.

Narcotics traffickers, with their unlimited financial resources, as well as weapons and private armies in their home countries, should be seen as capable of mounting violent operations against U.S. citizens, businesses, and allies anywhere they choose—including within the borders of the United States.

It would be a colossal error to assume these men are constrained in their actions by the borders of the nations that have become their headquarters and that, in many cases, they have helped to corrupt. Terrorist operations on their behalf conducted on American or allied soil would not have the component of fanatacism often associated with terrorist acts, but rather, they would likely be characterized by the detached professionalism of an expensive, well-planned shooting or bombing paid for by organized crime. Some acts of narco-terror might be discernible from gangland violence by the identity of the targets—law-abiding people engaged in the struggle against narcotics. Another distinction between organized-crime murders and possible narco-terror hits is the utter absence of ethical codes among drug barons. Unlike traditional Mafia family revenge killings, in which the relatives of the opposing factions are regarded as noncombatants, Latin American dealers in cocaine have repeatedly demonstrated they observe no such conventions. So an outbreak of narco-terror inside or outside the borders of the United States could involve the kidnapping, maiming, or murder of the families of government officials, corporate executives, or the easiest of revenge targets—American tourists.

With ordinary criminal gunmen available for hire around the world, narco-traffickers would not have to expose themselves or their associates to risk in order to punish the United States. Almost as easily as your own bank can wire money to you overseas, narco-traffickers would be able to send money and targeting information to contract killers around the world. By using what are called "cutouts," or layers of intermediaries—some of whom have no knowledge of the source of the contract—the drug lords would sharply reduce the chances that their role in such murders could ever be proved. Since the narco-traffickers have *billions* of dollars,[68] power to match, and a profound desire to protect all of that, they should be seen as possible employers not only of the gun and the bomb but also of chemicals, biologicals, and radiologicals, as well as of attacks on infrastructure. To convince the President, a governor, or a mayor to back down from aggressive law enforcement, it would not be out of character for drug lords to engage in super-violence terrorism—taking hundreds of lives—to bring home their message to the government.

The failure thus far of the United States or its allies to conduct sustained, comprehensive operations against the international narcotics industry—actually waging war—means the narco-traffickers have not been fully tested. If the time ever should come that the war on drugs transcends rhetoric, and becomes a genuine national security priority, then the challenge to the drug lords will be laid down. When the day arrives that adequate resources are added to the hard work and genuine heroism of agents of the Drug Enforcement Administration, the FBI, and local police departments, *then* the risk of narco-terror revenge against U.S. and allied interests will arrive, screaming for immediate action. But waiting until that time to plan and prevent would be an error of tragic proportions. Local, state, and, most of all, federal officials must take seriously the need to conduct high-quality intelligence operations against drug dealers—not only to arrest them —but to intercept any attempt by them to carry out terrorist acts.

There is no reason to limit the possibility of such violence to overseas-based narco-terrorism. Domestic drug dealers with enough at stake might resort to terror tactics as well. They would have the option of carrying out attacks on their own or paying others to do it for them. Terrorism could be used as leverage to try to get a prosecutor to drop a charge, a judge to soften a sentence. Farfetched? Remember 241 U.S. Marines killed in Beirut in 1983 by one Shiite fanatic driving a truck bomb? His act was key to driving the United States out of Lebanon. Why shouldn't narco-traffickers believe that they, too, could mold American policy by credibly threatening mass murder or doing it once and threatening it a second time if the government refuses to give in?

If the idea of foreign terrorists driving around the United States building their bombs, choosing their targets and preparing their attacks sounds unlikely, remember, it's already happened. The Japanese Red Army terrorist who was captured on the New Jersey Turnpike with three live bombs in April of 1988 had logged *seven thousand miles* on a second-hand car he bought in the Bronx a month before his arrest by a suspicious state trooper at a highway rest stop. Terrorist Yu Kikumura drove from New York City to Missouri, Kentucky, and West Virginia and back to the New York metropolitan area, where he was stopped before he could plant the powerful bombs he appears to have made himself, perhaps in his car, or in a trailer he rented briefly during his road trip. If a lone Japanese Red Army bomber can roam the nation undetected for a month, assembling the components of his bombs and preparing his assault, why not others bent on larger targets using bigger bombs, biologicals, or chemicals? Sadly, the components are easy to purchase, as are the manuals which instruct in their use as weapons. Here is an area where new controls on the availability of bomb components, as well as materials needed for radiological, chemical, and biological devices, are urgently needed to reduce the risk of such weapons being made by terrorists. These laws must also be uniform. Within the United States and Canada, that means federal legislation. In Western Europe, it means adoption by all European Community governments of identical laws—unthinkable ten years ago, perhaps, but in the contemporary political-economic environment, certainly within the realm of the attainable. Nonmember governments of the European Community, including Communist nations, will be able to further establish themselves as legitimate trading partners by enacting and enforcing the same laws. It would be naïve to expect complete compliance with such new antiterrorism laws, but even partial enforcement by all European states would have the effect of making the terrorists' life much more difficult. Even state-sponsored terrorists must develop additional infrastructure and lines of supply, in the event that their primary connection is somehow compromised or withdrawn. In the real world, terrorists must rely on outside help, including access to the components of their weapons and other tools of their work. Dr. Marius Deeb, a scholar on the Middle East with insights into terrorism, believes, "The best opportunity for disrupting the plans of terrorists over the long run is to continue to deny them access to infrastructure. That may not sound very dramatic, but it leaves the terrorist with no reliable base for his operations and so reduces the risk of such attacks."

A Matter of Character

A great power that publicly knuckles under to terrorists, as America did with Iran and Syria, should expect to be considered a target for further intimidation—until it reestablishes its reputation as too tough to tackle. The United States of America simply has not done that. Instead, there is a perpetuation of the image of America as a nation that is gutless. The unwillingness of the government to take effective military action against terrorists or the states that support them speaks volumes to America's adversaries, whose only appreciation is for power that is exercised. Terrorists, on the other hand, have an institutional-

ized passion for risk taking, even a need for reaffirming their machismo. Additionally, there is reason to assume terrorists are becoming
even more indifferent to the suffering of those who get in their way,
less likely to have even a moment's hesitation before perpetrating an
atrocity against unarmed, innocent civilians.

Colonel Stuart Perkins, a senior CIA analyst, told a conference on
terrorism at George Washington University, "There is a kind of natural selection process under way in terrorism; as security forces capture
or kill terrorists, we are left confronting ever-more-violent personalities."

An internationally reknowned expert on violence, Dr. Simon Dinitz, a professor of sociology at Ohio State University, warned in an
interview that the "natural selection" to which Perkins referred is
"most likely to produce terrorists willing to commit the most awful
kinds of crimes against innocents"—people whose character traits
contribute to using weapons of super-violence and mass slaughter.[69]

That suggests that coping with the expanding terrorist threat will
require bold, thoughtful, and creative leadership. But if recent history
is any guide, there is abundant reason to worry.

CHAPTER THREE

TECHNO-TERROR

A Middle East Scenario

TO: Secretary of State
FROM: NSC New East/Asia Bureau
RE: Intelligence Update Syria
DATE: January 30, 1992

Background

Following the death of President Assad of Syria, his brother, Rifaat al-Assad seized power from his more moderate competition. Initial assessments indicate that Rifaat is considerably less canny than Hafez al-Assad. (Onsite report characterizations vary from unstable to lunatic.)

Rifaat has been linked to Syria's drug trade, which finances its terrorist operations. His chief backer in Syrian intelligence is thought to be Major General Mohammed Kholi, linked by the CIA to several recent terrorist operations. Through Kholi, Rifaat is building support in several radical Palestinian groups.

Intelligence Alert

Recent intelligence indicators point to some disquieting undercurrents which, to date, have not been pieced together. West German sources have passed along rumors that two canisters of nerve agents—labeled as industrial chemicals—were passed through a Munich exporting house for re-shipment to an unknown destination. Sources in Lebanon report movement of small teams of probable saboteurs through Palestinian refugee camps. The interagency assessment is that plans for a new attack—possibly in Europe, possibly in Israel—may be under way.

Action Steps

We are continuing to monitor this situation and have passed this intelligence to our counterparts in the Middle East and Europe. Interpol has been advised.

TO: Secretary of State
FROM: NSC Near East/Asia Bureau
RE: Intelligence Update—Red Alert
           Status
DATE: February 2, 1992

Incident Report

UPI reports this morning flashed the arrest of two Arab men leaving a parked minivan outside the Knesset. Investigation revealed a suspicious canister, which on further analysis was found to contain nerve agents. Israeli bomb experts successfully defused the device.

Intelligence Alert

Intelligence (see memo dated January 30) indicates that this may not conclude the incident. There is a possibility that a second canister of nerve agent may be secreted somewhere in Israel. The Israeli Cabinet is meeting today in emergency session to prepare a response. At the moment, we are hoping that it will entail their standard counterterrorism strike on Syrian positions in Lebanon. Were a successful second chemical attack to be launched, however, the Israelis would likely resort to full-scale mobilization.

Action Steps

All appropriate contacts are being used to urge Israeli restraint, stressing the lack of conclusive evidence of Syrian involvement. It should be noted that Israel may not feel it needs a smoking gun, given the circumstantial evidence pointing to Syria.

A memo will be on your desk this afternoon with potential contingencies and options to head off another war in the Middle East. Now that the barrier of mass destruction has been crossed, we must move quickly to quash any possibility of an Israeli nuclear response, with all of the attendant risks of eventual U.S.-Soviet confrontation. We will also consider options to neutralize Rifaat—whom we believe to be the author of this fiasco—without provoking the Soviet Union. We would urge an immediate hotline communication from the President to General Secretary Gorbachev.

It is ironic that even as the prospect of direct superpower confrontation grows more distant, the possibility for devastating attacks from unconventional quarters and unwanted escalation is increasing. All around the world, we are seeing the rise of well-armed and determined regional adversaries. The lengths to which they will go to achieve their policy goals—and sometimes even what those goals are—almost defy Western comprehension.

However, contemporary terrorism offers few grand visions of a better world. Only a short time ago, we thought of terrorists as the disaffected children of Europe, the displaced refugees of the Middle East, or the disillusioned peasants of the developing world with frustrated rising expectations. Once we comforted ourselves with the reassuring notion that they had legitimate grievances that could be addressed with societal remedies.

Today's terrorist activities have as much to do with the *realpolitik* of international conflict as with the frustrated idealism of individuals. The ability of small nations to attack large ones, capitalizing on nihilistic mercenaries who employ the tactics of terror, has become painfully obvious. This brand of violence is so effective that it is becoming the instrument of choice for states which benefit from disruption and political paralysis in the West. Today's terrorist tends to be a professional (trained by hostile states) rather than a bomb-throwing amateur, well able to exploit a range of modern technologies from jet transport to satellite communications to heat-seeking missiles and, it is feared, the dispersal of radioactive, biological, or chemical materials.

The hijacking of a Kuwaiti airliner in 1988 by Shiite terrorists is an illustrative case of growing technological sophistication. In that episode, the terrorist team included at least one veteran of a hijacking, as well as a pilot qualified to fly the aircraft. From the outset, the hijackers reportedly blocked entry points on the plane and wired the 747 with explosives. Their careful planning, command, control, and communications rendered the jumbo jet impervious to rescue.[1]

Similarly, the bombing of Pan Am Flight 103 over Lockerbie, Scotland, later that year, using a multiphased trigger that sensed barometric pressure, takeoff and landing cycles, as well as time, demonstrated genuine technical expertise. There is evidence to indicate that both of these operations may have been planned by or with a hostile state, possibly Iran or Syria. This too is part of the new threshold of violence. Terrorists are increasingly combining a new sophistication in planning and technology through their existing political links with, or direct support from, states such as Iran, Syria, and Libya. With national intelligence services of enemy nations providing the where-withal and planning assistance, it is no longer clear what the political or technical limitations of terrorists will be.

Over the past two decades, we have witnessed a steady escalation in the weapons of terrorist wars. In the 1970s, the instances of missile attacks, for example, were isolated and few in number. Most of them used a Soviet light antitank missile, the RPG-7, or the relatively crude heat-seeking ground-to-air missile, the SA-7 or STRELA.

The handful of incidents using antiaircraft weapons includes a foiled attack in September 1973, when PFLP members were arrested outside Rome's airport with STRELAS; a misfire in January 1975, when two unknown terrorists launched an RPG-7 rocket at an El Al plane at the Paris airport; and in January 1976, when PFLP members were arrested with STRELAS, thought to have been provided by Libya and Uganda, outside the Nairobi airport. In September 1978, an SA-7 may have been successfully used by black nationalist guerrillas in shooting down a Rhodesian airliner, a crash in which thirty-eight people died.

In the 1980s missiles have become more sophisticated and much more available. Aging precision-guided missiles can be purchased virtually "over the counter" on the lucrative international arms markets, and have proliferated throughout the Third World—to governments, as well as to subnational groups. In 1985 members of the Libyan-linked El Rukn, Chicago street gang turned terrorists, were arrested as they tried to buy a missile to shoot down a jetliner at Chicago's O'Hare Airport. Afghani Mujahadin regularly used the American Stinger antiaircraft missile with devastating results against Soviet helicopter gunships and cargo planes. When the Israelis raided the PLO headquarters in Beirut during the Peace for Galilee operation in 1982, they discovered some three thousand RPG-7s and SA-7s in crates, ready for distribution.

If sophisticated weaponry is becoming more available, so too have terrorists become far more adept in their ability to analyze and assess highly sophisticated targets. Victim states of terrorist assaults have barely been able to cope with yesterday's brand of hijackings and assassinations. Now, they face the prospect of superviolent terrorists whose arsenals could include weapons of mass destruction and whose capabilities may reach into the core of modern civilization.

The decades ahead promise to immerse the United States in unconventional combat against which the usual tools of war—tanks, missiles, nuclear weapons—may offer few defenses. Terrorism has become warfare on the cheap.

For the more powerful sponsors like the Soviet Union, which is currently less active in terrorism, such attacks can be plausibly denied, which minimizes their risks of large-scale conventional or even nuclear confrontations. For the relatively weaker states, which are currently more active in sponsoring terrorist events, the tactics of terrorism allow them to achieve high leverage at an affordable cost. Nations such as Syria or Iran cannot compete economically or militarily with the United States on a more conventional battleground. Through terrorist proxies, however, they can inflict real damage on the United States and its allies—a threat potential for which we are shockingly unprepared.

Techniques for Mass Destruction

Speculation about whether terrorist groups would ever dare to use extreme weaponry such as nuclear explosives or biological, chemical, or radiological agents that can inflict mass destruction is often dismissed as sensationalist. It is argued that the lack of availability of nuclear materials and the universal horror surrounding the use of chemical or biological weapons would deter their use. The unfortunate reality is that the materials for such weapons have proliferated widely, that the expertise required is actually within their grasp, and that horror is the name of the terrorism game.

Nuclear materials, including plutonium, are ubiquitous. While plutonium-239 and other fissile materials (the ingredients of atomic bombs) are well guarded in established nuclear states, the stockpiles in newly emergent nuclear powers may be considerably less secure. Some nuclear power plants, which are both visible targets for sabotage as well as a source of hot radiological waste and plutonium, are surprisingly vulnerable to attack. Radioactive materials outside, and sometimes even inside, the NATO alliance are not always handled with extreme security precautions.

Taboos against the use of chemical and biological (CB) weaponry are also largely illusory. Such weapons are already being used today by certain states in the Third World. There are "have and have-not nations" in the current international order in which pariahs or rogue states may have little to lose by employing weapons of mass destruction. States like Libya may opt to fall back on chemical, biological, or radiological weapons to achieve their goals. Of the three, biological weapons—which leave few, if any, fingerprints—are the most insidious.

The use of CB (chemical and biological) weapons is as old as creation. Evidence exists that incendiary chemicals dubbed "Greek fire" were used as early as 1200 B.C. In 429 B.C., during the Peloponnesian War, the Spartans burned pitch and sulfur to release noxious gases under their enemies' city walls. A form of "Greek fire" was used during the American Civil War, causing Confederate General Pierre Gustave Beauregard to exclaim that the Yankees were shooting "the most destructive missile ever used in war."[2]

Nor is biological warfare purely a contemporary phenomenon. In 1347 the Mongols hurled the decaying bodies of plague victims over the walls of Genoese defenders, who carried the Black Death back with them to Europe. In North America in the eighteenth century, British military leaders offered a gift of smallpox-infected blankets to the Indians, causing thousands of deaths.[3] In the 1930s, in a horror story that has only recently came to light, the Japanese subjected prisoners of war to typhoid, anthrax, cholera, and plague organisms to test biological munitions.[4] Ironically, it is only because of those inhuman scientific experiments that we have some limited knowledge about lethal doses.

The extortion potential will always be high where the capacity for massive violence is present. Such CB agents may grow increasingly attractive as a kind of "poor man's atomic bomb." They are inexpensive, readily obtainable, and unstoppable, except for those who are prepared right now for such attack. Successful extortion may not require actual use of such weapons by terrorists. The declared or documented possession of mass destruction agents by a terrorist group would focus widespread publicity on the group and create for it the most powerful political leverage.

To date, terrorist groups or individual fanatics have only experimented around the edges of mass destruction weaponry. But their interest in and awareness of the potential of such weaponry is obvious and ominous. What is also clear is that the political as well as technological barriers to massively disruptive attacks are eroding.

In the past, it seemed likely that even if the technological hurdles were surmounted, terrorist groups would be refused safe haven if they went too far. It was reasoned that no state would want to be associated with madmen or criminals or risk retaliation for harboring terrorists. Moreover, it was believed that the terrorists themselves were more interested in the theatrical value of the event than in the number of fatalities. Many, particularly in the early seventies, espoused principles of social justice and political reform. As long as terrorists maintained an aura of social revolution, any action which threatened the lives of thousands of innocent people would have been difficult to defend.

As a form of warfare, however, the model of terrorism has become less convincing. Since nations have begun to sponsor these events, the problems of safe haven are less at issue. While terrorists continue to be very interested in theatrics, the international media is growing inured to the routine tactics of terrorism—hijackings, kidnappings, and bombings. At that level of violence, it is very difficult to attract the requisite front-page headlines. Over many days and weeks, the pretext of social justice appears threadbare when Syrian-backed suicide bombers attack American installations or Bulgarians help orchestrate an attempted papal assassination. It has become far less clear who will do what to whom and with what effect.

No amount of speculation will settle the issue. While it remains an improbable dream, terrorists, as far back as the original West German Baader Meinhoff gang, have contemplated either stealing or fabricating an atomic bomb. Terrorist nations such as Libya have offered tens of millions of dollars to anyone who could obtain an atomic bomb. For them it was—and still is—the ultimate image of power over the large nation-state.

Terrorists and antiterrorists alike have given a lot of thought to acquiring such weapons. Even if mass destruction were as highly unlikely as many believe, its potential consequences should not be ignored. The time to start thinking about and planning against it was long ago. Prudent government officials must act now.

Nuclear Terrorism

A U.S. Task Force on Nuclear Terrorism concluded in 1987 that building a crude nuclear device, although difficult, is well within the reach of a terrorist group that can recruit three to four qualified specialists. The team need not even have prior experience in weapons design but would require only chemical high explosives, which are essentially trivial to obtain, and a sufficient quantity of fissile nuclear materials.[5]

Designing an atomic weapon is not as mysterious a task as we once had hoped. Enterprising students at MIT, Harvard, and Princeton have independently "designed weapons" on paper. A student-led course in nuclear-weapons design was proposed, but not given, at the University of Connecticut. To the physicist, the most important piece of information about atomic devices was learned at Alamagordo, New Mexico, in 1944: supercritical masses of fissile materials explode.

In July 1975 the City of New York was the victim of the ultimate blackmail threat. The note it received read as follows: "We have successfully designed and built an atomic bomb. It is somewhere on Manhattan Island. This device will be used at 6:00 P.M. unless our demands ($30 million in small, unmarked, out-of-sequence bills) are met."[6]

What made the threat so worrisome was the drawing that accompanied the note. It showed some sophistication by someone with more than a passing acquaintance with nuclear physics. In this case, however, no one claimed the dummy ransom package that was placed at the drop site.

It would be foolhardy to suppose that nuclear threats will inevitably be hoaxes, or that a small dedicated group would never take advantage of any tool within its grasp. The nuclear explosive does not necessarily need to be state-of-the-art. High reliability and accuracy may be essential for generals, but criminals motivated by greed, or terrorists seeking political power, need only build a crude device that will explode and spawn the characteristic mushroom cloud.

While hardly an everyday occurrence, incidents of nuclear terrorism dot the political landscape. In 1979 documents discovered only hours after the downfall of Ugandan dictator Idi Amin disclosed a nuclear plot under his direction. Code-named "Operation Poker," the plot involved building nuclear bombs small enough to fit into suitcases, which would be carried worldwide into Ugandan embassies by teams of suicide-diplomats. Reportedly, Amin was actively recruiting help and expertise from terrorist groups. Certainly the absurdity of the plot reflected Amin's megalomania; building a nuclear device so tiny would have required technical skills far beyond the capacity of any small state or terrorist group.[7] But his obvious awareness of the enormous leverage of the threat should give us pause.

More recently, evidence surfaced in 1984 that linked the PLO with an Iraqi effort to purchase three atomic bombs.[8] In 1985, a previously unknown group, the Armenian Scientific Group, sent letters to Turkish newspapers threatening to destroy three major Turkish cities with small nuclear devices.[9] In the United States alone, there have been about eighty nuclear weapon threats although, with a few exceptions, all have been fairly obvious hoaxes.

Access to the proper materials and components will remain the primary obstacles to nuclear weapons terrorism. Nuclear reactors are probably the most available but least useful sources of fissile materials. The most common reactor worldwide is the light water reactor, which employs low-enriched uranium as fuel. But low-enriched uranium is not in itself usable in a weapons mode. Although the reactor waste contains substantial quantities of plutonium 239—the weapons material of choice—it cannot be separated out without sophisticated handling and chemical processing, which are out of reach of any terrorist group.

Although one cannot totally rule out theft of weapons-grade fissile materials or even a nuclear weapon, the safeguards against such a contingency, at least among the established nuclear powers, are extremely tight. In 1984, for example, a shipment of 250 kilograms of plutonium oxide (an efficiently designed bomb would require only a small fraction of that amount) from France to Japan was subject to extraordinary security precautions: the ship could carry no cargo other than the plutonium; it could make no intermediate stops; it was escorted on parts of its journey by French, U.S., and Japanese warships, and it was tracked continuously by U.S. military satellites.[10]

Soviet precautions against nuclear diversions are, if anything, even more stringent, especially for commercial nuclear wastes. Moscow is a keen supporter of nuclear safeguards, which it enforces strictly on its own territory and that of its customers.

Nevertheless, the potential for access to fissile materials has in recent years become somewhat more worrisome, because of the growth in the international market for plutonium, both for weapons and commercial purposes. In the private nuclear power sector, about forty-five tons of plutonium are discharged each year in the spent fuel of commercial nuclear power plants. If present reprocessing plans are carried out, by the late 1990s the amount of plutonium separated for civilian uses worldwide will exceed two hundred tons.[11] That means that more than four hundred thousand pounds of plutonium will be shipped in commercial transit or protected by private companies, which will inevitably raise questions about how well they are being safeguarded. What they would *deserve* is the same kind of security that surrounded the shipment from France to Japan.

The technology for nuclear weapons development has proliferated widely. Of the Third World countries, only China, India, Israel, and Pakistan have so far developed all the necessary technology. But it is only a matter of time before nuclear balances become a factor to be reckoned with in the international arena. Stockpiles of nuclear materials and weapons in Third World states may be vulnerable to terrorist assaults. Libya's Muammar al-Qaddafi has frequently threatened to steal an American nuclear weapon from secure storage areas in Europe and attempted to have one stolen by a renegade CIA operative. Others may find it far easier to seize a weapon in a nuclear threshold state where the level of security would likely be far lower.

Once the plutonium has been obtained, the creation of an atomic device is within reach of a technically knowledgeable nation. (No nation that has tried has ever failed.) Determined buyers have always been able to acquire nuclear components. While nuclear exports are routinely subject to review by the International Atomic Energy Agency (IAEA), there exists an extremely lucrative and secretive underground nuclear commerce that has circumvented international control.

Probably the most astonishing case of nuclear smuggling took place between 1977 and 1980, when a West German businessman shipped an entire nuclear plant to Pakistan in sixty-two truckloads and provided a team of West German engineers to supervise its construction. Unauthorized exports of U.S. krytrons (high-speed electronic switches) have been intercepted en route to Israel and Pakistan.[12]

Terrorist groups with the funds and the desire could dive into the netherworld of trade in illicit nuclear commodities, using the same subterfuges that national governments have employed with varying degrees of success. On the other hand, it might not be necessary for a terrorist group to steal or smuggle any materials. Newly emergent nuclear states, some of which routinely support terrorist groups, may one day find it useful to sponsor a nuclear attack through their terrorist proxies.

Israel clearly had this possibility in mind when it launched a preemptive attack in 1981 against Iraq's French-built Osirak nuclear facility, then under construction. Israel's rationale was not only to prevent Iraq from acquiring a nuclear weapons arsenal but to deny Iraq the ability to clandestinely deliver a nuclear device on Israeli territory. A nuclear bomb in Tel Aviv or any major city could constitute a virtually anonymous act of war. Such unconventional nuclear threats could unfortunately become a serious possibility, even in the age of *glasnost* and decreasing superpower tensions.

By and large, only the most sophisticated and determined terrorist groups will be able to surmount the hurdles involved in acquiring the fissile materials, components, and expertise to construct and handle a nuclear device. By contrast, the problems associated with simply dispersing radiological materials are trivial. Radioactive substances exist in abundance, found in hospitals and industrial facilities across the industrialized world and in pools of highly toxic nuclear waste around the globe.

Some examples of radiologicals include iodine 131, plutonium 239, cobalt 60, cesium 137, and polonium 210. Iodine 131 is found in nearly every hospital and diagnostic laboratory. Plutonium 239 is a plentiful byproduct of nuclear reactors, although in its pure weapons form it is very difficult and dangerous to obtain. Cobalt 60 is available in sizable amounts in medical centers and industrial X-ray facilities, where it is used for cancer research and therapy. Polonium 210, also extremely dangerous, is available in small amounts for laboratory experiments under license by government agencies.

The effects of radiologicals can take quite a long time to mature—the ensuing cancers and related illnesses may not develop for many years after the initial attack. For this reason, it is not typically classed as a weapon of mass destruction; its horror value, as measured in terms of immediate fatalities, is limited.

All the same, the threat to disperse radiological materials could be a very potent one. In 1986 a radiological threat to contaminate water reservoirs in New York City with plutonium chloride frightened many responsible officials. The threat was considered to be serious because the perpetrators clearly knew enough to understand that plutonium chloride is a salt that is soluble in water.

In a crisis game run at the Center for Strategic and International Studies, a Washington, D.C. think tank, a different kind of radiological threat was considered: Middle Eastern terrorists hijacked an airplane that was seeded with cobalt 60—a nasty gamma emitter. The passengers on the plane were literally "cooking" during the hours of desperate negotiations. Scientists informed the simulated National Security Council that as the hours passed, more and more rows of passengers, farther away from the radiation source, would receive a lethal dose.[13]

Moreover, radiological agents would be useful for "area denial." The half-lives of many dangerous radioactive materials are comparatively long, impeding access to critical areas for an extended period. Suppose, for example, that a terrorist group was able to spread cobalt 60 within the World Trade Center in New York, Harrods department store in London, or the Bourse in Paris. Depending on the extent and effectiveness of the attack, these vital business, shopping, and financial centers could be forced to shut down for years. Rehabilitation would depend on whether the building could be cleared of the radioactive material and whether the value of the contaminated area exceeded the statistical risk of any lingering long-term physical threats. Financial loss could be staggering, with insurance coverage questionable.

Chemical and Biological Agents

Chemical attacks by terrorists will almost certainly be driven by the proliferation of chemical arsenals among their state sponsors.

Western intelligence services estimate fifteen to thirty countries now have or are actively working to possess chemical munitions. In the case of chemicals, it is not so much a matter of technological innovation as it is mere availability. The internationalization of the chemical industry—petrochemicals, fertilizers, and insecticides—has put chemical weapons capabilities within reach of Third World countries and their terrorist protégés and virtually out of reach of any meaningful control.

The episodic use of chemical agents by Egypt during the Yemeni Civil War during the sixties has been followed by a spate of other incidents in the late seventies and eighties. Some claims are in dispute, notably in Laos, although the United States Government steadfastly maintains that Yellow Rain, a fungal toxin which causes people to bleed to death internally, is not a natural occurrence but a cruel Soviet chemical-warfare experiment. Other incidents, such as the use of chemical munitions in the Persian Gulf and Afghanistan, are unquestionable.

The specter of chemical warfare was brought home to Israel when munitions containing nerve agents were discovered among the Egyptian stockpiles captured in the Sinai Desert. In 1973 reports indicated that Egypt was preparing to attach chemical warheads to its Soviet-supplied missiles and this concern grew especially serious when analyses of captured Soviet equipment revealed that it had been designed for fighting in contaminated environments.[14]

Following the Soviet Union's invasion of Afghanistan in 1979, rumors surfaced that experimental new chemicals were being tested. An Afghan pilot described the use of chemicals that made the skin so soft that a person's finger could easily push right through it.[15] Defectors report that Cuba may be stockpiling chemical munitions. The Sandinista regime in Nicaragua has been using herbicides as an antipersonnel weapon against the rebellious Mesquito Indians.

Iraq, Iran, and Libya are actively developing chemical weapons facilities. Libyan claims that its massive complex will produce pharmaceuticals is belied by the ring of antiaircraft missiles surrounding the plant. Iraq's chemical-weapons program, under way for at least a decade, includes several laboratory complexes around the country. And there is growing evidence that Syria is producing nerve gas in a facility located far to the north of Damascus. The speculation is that Syria may be attempting to design nerve-agent warheads for its highly accurate, Soviet-supplied, intermediate-range ballistic missiles.[16] Should such warheads ever be assembled, preemptive action by Israel might well be expected.

With the apparent loss of any lingering ethical or political restraints, the fabrication of such chemical munitions is a comparatively minor task. There are literally tens of thousands of highly poisonous chemicals. Among the most toxic are the organophosphorus compounds, the so-called nerve agents. They have been described as "doing to humans what insect sprays do to bugs."[17] Indeed, many organophosphates are commercially available as insecticides.

Nerve agents enter the body through inhalation or through the skin. They are intended to interfere with the electrochemical transmission of nerve signals, the messages sent from one nerve ending to another. If not counteracted with atropine immediately, the nerve agent causes the body to go into spasms, with death following between fifteen minutes and two hours later. Nerve agents, which were first developed by the Nazis, include Tabun, Sarin, and the more toxic VX nerve agent stockpiled by the U.S. Army. The amount of VX that one could place on the head of a pin would be sufficient to produce individual death.

Terrorists have long had more than a passing interest in the extortion potential of chemical warfare. In recent years Israeli security agents and police found canisters of a potent poison, presumed to have been brought in by terrorists, at a safe house in Tel Aviv. In 1975 German entrepreneurs were apprehended in Vienna, attempting to sell Tabun to Palestinian terrorists. Between 1978 and 1979, approximately four hundred kilograms of intermediate compounds that could be used for manufacturing organophosphorous nerve agents were discovered in a terrorist safe house in West Germany.

One of the most worrisome threats occurred in the United States in 1974. Authorities received taped messages from an anonymous individual nicknamed the "Alphabet Bomber." In one message, the individual claimed to have nerve gas, which he described in scientifically accurate terms, and warned that he was coming to kill the President. Whether or not he had finished assembling the nerve agent remains an open question. Some reports suggest he had. Others suggest that he had assembled all but one of the critical ingredients and had made arrangements to pick up the remaining substance on the day he was arrested.[18]

Among other possible chemical options are blistering agents, such as mustard gas, first used in World War I and, more recently, against Iranian troops and civilians by Iraq. A yellowish oily liquid, mustard gas is dispensed as a fine spray that sticks to everything it touches. It raises painful blisters that take much longer to heal than ordinary burns. Blistering agents attack the eyes and burn the lining of the lungs, often killing the victims. In 1975 terrorists successfully stole canisters of this agent from U.S. stocks in West Germany.

Far more lethal alternatives are toxins, the poisonous by-products of microorganisms, plants, or animals. Toxins actually fall somewhere between chemical and biological weapons; they are synthesized from living material but are not living themselves.

Probably the best known toxin causes botulism, which is found virtually everywhere (improperly sealed cans of tainted meat are classic sources). The virulence of the toxin is incredible. When compared with the most dangerous nerve agents, botulinal toxins are a thousand times more effective. The average lethal dose is probably as low as a few tenths of a microgram. Could terrorists find a use for botulinal toxin? Apparently one group thought so. In a raid on a Red Army Faction safe house in 1980, French police found flasks of the unpurified toxin stored in the bathtub.

One of the most lethal plant toxins is Ricin, extracted from the castor bean, which coincidentally is also the source of castor oil. Processed one way, the castor bean is a purgative; processed another way, it is a deadly poison.

The most well-publicized cases of Ricin poisoning occurred in 1978 against a pair of Bulgarian exiles. Each was attacked by Bulgarian Secret Service agents using umbrellas with an ingenious spring device that fired tiny steel pellets (the size of a pinhead) with microscopic grooves that contained Ricin. One of the victims died. French doctors discovered the pellet lodged in the back of the other man and surgically removed it just in time to save his life.

The problem with such attacks is that the cause of death is not always obvious. There are still serious people who believe that the outbreak of Legionnaires' disease in Philadelphia was the result of a malevolent attack. Various chemicals or biologicals were considered at the time to be likely candidates, particularly Ricin. Even if it was not a deliberate attack, which is quite likely, it provided a case study in how to launch such an attack.

Indeed, a situation approximating the Philadelphia scenario was simulated in 1978 in West Berlin at a multinational conference on terrorism. In that exercise, terrorists sought to bring down several governments in Europe by simultaneously planting aerosols of Ricin in various major European hotels at which political or industrial meetings would be held. The results of the exercise were not encouraging; the simulated European governments handling the simulated crisis literally collapsed. Former government officials and well-placed industrialists did not have a clue as to how to handle such an event.[19]

More ominous still is the untapped potential for biological weapons. Suppose a terrorist group wanted to wreak utter havoc among the twenty-one million residents of metropolitan New York City. One of the effective modes of attack would be with biological agents. Given the unrestricted availability of the necessary information, the relatively small resources and skills needed, as well as an ability to test the product, the mortality levels from a biological attack could possibly exceed that of a large nuclear explosion.

For example, under good meteorological conditions, with a light wind, a small boat could release anthrax spores along New York's twenty-five-mile inland waterway in about three hours—traveling from Battery Park at the southern tip of Manhattan to City Island at the entrance of Long Island Sound. The cloud of anthrax spores would drift over densely populated areas, leading to serious illnesses if inhaled. Even if only half of the inhabitants were exposed to the spores, even if only half of those exposed developed pulmonary anthrax, and even if only half of those cases result in death (all conservative estimates), more than six hundred thousand people would die.[20]

Biological agents include tiny microorganisms—fungi, bacteria, or viruses—which are cultured in concentration. Among the most serious viral agents are those that produce smallpox, yellow fever, and influenza. Bacterial agents include anthrax, plague, or typhoid fever. Although biological weapons are more dangerous for the handler because they are designed to be infectious and are often extremely contagious, their effects are also far greater. Only a small quantity is sufficient to devastate a crowded urban area, killing hundreds of thousands, even millions, of people. But the truly insidious part of biological weapons is the initial difficulty defenders have in determining whether they are under attack or are merely being struck by a natural epidemic.

Pentagon officials claim that ten nations—none of them U.S. allies —have developed a biological capability or are mustering the scientific know-how to genetically engineer exotic new germs.[21] These include Iraq, Egypt, Iran, and Syria. There is little question that a determined state could put together the requisite components of a biological weapon without great difficulty. Indeed, it has been suggested that a university-level technician could produce biological agents in a basement laboratory of only moderate sophistication, a scenario which could put biological weapons capability in the hands of terrorists as well.

Probably the most worrisome example of the potential of biological warfare occurred in the Soviet Union in 1979. U.S. intelligence sources maintain that during early April an accident occurred, at a suspected biological research facility at Sverdlovsk, which released as much as a kilogram of dry anthrax spores into the air. The Soviets have denied the charge for nearly ten years, claiming that the epidemic was due to the sale of tainted meat on the black market.

Despite a detailed refutation by Soviet scientists in 1988 at the U.S. National Academy of Science, there remain loose ends in the Soviet account that do not fully explain the incident. According to reports by local doctors at the scene, the individuals admitted to the hospital displayed symptoms of high fever, bluish ears and lips, choking, and difficulty in breathing. The symptoms were of pulmonary anthrax, which implies that the disease had been spread by air. Had the symptoms been those of skin or gastric anthrax, they would have been more consistent with the story of tainted meat that had been handled or eaten.[22]

Subsequently, the Soviet military took over the hospital building, evacuating the staff members and their families, and buried the dead in specially prepared caskets. The land around the research facility was graded and covered with asphalt. Nearby buildings and factories were disinfected inside and out. A five-by-seven-kilometer area around the plant was disinfected by overhead spraying, precautions that would also seem to have more relevance in counteracting airborne anthrax than tainted meat.[23]

Terrorist and dissident groups have long evinced an interest in biologicals, even though the actual threats have thus far been extremely limited. Robert De Pugh, the leader of the Minutemen—a militant right-wing American group—has been quoted as saying:

"The first batch of nerve gas I ever made—of course, it's a kind of liquid, not a gas—I figured what I thought would be the minimum lethal dose for this dog. I just wanted to see if I had the thing right, you know, and I figured the minimum effective dose, and then I cut that by ten, and I put it on the dog's nose and the dog walked six steps and dropped dead." De Pugh operated out of the Biolab Corporation, which he owned, in Missouri. The group claimed it planned to disperse a virus that De Pugh had developed by sprinkling it on the floors of major airline terminals.[24]

In the early seventies, the U.S. Army was reportedly alerted to a plot by the Weathermen to steal a biological weapon from Fort Detrick in Maryland—by blackmailing a homosexual officer—in order to poison the water supply of a major city.[25]

The biological attack that perhaps came closest to fruition, however, was disclosed in 1972, when two teenagers were charged with conspiracy to commit murder by introducing typhoid bacteria into the Chicago water supply. One of the teenagers—then a nineteen-year-old—had apparently developed the culture in a school laboratory, where a quantity was found. The two men had formed an extremist group called RISE. Allegedly, the members of the group were to be inoculated against the diseases, enabling them to survive the infections to form the basis of a new master race.[26]

For a variety of reasons, biological agents have not historically been generally regarded as a weapon of choice. In the past, the strategic utility of biological weapons was thought to be limited because the agents best suited for use—those that could be effectively disseminated, work quickly and somewhat controllably—were prohibitively expensive. Too, the difficulty of safely storing biological munitions and the likelihood that they might backfire—infecting friends as well as enemies—mitigated against their development or use. These limitations led President Nixon in 1972 to discontinue production of biological weapons and accept an international treaty banning the use and possession of biological agents and toxins.

Today, stunning advances in the field of biotechnology—advances that have brought into common parlance terms like genetic engineering and recombinant DNA—have changed the picture on biological warfare. It is now possible to synthesize biological weapon agents tailored to specification—fast-acting incapacitants developed to fit climate conditions or mixed to complicate identification or circumvent antidotes that the other side is suspected to possess. "Designer" biological weapons raise horrifying prospects, such as the creation of bacteria to attack specific human organs or even to kill members of one race while sparing those of another.[27]

New agents can be produced in hours, while antidotes may take years. New technology can also yield biological weapons against which the attacker could immunize himself in advance. This would tend to enhance biological weapons' military advantage over chemical weapons such as nerve agents, against which neither side is immune.

The seed stocks of biological agents can be fermented into large production quantities in three to four weeks. After a production run, the equipment, operating on self-cleaning principle, destroys within an hour or two whatever residue there might be, making it impossible to prove that a given substance has been produced. Biologicals can be truly anonymous weapons of attack.[28]

The ease of obtaining biological organisms was demonstrated in 1984 when two Canadians, posing as microbiologists from the Canadian firm ICM Science, ordered pathogens over the telephone from a laboratory in Maryland. The American Type Culture Collection of Rockville, Maryland, routinely stocks biological cultures of all varieties for research and clinical purposes. When ATCC routinely sent a copy of the sales invoice to ICM Science, the large quantity of tetanus ordered caught their attention. ICM Science recognized that it had not ordered the cultures and had no employees by the names given. When the two men placed another order, this time for botulinal toxin, the FBI was able to apprehend them when the bogus toxin was picked up.[29]

Recently, Senator John McCain (R-Ariz.) alleged that cultures of the tularemia bacteria had been shipped to Iraq from the Rockville laboratory.[30] It is widely assumed that Iraq will incorporate the bacteria stock, which can be more lethal (by weight) than anthrax, into its emerging biological weapons arsenal.

Ironically, it was the U.S. Army that first tested the way in which biological agents could be disseminated. In the late 1950s and early 1960s, government personnel conducted experiments to gauge the effects of biological attacks in the United States. Using a nonlethal substitute for dry anthrax, they dropped light bulbs full of the powder in the subway system of New York City. The enormous winds created by the onrushing trains distributed the powder through the tunnel system. Measurements taken indicated that hundreds of thousands of people would have died, had the attack been real. On the other side of the country, anthrax simulants were dispersed with aerosols in San Francisco Bay. Other tests involved the dispersal of pseudotoxins, using cleverly designed attaché cases, at buses and airports, and with boats equipped with aerosol sprays in inland waterways. In all, the Army found that such a series of attacks might yield tens of millions of casualties.

One of the most frightening biological scenarios involves the AIDS virus, for which there are no vaccines or cures. AIDS inspires fear and panic, even though its transmission patterns are limited. Suppose, however, that a terrorist group threatened to contaminate the drinking water of major U.S. cities with the virus. Even if the likelihood of contagion were minuscule, the ensuing panic and political uproar would be tantamount to a large-scale invasion. In fact, biologicals could be dispersed with some degree of lethal effectiveness almost anywhere people congregate in large numbers or they could be inserted into production lines at factories turning out packaged prepared foods, the same foods that come in "tamper-proof" containers.

What makes the prospect of biological weapons so nightmarish is the catastrophic power of even modest attacks, particularly in comparison to other super-violent weapons. For nuclear threats with a small subkiloton device, the fatalities, even in a major urban center, would be on the order of several hundred thousand. A chemical attack with the best agents available would probably not exceed a few thousand fatalities. But for biological weapons, the numbers could run theoretically into the millions, making biological attacks one of the most serious and truly frightening possibilities the world may face.

Hidden Vulnerabilities

Terrorists need not use atomic bombs and chemical or biological agents to bring about utter devastation in the United States. They are becoming more technologically adept, not only in the weapons available to them but also in their ability to analyze and assess more complex infrastructural targets. Among the Western democracies, the United States may be the choicest target for such attacks. From its electrical transmission networks to its banking and computer centers, America is staggeringly vulnerable to techno-terrorism. The arrest of a Japanese Red Army terrorist, Yu Kikumura, transporting three disguised bombs on the New Jersey Turnpike in 1988, should explode any lingering illusions that it can't happen in the United States.

The horrifying prospect of infrastructural attacks causes many officials simply to throw up their hands. The technology interconnections upon which we depend, minute by minute, have become such an integral part of our lives as to be virtually invisible. These systems—power, telecommunication and computer networks, transportation and potable water systems, oil and natural gas systems—are inextricably interlocked. The failure of any one system can mean the cascading disruption of many others. Failures or problems in one area can propagate along and across other networks with devastating effects.

This vulnerability is largely the result of the way in which America's technological infrastructure evolved—in a patchwork-quilt pattern, with little continuous planning and no provision for survivability against attack. Absent any notion of malevolent threat, it made good economic sense to route all technological links over the easiest paths. But this means that highways, canals, railways, power lines, pipelines, and telephone wires today inevitably come together at natural gateways and crossroads. That creates nodes of vulnerability which, if cleverly attacked, could cripple U.S. society.

Thousands of miles of electric power lines and petroleum pipelines represent exposed targets; publicly available maps show where they may be severed to isolate entire regions of the nation. A handful of people could turn off three quarters of the oil and gas supply to the East Coast without ever leaving the state of Louisiana. The loss of three major domestic pipelines would interdict half again as much oil as the maximum import shortfall in the 1973 embargo. Indeed, just one pipeline system, dependent on a single control center, carries half the barrel miles of refined products shipped in this country.[31]

Similarly, many electric power substations are in remote, unprotected areas; damage to them could disable a network for an extended period. Some heavy electrical transformers are no longer stockpiled and require more than a year to replace. Imagine a strategically vectored attack that left New York City without power for even a week, much less several months. It is not difficult to imagine night-marish but realistic scenarios far worse than what did occur in the 1977 blackout caused by a lightning strike: looting on a massive scale, fires started at random, and jittery National Guardsmen shooting into crowds of panicked people. The sanitation, food, mass transportation, and water systems, all dependent on electric power, would collapse. Indeed, in 1977, even routine law enforcement procedures were sty-mied because the electric typewriters in the New York Police Depart-ment could not work. Hundreds of cases were thrown out of court for lack of adequate arrest records.

Carefully placed pressure mines on major bridges could knock out critical rail links. It was quietly noted, for example, that if the 1981 Air Florida crash in Washington had hit the nearby rail bridge instead of the river, all north-south rail traffic along the U.S. Eastern Seaboard would have been disrupted for an extended period.

In any technologically based democratic society, some degree of risk must always be accepted. The cost of protecting against every natural, accidental, or induced disaster would be prohibitively high. Californians protect their schools and hospitals against the anticipated intermediate earthquake, not the feared massive one. Flood precau-tions are not designed to contain the once-in-a-century flood. In gen-eral, our emergency procedures and security measures are based on a central assumption: the effects of most disasters are isolatable, tempo-rary, and reversible.

The danger today stems from induced disasters of vastly different magnitude. The vulnerability of society's life-supporting physical net-works literally invites focused sabotage and the low-intensity warfare of terrorist attacks. If successful, such assaults could exceed the self-healing limits of society.[32]

Unfortunately, the potential for such attacks on the infrastructure is not confined to the realm of speculation. Electric power facilities have been a magnet for terrorist attacks for more than fifteen years. In the United States, the New World Liberation Front—a consumer protest group in the Pacific Northwest—targeted the Pacific Gas and Electric Company at least ten times during the 1970s. They were never very well coordinated, leading police officials to the conclusions that the group either didn't intend to hit vital nodes or just didn't know how. In a raid on an FALN (Puerto Rican separatist group) safe house in 1980, police found detailed plans of the electrical power system of Madison Square Garden in New York, where the Democratic Party's convention was about to convene, possibly signaling a plot to black out the facility and disrupt the American electoral process. Assassinations under cover of imposed darkness could have followed amidst the sudden chaos.

Puerto Rican extremists have targeted electric utilities on their home ground as well. In 1980 other Puerto Rican separatists, the Macheteros, claimed responsibility for an explosion in the Palo Seco electrical plant that shut down the island's entire electric distribution system and cost millions of dollars to repair. Similarly, in 1981, the Macheteros said they set off the bomb blasts that knocked out electricity to twenty thousand customers.

In 1978, in the Philippines, the Moro National Liberation Front blacked out almost one half of the island of Mindoro. In November 1980, in Chile, members of the Movement of the Revolutionary Left (MIR) bombed nine high-tension towers, cutting off power in Santiago, Valparaiso, and Viña del Mar. In Italy, Red Brigades have been targeting the power grid with varying degrees of success. Following the assassination of Aldo Moro, they unsuccessfully attempted to black out Rome. This was nevertheless an improvement over their performance two years earlier, when the electromagnetic field around the power lines created a charge on their own bomb that blew up the would-be saboteurs.

The bottom line is that electric power facilities, precisely because they are an embracing system upon which almost all other services depend, have become a target of choice for terrorists worldwide. There are few damage-control options once an electric facility has been taken off line. The problem extends beyond light and heat. In the most extreme case, a major and lengthy power failure could paralyze computer networks, food supply chains, sanitation and water systems, fuel, and transportation.

A few terrorist groups have made attacks on the infrastructure their particular specialty. The Shining Path in Peru has managed to black out the capital, Lima, on several occasions. In 1984 the group blew up a strategic railroad bridge east of Lima, cutting off food and mineral shipments.[33]

In 1978 a leftist Japanese group cut the cables leading to the control tower at Tokyo International Airport, forcing the control tower to stop all takeoffs and landings. A much more sophisticated attack occurred in Japan in 1985. Acting with military precision, helmeted terrorists simultaneously attacked thirty-four nodes of the national railway system, shutting it down and idling eighteen million commuters. It soon became clear that members of the group, the Chukaku-Ha or Middle Core, knew precisely what they were doing. They systematically sought out and destroyed the electronic cables that ran alongside the tracks and directed the trains' movement. According to press reports, they then tried to increase the panic by jamming police communications with a special radio transmitter.[34]

One of the most worrisome types of infrastructural attacks involves nuclear power reactors. A powerful bomb set off in a reactor could conceivably rip open the highly radioactive core and crack the outer shell of the plant, leading to release of radiation.

Nuclear power plants and violence are no strangers. Over the past twenty years, some one hundred fifty-five bombings and other attacks have taken place at the site of civil nuclear installations, mostly in Europe and the United States. The U.S. Task Force on the Prevention of Nuclear Terrorism concluded: "A reactor incident brought about by terrorists, even one releasing significant amounts of radioactivity, is by no means implausible and is technologically feasible."[35]

Unexploded bombs have been discovered at nuclear power plants in Sweden, Spain, the United Kingdom, France, Italy, and Belgium, as well as in the United States. In 1973 an Argentine reactor was stormed by armed revolutionaries and its staff held hostage. Fortunately, in that instance, the action was largely symbolic—the group raised its flag over the reactor and painted slogans on the wall. But, for a time, they had absolute freedom of access to the facility. In France in 1975 a terrorist group breached security—a chain-link fence—at a nuclear power plant in Brittany, setting off two bombs around the facility. In 1977 the Basque terrorists in Spain—the ETA—unsuccessfully attempted to overpower the guards at the Lemonitz nuclear facility. The group later claimed that it planned to use blasting powder stored at the site to blow up the reactors.[36]

There have been a few unsettling references to nuclear sabotage possibilities. A communiqué received in March 1980 by the newspaper *El Espectador* in Bogotá stated that armed action would be taken in the United States if any military action were launched to end the terrorist occupation of the Dominican embassy in Bogotá. The warning, made by several revolutionary groups, warned: "You must remember, U.S. gentlemen, that you have never experienced war in your vitals and that you have many nuclear reactors."[37]

Following the mass murder by truck bomb of the U.S. Marines in Beirut in 1983, the U.S. Government commissioned a study of the potential damage that truck bombs of various sizes could cause at various distances from a power reactor. The Sandia National Laboratory, one of the foremost nuclear weapons research centers in the country, concluded that unacceptable damage to vital reactor systems could occur from a relatively small charge at close distances but also from larger but still reasonable-size charges at large set back distances (greater than the protected area for most plants). Although the danger was greater than had been originally thought, the Nuclear Regulatory Commission suspended action on these results only two weeks after the study was published. The costs of protecting privately owned nuclear power plants outside the already large perimeter of the facility would simply be prohibitive.[38]

For the future, we must be concerned that new applications of technology will create new risks. For example, the data processing and telecommunications linkages which underpin the economy are vulnerable to terrorist-induced catastrophic collapse. The four major electronic funds transfer networks alone carry the equivalent of the federal budget every two to four hours. These almost incomprehensible sums of money are processed solely between the memories of computers, using communications systems that are vulnerable to physical disruption or electronic tampering.[39]

Even computer software is dangerously open to sophisticated terrorist attack. A new and frightening variant of computer hacking is emerging. The so-called "computer virus" can alter computerized records, destroy data, and control systems. Its potential to wreak havoc in the government, financial, business, and academic sectors has become a matter of national security.

Computer viruses are actually lines of code hidden within normal programming instructions. Like its biological counterpart, a computer virus can be highly contagious. It has the capability to clone a copy of itself instantaneously and then to bury that copy inside other software programs. All infected programs also become contagious, and the virus passes to other computers over telephone lines. A single strategically placed computer with an infected memory—for example, a central banking computer—could rapidly infect thousands of smaller computers.

Viruses can be programmed to act immediately or to lie in wait for a predetermined trigger. A typical network attack takes only hours to spread throughout a system; in one as-yet-undisclosed case—an IBM —seconds. But the virus can persist indefinitely, stored on backup tapes or other media. It can be accidentally or deliberately revived many years after insertion, indeed, even after it appears to have been eradicated. The widespread use of software backups to protect against system failure may actually provide safe harbor for such viruses rather than a sound defense against them.

In biological terms, a computer virus is a disease that is a hundred percent infectious spreads instantaneously at the moment of contact and has no detectable symptoms until the moment it strikes. Like the biological organism, there are no known vaccines against it. A carefully engineered computer virus has the potential to bring down whole computerized networks for a significant length of time, paralyzing vital sectors of the economy and of the defense establishment or any other computer-dependent part of life in the modern world.

The existence of such viruses no longer belongs in the realm of science fiction or mere paranoia. Computer viruses have been discovered in personal computer programs at corporations such as IBM, Hewlett-Packard, and Apple and at major university centers, as well as in Israel, West Germany, Switzerland, Britain, and Italy.

A few years ago, a West German student played a computer prank that highlighted the potential of computer viruses. He created a program that looked like an innocent Christmas card greeting. When it was run, however, it secretly reached into computer files and sent copies of itself to everyone who had exchanged messages with the individual who was now sending on the greeting card. The bogus Christmas card crossed five continents and flooded an IBM network with trash mail, bringing normal operations to a standstill. The chain letter replicated the mailing list, but did not infect the programs it encountered along its path. But it could have been programmed to do so. And, if it had, it would have created a worldwide disaster for the world's largest computer company.[40]

A more invidious attack by a computer virus was accidentally discovered in Israel in 1988. Designed as a weapon of political protest, the virus code contained a "time bomb" that would have caused all infected programs to erase their files on May 13, the fortieth anniversary of the demise of Palestine. The virus was discovered because of an error in its program which did not allow it to distinguish between uninfected and already infected programs. Because it continued to add copies of itself to infected software, in some cases up to twenty-three hundred times, the extra lines of software began to flood the disk memories. Although one or two lines of virus code would have been almost impossible to detect, the anomaly of so many lines of repetitive programming proved to be easier to spot.[41]

Nagging concerns about U.S. vulnerability to attack were dramatically realized in 1988 when a Cornell computer whiz, Robert Morris, Jr., created a virus program that disrupted operations in an estimated six thousand computers nationwide for over a twenty-four-hour period. Morris found a back door into the Arpanet—a computer data network that links three hundred universities, private research companies, and defense contractors. His program was designed to move undetected through the Arpanet—secretly and gradually making copies of itself, which would continue to move through the network. But a design error caused it to replicate wildly, ultimately jamming all of the networks it infected.

Fortunately, the virus was not instructed to damage operating systems or destroy information, only to consume unused memory banks in the network by reproducing data files. But the potential for damage was clear. What began as a student prank led to intensive interagency scrutiny of U.S. vulnerability to computer sabotage.

The damage potential of computer viruses is so enormous that it may be impossible to calculate. Suppose, for example, someone managed to hide a computer virus among the millions of lines of programming instructions in the strategic defense control systems. Experts claim that it is difficult enough to identify random bugs in the system; it would be virtually impossible to spot any Trojan horse lines of code. But, quite conceivably, a weapons system could be presabotaged to fail at a moment of crisis. Ultimately, the security of the West and the international balance of power hinges on our ability to prevent insertion of such a virus in computers that communicate or "talk" to other computers.

The United States and its allies are massively vulnerable to an entire spectrum of extraordinary attacks. Even assessing where our vulnerabilities lie is a herculean task, requiring years of analysis on the most sophisticated computers that are available.

Identifying the critical nodes of vulnerability on a complex network is not as simple as it may appear. For example, if we want to ensure that no terrorist group could shut down the natural gas system in the United States Northeast, our first preventive measures would not be taken in New York, Massachusetts, or Maine, but in Louisiana, more than a thousand miles away.

There are few cost-effectiveness studies that analyze how we might begin to go about the business of protecting ourselves. There is no well-honed crisis management apparatus to provide emergency relief to the millions of people who might be affected in the event of the disruption or destruction of our computerized communications systems. The potential for terrorist attacks on U.S. soil is an issue which few Americans wish to contemplate. But the government's seeming complacence that "It can't happen here" borders on wishful thinking. Our unpreparedness to cope with the aftermath of super-violence only raises the terrorists' ante in the event that threat becomes reality.

Most terrorist groups will continue to employ the usual weapons: machine guns, rockets, and bombs. Some groups, however, are becoming technically more adept. It is important that they and their sponsors be monitored carefully so as to deny them the opportunity of obtaining advanced weaponry and attacking critical targets. The consequences of miscalculating a sophisticated terrorist's intentions are absolutely frightening. There are no solutions based upon idealism alone. Governments and the public must learn to cope with both the old terrorism and the new.

CHAPTER FOUR

COPING WITH TERROR

Modern terrorism burst on the scene over twenty years ago with three shocking incidents—at Dawson Field in Jordan, where the PFLP blew up two planes in full view of the preassembled media, at Lod Airport, where the Japanese United Red Army and the PFLP massacred twenty-six people, and at Munich, where the Black September Palestinian group seized a group of Israeli Olympic athletes. The United States and its allies were stunned and largely unprepared. No one in political power was certain whether the attacks represented an excess of revolutionary zeal in support of legitimate causes or vicious nihilism. No one quite knew how to respond.

While the definitional problems remain, victim nations have slowly and painfully learned how to defend themselves against some forms of terror. Today, there is near-universal screening of tens of millions of airline passengers to prevent a handful of terrorists from strolling on board with guns or bombs. Concrete barricades, ill-disguised as planters, surround most major U.S. Government buildings to deter the odd suicide bomber.

And the United States is learning to reach out aggressively for new tools in the counterterrorism battle—for example, ways to bring terrorists to justice under our own system of law. The arrest by federal agents of Fawaz Younis—one of the terrorists who stormed a Royal Jordanian airliner in 1985 and blew it up on the tarmac—demonstrated the length of America's reach. During the year-long "Operation Goldenrod," Younis was carefully lured with promises of drugs

117

and women into international waters, where he was trapped and returned to stand trial in a U.S. courtroom.[1]

Physical security is another avenue of improved U.S. defenses.
Training programs, new building designs, and enhanced security measures have made American government personnel and embassies less
accessible targets of attack. The threat of retaliation is a third line of
active defense. Given the more bellicose U.S. position on punitive
response, terrorists and their state sponsors can be less certain that the
United States will accept victimization passively.

The critical question, however, is whether the United States is
prepared to deal with future mutations of threat. Terrorist tactics are
already changing. In 1983 the bomb that devastated the Marine barracks compound was the largest nonnuclear blast ever seen by FBI
experts. Equivalent to twelve tons of TNT, the bomb dug an eight-
foot crater through a seven-inch floor of reinforced concrete.[2] In 1988
the hijacking of the Kuwaiti airline, which the terrorists, through a
combination of tactics, rendered impervious to rescue, was the most
organizationally sophisticated act of international terrorism ever perpetrated. Months later, the Pan Am Flight 103 bombing demonstrated again the logistical and technical prowess that terrorists are
acquiring.

We should expect that terrorist acts will grow more lethal for
several reasons. First, governments willing to sponsor terrorism are
providing the wherewithal—intelligence, logistical support, weapons
—for attacks against new and more sophisticated targets. Their intelligence arms are far more adept at planning—and far more able to
pinpoint technical and political vulnerabilities in an opponent nation
—than single terrorist units. Religious radicals are also establishing
new boundaries for mass violence far beyond what their secular counterparts have historically been willing to inflict. Single-issue groups—
such as white supremacists, antiabortionists, or environmental groups
—are showing a far greater willingness to resort to violent tactics.

Second, the threshold for new forms of attack has already been
breached. Attacks on the technological infrastructure, poisonings of
municipal water supplies and medicinal supplies, thefts of radiological
materials, while not necessarily of terrorist origin, have created clear
precedents for future actions.

An effective counterterrorism apparatus must be geared toward
dealing with the next set of terrorist crises, not the last. Forward-

looking policy must be constructed on three interlocking layers: defense, deterrence and disaster management.

Defense involves increased vigilance in the effort to intercept and thwart attacks against us. We need improved intelligence and hardening of potential targets, such as improved intelligence and hardening of potential targets.

Deterrence entails visible readiness to respond to terrorist attacks. Effective law enforcement and retaliatory countermeasures, bolstered by new technologies, would enable us to conclude an incident on our own terms.

Finally, a disaster management apparatus is critical to managing the aftermath of a successful terrorist attack and preventing the terrorist from achieving lasting disruption.

Above all, we need policies that, while capitalizing on the full spectrum of capabilities, reflect the limitations inherent in dealing with terrorism. Terrorists retain all the advantages of the clandestine offense; they control the targets, timing and often the tempo of the event. The perception that the U.S. Government must be able to protect its citizens everywhere against everything lays the groundwork for our eventual humiliation. The reality is that the United States is neither omnipotent nor omniscient.

For the foreseeable future, terrorism will remain deeply embedded in the international system. No matter what is done or how well it is done, we will not always be able to prevent terrorist attacks or loss of life. We may not always be able to identify or apprehend the perpetrators.

The United States can, however, learn to cope with terrorism with a great deal more sophistication. The best defense is to avoid the panic, hysteria, and overreaction the terrorists seek to foment. Readiness, tempered by realism, will be the key to our ultimate success.

Forging a Policy Approach

Although U.S. policymakers have spent a great deal of time trying to forge coherent and credible antiterrorism policies, the record over the past twenty years can be generously described as dismal. A number of different policy approaches were tested by the Nixon, Ford, Carter, and Reagan administrations. None has proven truly effective in meeting the terror challenge.

One common thread running through the various counterterrorism strategies was the search for "a silver bullet" against terrorism. The Nixon administration's miracle cure was a multilateral collective security system to deny terrorists sanctuary anywhere in the world. This approach assumed that states would treat attacks on other countries with the same seriousness that they treat attacks on themselves. In reality, this has never been the case. Some states suffer very little from terrorism and/or do not view it as an illegitimate tactic, sometimes because they use it themselves.

The Carter administration viewed terrorism as one symptom of much larger human rights issues—violence that had its roots in poverty, injustice, and political repression. This approach virtually ignored the evidence that terrorism was becoming part of the arsenal for low-intensity warfare—that states, not groups, were the prime movers of terrorist operations. But even if it were true, the United States could not single-handedly sweep away the historical injustices, or economic and social tragedies that give rise to terrorism. Indeed, the Carter administration's greatest success—the Camp David accords—did nothing to diminish the explosive power of an Islamic revolution that sparked a wholly new wave of terrorist violence.

The Reagan administration took counterterrorism policy in precisely the opposite direction, seeking to deter all comers with a strong retaliatory posture. Although President Reagan promised a swift and devastating response against terrorist actions that violated the norms of civilized conduct, the Administration was only occasionally able to carry out the threat, and never in a way that deterred very much for very long.

Reagan's cinematic machismo proved to be as unworkable, in practice, as President Carter's compassionate approach. The use of force is simply not applicable in every terrorist incident. One may seize an opportunity, as the United States did in intercepting the hijackers of the *Achille Lauro* cruise ship in the Mediterranean, but the window of opportunity is not always open. The exercise of military force generally requires a fair amount of luck. Had the hijackers of the *Achille Lauro* thought to bring along a few hostages to ensure their safe passage, the denouement of that episode could have been considerably different.

Another common thread in counterterrorism policy is that the United States must never "give in" to terrorists—the "no-concessions" approach. Whether or not a no-concessions policy is effective has never actually been tested, since it has never been followed in practice. Every administration has been reluctantly drawn into negotiations with, and on occasion concessions to, terrorist groups.

Although the Nixon administration declared that the United States would not pay ransom monies or urge other countries to release imprisoned terrorists in exchange for kidnapped Americans, it repeatedly condoned concessions by third parties—U.S. corporations, for example—and granted ransom and safe passage demands in several internationally significant hijackings. President Ford's administration privately assisted in the negotiations and payoff to Tanzanian terrorists holding three U.S. students. President Carter ultimately granted substantive concessions to Iran for the release of the embassy hostages, while President Reagan entered into the complex and disastrous arms-for-hostages barter.

Why has it been so difficult to develop an effective counterterrorism policy? Part of the problem lies with U.S. leaders. Each administration has foolishly promised counterterrorism miracles, deluding itself and the public that the terror phenomenon is amenable to a U.S.-imposed solution. Nothing could be farther from the truth. As Ambassador L. Paul Bremer III put it: "This is a game of drag bunts and stolen bases, not home runs. There will be no treaties of unconditional surrender and probably no treaties at all. The best-laid diplomatic, economic, legal and even military plans will only contain terrorism, not defeat it."[3]

Terrorism is so broadly defined as to encompass almost every form of violent action short of large-state conventional warfare. But a frustrated Cuban hijacker is not the same as a Shiite radical, who is different from an Armenian vigilante or a Puerto Rican nationalist. By describing the many phenomena at times called "terrorism" as a single entity, we have created an almost insurmountable policy problem. No single approach to terrorism is inherently wrong, just inherently inadequate to deal with every incident and every foe.

No matter how profound the indignation, the United States must balance its counterterrorism options within the nation's larger foreign and defense-policy interests. Terrorist activities do not stand in splendid isolation as America's premier foreign policy concern. Just as our counterterrorism goals are not identical with those of other nations so, too, do counterterrorism options vie with other U.S. policy interests of equal or greater concern. The government's displeasure with Egypt over its release of the *Achille Lauro* hijackers was publicly tempered because of Egypt's critical role in the Middle East peace process. In the 1986 La Belle disco bombing in Berlin, which prompted U.S. bombing raids on Libya, the evidence of *Syrian* complicity was conveniently ignored, since any retaliation against Syria could have had wider implications for the U.S.–Soviet relationship. Syria, a Soviet client state, was host to hundreds of Soviet radar and missile technicians who had just set up a state-of-the-art air defense system.

Finally, we will remain vulnerable to terrorist attack because of who and what we are: an open society with an unfettered media. Terrorists rely on the reach of modern telecommunications to create a horrifying media spectacle for an international audience, both to bolster their own perceived prowess and to make the victim government appear weak or incompetent. The elimination or diminution of media coverage could be a truly effective counterterrorism measure. But the most basic traditions and beliefs of democratic societies make this approach not only unthinkable but abhorrent. Were this goal pursued, the fundamental tenets of our democracy would be held at risk.

This should not imply that there are no workable counterterrorism strategies. In the past, however, U.S. policymakers have tended to confuse ends and means, substituting tactics such as multilateralism, economic assistance, or threats of force for counterterrorism policies. Having made the general point that the United States opposes terrorism, there does not appear to be any compelling reason to limit our options in support of any single counterterrorism approach. The fact is that the United States will need every trick in the diplomatic and military arsenal to oppose terrorism effectively.

Reserving its options permits the United States the luxury of using them without compromising any standing doctrine. Tough rhetoric can be a useful tool, but quiet, behind-the-scenes negotiations have proven just as effective. International cooperation is a valuable approach, but so too is friendly intercession by neutral third parties.

It may be that the best declaratory policy is *no specific* policy at all, but rather an expanded menu of tools and tactics for use in each unique situation. This requires, at the tactical level, more imagination and more flexibility. Combating terrorism encompasses a wide range of organizational and operational talents including:

- legal and diplomatic options
- constantly improved intelligence
- technological tools to cover a range of current and potential modes of attack
- military capabilities across the spectrum of low-intensity warfare
- covert options
- improved crisis management and emergency preparedness apparatus

All of these options are essential components of a counterterrorism arsenal, though the opportunities they present can be overridden by the limitations of their use.

Law Enforcement

Although terrorism is, in some sense, supercriminality, it is crime nonetheless for which society has penalties and sanctions. The law helps to strip the bravado from terrorist crimes, looking only at the ugliness and brutality of the end result.

Effective law enforcement is an indispensable—perhaps *the* indispensable—tool in the counterterrorism arsenal of free societies. When it works, it reflects the democratic system at its best. The problem is that it doesn't always work well against all classes of terrorism.

For domestic terrorism, the issues are relatively straightforward. The United States has both the means and the authority to respond decisively, both before and after a terrorist event. The FBI and local law-enforcement officials have achieved a notable success rate against both left- and right-wing groups. The Weathermen, Symbionese Liberation Army, Posse Comitatus, FALN, Aryan Nations, and United

Freedom Front have faded in turn from the front pages, due in large measure to high-quality police work.

Over the past six years, organizational and operational capabilities have been substantially upgraded, beginning with the creation of the FBI's Hostage Rescue Team (HRT) in 1982. Each member of that fifty-man team receives specialized training in emergency medical procedures, diversion and entry techniques, weapons and tactics for use in seige or hostage incidents. The HRT has been in place at the Los Angeles Olympic Games, the 1984 and 1988 Democratic and Republican presidential conventions, the Statue of Liberty Rededication, the Pan American Games in Indianapolis, the 1987 Cuban prisoner uprising in Atlanta, and the Seoul Olympics.[4]

Another organizational innovation is the joint terrorism task-force concept to smooth over jurisdictional problems among federal, state, and local officials. There are currently nine formal task forces throughout the United States, in Boston, Chicago, Illinois, Houston, Los Angeles, Newark, New York, Philadelphia, and Washington, D.C., which are staffed and supervised by police detectives, state troopers, and FBI agents. All police officers on the task forces are deputized as U.S. marshals and receive the same security clearances as FBI agents. Terrorism task forces have been critical in several major terrorism investigations, including the United Freedom Front, the Armed Resistance Unit, and the May 19th Communist Organization.[5]

Terrorist attacks on American citizens or assets abroad, however, pose an entirely different set of law enforcement dilemmas. Questions of access, jurisdiction, and national sovereignty invariably complicate a response. For its part, the United States has made a great deal of headway in unshackling the legal restraints on law enforcement officials. Indeed, until recently, the murder of U.S. citizens overseas was not a punishable offense under U.S. law. As late as 1985, the Attorney General was unable to bring indictments against those suspected in the slayings of two Americans in El Salvador because they had violated no American law.[6]

Some of the obvious legal gaps in the fight against terrorism have now been closed by legislation including:

- the 1984 Act to Combat Terrorism, which approved ratification of the UN Convention Against Aircraft Sabotage, the UN Convention Against the Taking of Hostages, and authorized the Secretary of State to pay rewards for information leading to the arrest of terrorists.

- the Foreign Assistance Authorization Act of 1985, which expanded the authority of the Federal Aviation Administration to inspect airports outside the United States and to issue travel advisories (posting a published blacklist) for airports that fail to meet minimum security standards. It was only after the United States threatened to name Athens a security risk that Greece made security improvements. Fear of losing U.S. tourist dollars was the clear motivation.

- the Omnibus Diplomatic Security and Antiterrorism Act of 1986, which made the murder or assault of an American overseas a U.S. felony and upheld the principle of extradition of terrorists by *legal or other means* to the United States for prosecution (other means generally taken to imply forcible abduction). Other provisions of the act included efforts to enhance the security of U.S. diplomatic facilities and personnel abroad, as well as to set international standards for seaport and shipboard security.

Strong U.S. legislative support has helped to increase the resolve of other nations to pursue legal remedies against terrorists. Despite political pressures for appeasement and threats of terrorist retaliation, increasing numbers of terrorists are being caught and publicly tried worldwide. In London, Nezar Hindawi received a life sentence for his attempt to use his unwitting pregnant Irish girlfriend to blow up an Israeli jumbo jet in the air. In Paris, George Ibrahim Abdallah received a life sentence for his role in the murder of a U.S. Army attaché, despite shocking attempts by the French prosecutor to press for leniency. In Madrid, a Palestinian terrorist was sentenced to forty-seven years for directing the June 1986 bombing attempt against an El Al plane. In Washington, Fawaz Younis was convicted for the 1985 hijacking of the Royal Jordanian airliner.

Clearly, legal remedies against international terrorism are worth pursuing. The problem is that jurisdictional questions cut both ways. While the United States can foster a climate conducive to legal apprehension and prosecution of terrorists, it cannot impose its will on an unwilling foreign government or unilaterally authorize its officials to operate on foreign soil. Even friendly governments have balked at holding terrorists for prosecution, much less extradition, stemming from a profound fear of retaliation.

For example, after the series of kidnappings began in Lebanon in the early eighties, U.S. authorities learned that one of the ringleaders was in France. When the United States asked informally for custody, French authorities alerted Imam Mugniyah, one of the most powerful of all terrorist leaders; he was able to slip away. In 1983 U.S. and British intelligence officers exposed a plot by a terrorist, who was probably a member of Abu Ibrahim's May 15 group, to place a suitcase bomb on a flight out of Athens. The Greek government, however, allowed him to leave on a flight for Algeria before the United States could formalize an extradition request.[7] In the 1986 *Achille Lauro* case, the Italian and Yugoslav governments spirited the mastermind of the operation, Muhammed Abul al-Abas (disguised as a Yugoslav flight attendant), out of their territories as quickly as possible.

In 1987 the German government was extorted into refusing extradition to the United States of Mohammed Hamadei, a terrorist accused of participating in the hijack of TWA Flight 847 to Beirut and the murder of a U.S. Navy diver during the incident. Hamadei's Hizballah terror gang "family" in Beirut engineered the kidnapping of two West German businessmen. Their pressure on West Germany was so effective that the German government agreed to consider trying twenty-three-year-old Hamadei in juvenile court, exposing him to a maximum sentence of only ten years.[8] Under pressure from the United States, he was convicted in May 1989 and sentenced to serve a life term.

One senior West German official who lobbied for extradition of Hamadei to the United States, Alexander Prechtel, is a veteran terrorism prosecutor and federal court spokesman. He has warned that bringing the full force of the judicial systems of the West into the war against terrorism will not be an easy task. Along with different political and economic considerations, the allies are also afflicted with sometimes conflicting bodies of law.

Prior to the release by Hizballah terrorists of Rudolph Cordes, a West German hostage who was seized in Beirut to pressure the German government into refusing extradition of Hamadei to the United States, Prechtel admitted, "We fear that what may happen with

Cordes may give terrorists the idea that our country is not as tough as it once was, and so they may be tempted to try again at some point to intimidate our government. There is, in this, a serious danger for the future of our efforts to deter terrorism and to establish the expectation of sure and strong punishment." (Immediately following Cordes' release, unconfirmed reports, which the German government denied, said the hostages' employer had paid Hizballah as much as five million dollars in ransom.)

Precisely because the ability to gain access to terrorists through diplomatic channels is often blocked, the U.S. Government has attempted to take matters into its own hands with the policy of forcible abduction. The court is supposed to turn a blind eye to the issue of how a defendant came before it, judging the criminal case only on its merits. This approach, however, has several limitations.

First, it tends to be more symbolic than realistic. As a practical matter, it takes months, perhaps years, of concerted effort to set the bait for even a single terrorist. In general, terrorists tend to take sanctuary with their state sponsors, making covert U.S. operations in hostile territory a risky business. Efforts to lure the bigger fish out of hiding and into a U.S. net may be substantially more difficult. Fawaz Younis was not one of the most notorious international terrorists, merely one of the most viable targets, since he was living openly in Beirut and running short of money.[9]

Second, forcible abductions will inevitably raise questions of due process. When federal agents slammed Younis to the deck of the boat on which he was captured, they were apparently unaware then, and during the interrogation which followed, that both of his wrists had been broken in the fall. In the decision by U.S. District Judge Barrington Parker to throw out the Younis confession, the judge blasted the FBI writing that "In an uncertain physical condition, in an oppressive environment and subject to relentless interrogation, Younis lacked the will necessary to waive his U.S. [constitutional] rights."*[10]

---

* Although issues of due process will inevitably cloud the legal issues in cases of forcible abduction, however, there is a body of law to support the principle. In *United States* vs. *Reed,* the defendant, convicted in absentia for mail fraud, was lured out of hiding in the Bahamas and arrested. Reed later claimed in court that the CIA agent held a cocked revolver to his head and threatened to "blow his brains out" if he moved. Reed's defense attorneys argued that his "abduction at the hands of government agents breeds contempt for the law, mocks our stated concern for human rights,

Finally, it is clear that the ability to apprehend and prosecute terrorists will hinge on international cooperation. Here, the problem centers on the sometimes vague distinction between terrorism and political crimes against an established tyranny, with which most democratic nations tend to sympathize. Even the United States has not been exempt from charges that it offers safe haven for terrorists. Indeed, Great Britain complained for years about the reluctance of the United States to extradite members of the Irish Republican Army.

Similarly, no country has yet agreed to extradite terrorists to the United States, possibly risking retaliation upon themselves. Indeed, some make it difficult as possible. In the Younis case, American planners, fearing interference, arranged to convey Younis across four thousand miles without entering the sovereign waters or territory of any other country.[11]

Because terrorism cuts across national boundaries, there can be no lasting unilateral solution. Indeed, just as international terrorism would not be possible without the active collaboration of hostile governments, so, too, efforts to combat it will not be possible without collaboration among victim governments. The record in this area, however, leaves substantial room for improvement.

Back in the early seventies, when terrorism was just beginning to emerge as an international problem, the United States approached the United Nations and its sister agencies for multilateral cooperation against terrorism. While the UN has formally condemned specific acts of terrorism—defining airline hijackings and sabotage, attacks on diplomats, and hostage taking as crimes of international significance—none of the conventions contain enforcement mechanisms with any teeth. Indeed, no UN action has ever been taken against any state which has actively violated UN antiterrorism conventions.[12]

Eventually, the United States turned to the Summit Seven—the heads of state of the seven major Western industrialized countries—the United States, Canada, West Germany, France, Italy, Japan, and

and jeopardizes our standing in the international community." The court rejected this argument crisply, noting that: "Appelant Reed, a fugitive from justice, with no respect for the law whatsoever is hardly in a position to urge otherwise." (E. Anthony Fessler, "Extraterritorial Apprehension as a Proactive Counterterrorism Measure," in Neil C. Livingstone and Terrell E. Arnold, *Beyond the Iran-Contra Crisis* [Lexington, Mass.: Lexington Books, 1988], p. 244.)

the United Kingdom—who meet annually on economic, and political matters. At each of their annual summits, the leaders have condemned a host of terrorist evils, including hijackings, hostage takings, state-supported terrorism, and abuses of diplomatic immunity. All have promised cooperation—but to little effect. In most cases, the declarations that follow the summits do little more than signal political resolve rather than endorse specific actions.[13]

Despite dozens of potential candidates, the seven have applied counterterrorism principles in only one incident. All flights to and from Afghanistan were halted because the Afghan regime provided sanctuary to the hijackers of a Pakistani aircraft. The sanctions proved to be a relatively painless undertaking for everyone except the Afghanis.

Where sanctions entail mutual hardship, however, action by the Seven has been less forthcoming. Probably the low ebb in transatlantic relations came just prior to the U.S. raid on Libya. During the winter of 1985, U.S. Deputy Secretary of State John Whitehead crisscrossed Europe to persuade the allies to join the United States in penalizing Libya for its sponsorship of terrorism, notably the 1985 airport massacres in Rome and Vienna. Although the Europeans agreed not to undercut U.S. economic sanctions—a policy that could not be implemented in practice—their response was tepid at best.

One of the problems in trying to use the Seven to launch an antiterrorism campaign is that it is inherently unwieldy and slow to act, with no permanent staff to monitor either sanctions that should be imposed or the actual effects of such sanctions. Too, terrorism is only one of the issues on an annual agenda that includes trade, economic, and political questions of equal if not greater importance.[14]

Consequently, by the mid-eighties the United States began to turn its attention to other forums, such as NATO and the European Economic Community, to broaden the framework for international cooperation. Although Congress directed the President to consult with the NATO allies, its membership was also reluctant to act, reminding the United States that NATO's charter did not create a mandate to respond to terrorism questions.

The European Economic Community and its subgroups have yielded some interesting prospects for cooperation. Several of the members, particularly France, appeared to be more comfortable with the EEC as a channel for collective counterterrorism. The advantage, at least from the European perspective, was that any collaboration with the United States was necessarily informal, since the United States is not a member of the organization. Thus, Europe has a relatively greater voice in the deliberations, which are freer of any linkages to U.S. policies.

In practice, the EEC has managed to take a harder line against terrorism than its international counterparts. When Britain tried to orchestrate a European response to Syria's involvement in the sabotage of an El Al flight, the EEC members eventually came on board, staging a show of Western solidarity that induced Syria's Assad to retreat from the terrorism scene for a time.[15] The clever and contemptuous Assad was stunned by the show of genuine Western unity.

From the U.S. point of view, working through the EEC is less than optimal. As a nonmember, the United States cannot directly participate in the dialogue or the decision-making process. In 1987, however, a meeting between the EEC and Summit Seven leadership offered a potentially critical breakthrough in counterterrorism collaboration: creation of a new joint venture between the two that would endow the United States with full membership privileges.

Probably the single most limiting factor in the war against terrorism is the lack of solidarity among victim states. There are important issues on the multinational agenda which have yet to be resolved, including a broader and more routine sharing of intelligence information, consistency in the enforcement of existing international agreements and alignment of national laws on extradition and prosecution.

At the enforcement level, there are many such critical operational steps that will assist in the battle against terror. At the foreign policy level, the prospect of joint action remains elusive. Perhaps we should not expect too much progress in this area. What is often ignored in the United States is that the price of proactive multilateral action is often unequally shared, with Europe bearing a disproportionate amount of the cost and risk. Where joint sanctions or other penalties can be imposed against state sponsors, a powerful signal will be sent. But the United States cannot take for granted that shared counterterrorism aims will automatically yield joint action. Public declarations by American presidents praising any improvement in allied cooperation could be of serious benefit—or detriment. The United States *must* improve not only its appreciation of allies' problems but also, its *con-*

sultation with allies prior to any public statement and *virtually* all actions.

Improved Intelligence

Intelligence efforts designed to thwart terrorist attacks are obviously another critical component of counterterrorism. Without an effective intelligence apparatus—to provide insights about the terrorists, their aims and motivations, alignments, leadership and organizational structure—a hardline policy of counterterrorism can only be rhetorical.

During the 1970s, intelligence capabilities in the United States were virtually decimated by legislative fiat—a backlash against the excesses of the past, such as the overthrow of the Allende regime in Chile and failed attempts to assassinate Fidel Castro. By 1980, the intelligence community had lost a quarter of its people; three quarters of its station chiefs overseas were eligible for retirement. Less than half of the CIA's intelligence analysts spoke the language of the country they were assigned to cover. An even smaller proportion had even visited the countries for which they had to have expertise. Information transmitted by satellite rather than human intelligence on the ground came to dominate (and limit) America's intelligence-gathering capabilities.[16]

America's lack of reliable information and sound analysis facilitated some spectacular blows against the United States. In 1979 it was clear to most knowledgeable observers that the decision to allow the ailing Shah to enter the United States might lead to some form of retaliation by Iranian radicals. Israel warned Washington that the U.S. embassy would be seized in Iran. Yet, the obvious step—to reduce the number of embassy personnel down to a skeleton staff—was not taken, with the result that Iran's Revolutionary Guard was able to net sixty-six Americans when it seized the embassy. In 1983, the U.S. Marine compound in Lebanon was virtually undefended, a sitting duck for terrorist attack. But the intelligence expertise which might have predicted the event and forced defensive changes had been wiped out in the Beirut embassy bombing a few months before; the

United States lacked replacement personnel or the wisdom to know
that replacements were urgently needed.

If the track record abroad has been less than overwhelming, the
United States has been a good deal more successful at home. When
terrorism is treated as part of a spectrum of domestic criminal activity,
the United States has both the authority and the means to respond
effectively. Since 1982, the FBI and other law enforcement agencies
have been able to interdict at least fifty-four terrorist attacks within
the United States.[17]

For example, in 1983 the FBI arrested a pro-Khomeini student
group as it was about to firebomb a theater in Seattle. In 1985 members of the Libyan-linked street gang El Rukn were arrested during
the purchase of a rocket intended to shoot down an aircraft at Chicago's O'Hare Airport. In 1986 the Royal Canadian Mounted Police,
working with the FBI, arrested five Sikh terrorists who conspired to
place a bomb on an Air India flight out of JFK International Airport
in New York.[18]

Within the FBI, analytical capabilities have been vastly upgraded,
including the Bomb Data Center, the Terrorist Research and Analytical Center (TRAC), and the Special Operations and Research Unit
(SOAR). The Bomb Data Center collects and distributes details of
bombings by terrorist groups and is involved in research and development in support of hostage-rescue activities.

TRAC analyzes the available data with a view toward the likelihood of attack and produces an annual incident summary, identifying
all terrorist acts which have taken place in the United States during
the preceding year.[19]

SOAR studies terrorists and other criminals for tactical and psychological insights. Located at the FBI Academy at Quantico, Virginia, SOAR profiles individuals and groups, gauging the dimensions
of threat. SOAR specializes in analyzing threat and extortion notes,
using the techniques of psycholinguistics. The unit has been im-
mensely successful in predicting the activities of right-wing hate
groups—white supremacists, neo-Nazis—as well as left-wing nihilistic
groups such as the United Freedom Front and other offshoots of the
old Weather Underground. SOAR was also directly involved—in cooperation with other elements of the FBI and New York and Chicago
police—in identifying and quashing the FALN (Puerto Rican separatist) networks in the United States.

Similarly, the International Association of Chiefs of Police has taken the problem of information sharing and intelligence systems to the municipality level. In 1986 the IACP established a committee on terrorism to exchange information and provide educational opportunities for its membership.[20]

Ongoing cooperation among law enforcement agencies internationally has also contributed to the improved track record. Interpol—the international police organization—stood back from the terrorism problem for many years, treating terrorism as political crime and therefore outside of its jurisdiction. In 1984, however, its membership reinterpreted Interpol's charter to open the door for an exchange of information on terrorism, and in 1986 Interpol created a specialized unit to compile information on terrorist groups and transmit this data to its worldwide network.[21]

Good intelligence and analysis are obviously a first line of defense. If we were able to thwart every attack, the problem of terrorism would be considerably diminished. Unfortunately, intelligence, no matter how diligent, offers no panacea against attack.

In many cases, prevention is largely a matter of sheer luck. The 1988 interdiction of a Japanese Red Army terrorist, Yu Kikumura, came down to astute observation by a local state trooper at a highway rest stop. Obviously, any hope that we can uncover every terrorist plot or penetrate every terrorist group is unrealistic.

Today, we may pay dearly for what amounts to little more than rumor or may rationalize a fortuitous arrest as a major intelligence coup. Intelligence collection and subsequent analysis often tend to highlight trends that are already evident to any informed observer, hence missing the critical activity beneath the surface. For example, the danger of serious terrorist attack looms largest when the noise level is *lowest*. When terrorist groups appear to be shooting or bombing everything in sight, they don't have the time, resources, or manpower to undertake major new operations. It is during the lulls that competent terrorist groups devote their limited resources to planning and logistics for truly devastating attacks.

Data collection and analysis alone will not be sufficient to predict those operations that the terrorists are at pain to hide. Looking for advance information about terrorist activities is often likened to looking for a needle in a haystack. The most menacing terrorist groups are closely knit cells that are difficult to penetrate under the best of circumstances. Even when the United States is successful, the survival time for reliable informants is not particularly long.

Thwarting terrorist attacks, however, is only one of the functions of a good intelligence apparatus. When it works well, the government appears prescient and powerful. But even when it doesn't, intelligence plays a critical role in the deft handling of a terrorist crisis. Among the key functions of intelligence are credibility assessments, technical assessments, and behavioral assessments.[22]

A first line of analysis is to assess the willingness of the terrorists to execute their threat. If the PLO threatened to use nerve agents, a credibility assessment should focus on the PLO's resolve to actually carry out such a threat rather than attempt to verify the existence of the nerve agent. By contrast, if an Iranian Shiite group made comparably serious threats, concern would center on their capability to execute it.

An important component of gauging the credibility of the threat is a sophisticated assessment of individual terrorist groups as well as trends within various terrorist movements. Quite simply, it is the kind of knowledge that one would want to possess about any potential adversary. It must be instantly available to national leaders in times of crisis and it must be absent of any ideological coloration.

A second area of intelligence gathering is technical estimations of threat, which in practice may be quite difficult. In the nuclear arena, designs and some details about nuclear devices exist in the open literature. Unless there are obvious flaws, it may take considerable time and effort to determine the magnitude of the threat. For chemical or biological threats, the situation is far worse. Such agents can be manufactured with relatively limited resources, while the control mechanisms for commercial purchase and transportation are often relatively weak. If such a threat were issued, the intelligence analysts would be called upon to evaluate the likelihood that the terrorist group did indeed possess such agents and had the technical sophistication to disperse them effectively.

Finally, after a threat is verified to be authentic, the intelligence community will be tasked with providing behavior assessments about the background and psychological profile of the group. Understanding the motivation, leadership structures, and control centers of each unique group is critical in planning and carrying out responsive countermeasures.

Information about past interactions with terrorist groups—their willingness to negotiate, compromise, allow deadlines to pass, or take violent actions—is an indispensable tool in preparing a response. What deters one terrorist group may incite another to carry out its threat. Studies of German youths who enter terrorist groups suggest that many have experienced failure in school or work.[23] Many are juvenile delinquents who are alienated from the society at large. By contrast, Middle Eastern religiously motivated terrorists believe that they are facilitating the arrival of salvation by participating in the struggle to expunge the "filth and corruption" of the West. Terrorists' personality profiles range from the psychotic to the psychopathic to the religious or politically fanatic. Our successful response may depend on accurate assessment of the character of the group.

In some cases, a policy of reactive retaliation may have the opposite effect of deterrence, and reinforce the mindset of the terrorist. This is particularly true for organizations composed of autonomous cells, such as the Maoist Shining Path of Peru, Red Army Faction of West Germany, or the Red Brigades of Italy. When small groups come under threat, the external danger has the effect of uniting the group against an outside enemy. One of the few generally agreed on psychological truths about such secretive, violent people states: "Terrorists whose only sense of significance comes from being terrorists cannot be compelled to give up terrorism. To do so would be to lose their very reason for being, to commit psychological suicide."[24]

For complex organizations, such as the PLO or the Basque separatists ETA, where the terrorist groups operate in parallel with mainstream political movements, the dynamics are clearly different. Dedicated to nationalist political causes, these groups can often be inhibited, where political remedies can be credibly offered.

For *state*-controlled terrorist groups, the circumstances for effective resolution are again different. Action against or negotiations with the group may have little effect, since they are operating at the behest of an adversary government. And if lost in a shoot-out, they can be readily cloned by their state sponsor.

How well we respond to terrorists depends a great deal on what we know about them. While the weapons may be the same, the terrorists are not. Issues of culture, demography, and individual psychology create an internal dynamic to each incident. Despite the efforts of psychologists, diplomats, and police, all too little is understood about analyzing and integrating these factors into the response calculus. While we must work much harder to succeed, we must also prepare the people for a possible failure.

Technology and Counterterrorism

Beyond law enforcement and diplomacy, there is a pressing need to bolster our technological response capabilities. The objective is to increase the ante for the terrorists—to raise the price of attack or to lower their probability of success—and to reduce the amount of real and perceived damage of successful attack.

Although terrorists are becoming more technologically sophisticated, so too are the potential counterterrorism applications. Technology plays a vital role both in hardening targets against terrorist attacks and in managing such incidents successfully. From early intelligence warning to improved physical barriers, from remote sensing devices to rapid entry techniques, technology offers innovative offensive and defensive approaches.

In the past, we have tended to rely on rough-and-ready measures —dump trucks laden with sand, concrete barriers, or sheer firepower. But the range of sophisticated counterterrorism technologies on the shelf, or on the horizon, is simply staggering. Solid-state television cameras, smaller than a quarter, can be invisibly hidden in advance to monitor a hijacking in progress. Long-range infrared devices, which detect motion and placement of individuals inside a hostage barricade, are also available. Fiber optics, tiny hairlike strands of glass with a lens cover, can generate television pictures of events on the inside of a terrorist operation. Indeed, during the hijacking of a TWA flight in Beirut, one American television network attempted to smuggle fiber optics on board the plane. As crass as it may sound, had they been successful, they would have scooped not only their competition but the U.S. Government as well.

Laser technologies offer a host of previously inconceivable capabilities. Using lasers aimed through the windows of an aircraft or the glass panes of a building onto such items as a piece of paper, one can actually listen in on conversations inside a hostage area. Similarly, lasers can be used as a means of communication to individual hostages by modulating the tiniest concentrations of organic vapors. Though a difficult matter to accomplish clandestinely, it is in principle possible to communicate instructions to an individual hostage, e.g., to move a foot to the right to allow sharpshooters a clear shot. But such techniques can also be used offensively—to envelop a target in sound.

Techniques have been developed to wall off communications around a particular target, such as a commercial airliner sitting on the ground. It is even possible to accomplish this selectively, so that the terrorists will not know that their other messages are being jammed. It was a good idea in theory, but it was impractical in application.

Other devices, including specialized explosives, high-powered sound, or lasers, can be used to disintegrate brick and mortar, to allow for rapid entry. Related techniques have been used for antipersonnel objectives—to create temporary mental confusion and loss of bodily controls. The phenomenon has long been recognized—even high-powered/low-frequency bullhorns can create similar effects. Until the arrival of Gorbachev, the Russians used microwaves against the U.S. embassy in Moscow to induce mental disorientation, fatigue, and low-grade illness.

Although the emerging technological arsenal provides some extraordinary capabilities, there is no room for complacence. Most any system can be defeated with careful planning and a modicum of sophistication. Just when we believed our airports were secure, plastic handguns or bombs planted in cargo bays emerged to outwit routine security precautions. Terrorists have learned that continually moving people around on a hijacked plane can confuse remote sensing devices.

There are weak links in any system that can be exploited by terrorists. Without a well-directed and adequately funded ongoing program of research and technology, we are perpetually in a reactive mode—always one step behind the terrorists' countermeasures.

There are four areas of research and development priorities for new technological countermeasures: meeting current levels of threat, meeting threats to the technological infrastructure, meeting low-probability/high-consequence threats, and threat anticipation. In each area, there are short-term and long-term research needs and several key problem areas for which there are no practical or known technical solutions.

Meeting Current Threats Current threats include bombings, hijackings, hostage-taking, and their variants. Technology can assist in three key areas: intelligence and surveillance, protection and safeguards, and incident response.

Intelligence and surveillance, provided by a combination of traditional police methods and sophisticated technical systems, tend to be well supported because of the overlap with the needs of private business. For the most part, in this area, systems and services needed to deal with terrorism overlap with those needed for coping with other criminal threats.

The image of a lone plant guard walking his beat is today largely illusory. In his place are increasingly elaborate systems of electronic checks, door controls, monitors, sensors, automatic telephone call systems, and computer programs that help the user make rapid crisis assessments. A huge security industry, which some experts predict will reach fifty to sixty billion dollars annually by the turn of the century, is devoted to access-control and crisis prevention.[25]

Nevertheless, it is not clear, particularly as terrorists grow more sophisticated, that counterterrorism can be regarded as a small subset of a larger security problem. The types of defenses to thwart criminals and terrorists may not be identical, particularly in the event of massively destructive attacks. More focused research for systems specifically applicable to terrorism defenses is still lacking.

Protection and safeguards technologies are today generally limited to barriers and various entry-screening devices. Metal detectors, while useful in locating small arms, have fairly obvious weaknesses, notably their lack of utility in detecting nonmetal firearms or high explosives in airline baggage. There are some new approaches, particularly in high-explosives detection, under consideration. One of the most promising is neutron activation, a technique employed by the Israelis. But the adverse side effect of the technology, which leaves the baggage slightly radioactive, implies that considerably more research must be done.

Response capability technologies can offer useful complements to conventional military or police methods. The near-term options under consideration include explosive disablement devices—firing a slug of ultracold material into an explosive to freeze its fusing mechanisms. Another option is liquid metal embrittlement—weakening the molecular composition of aluminum and magnesium metals to substantially reduce the amount of explosives needed to force entry through an aircraft door. The longer-term technological wish list might include more precise remote sensing devices to distinguish terrorists from their victims, low-profile antivehicle perimeters that shut down an internal combustion engine automatically, perhaps even techniques that can selectively impair brain functions or send commands (e.g., to put down the gun) directly to the brain.

Threats to the Technological Infrastructure   In this area, the lack of understanding about where key nodes of vulnerability lie and how to defend them is the primary research gap. Private-sector businesses are primarily concerned with their own tiny pieces of infrastructure, not with the integrity of the system as a whole. The technical characteristics and interconnections among various systems are so complex as to require highly sophisticated computer modeling and analysis, which can only be provided at the federal level.

Low-Probability/High-Consequence Threats   The question here is how much attention and funding we are prepared to devote to the off chance that we may be the victims of a highly destructive attack. In the United States, speculation about the threat of nuclear terrorism or the possibility of nuclear accidents led to the federal formation of the Nuclear Emergency Search Teams (NEST). NEST provides a rapid response capability, scientific knowledge and experience, a logistics and communications base, and specialized equipment in the event of a nuclear emergency. Unfortunately, no similar capability exists to respond to chemical, biological, or toxicological threats.[26] One of the primary obstacles, as well as an area of needed research, is instrumentation to detect and identify such agents. While some chemical-agent detectors and alarm systems are available "off the shelf," detectors for biological or toxicological agents are not readily available. This is particularly true for long-range detection. By the time we can discern an aerosol cloud approaching, it is far too late to prevent a crisis. The Los Alamos National Laboratory has developed lasers that are capable of selectively exciting aerosols of organic poisons, toxins, and live biologicals. But their value rests primarily in a military battlefield setting rather than protection of civilian lives. Technologies for neutralization, immunization, and detoxification are either rudimentary or non-existent.

The cleanup problems from such attacks pose potentially serious obstacles. For example, anthrax spores can survive for more than twenty years, potentially denying access to an area for an indefinite period. The British experimented with anthrax in the Helorides Islands in the *1940s* and have yet to clean it up despite the extensive use of flamethrowers.

Threat Anticipation   Finally, research is needed to attempt to identify future threats and possible areas of research and development for response. Already, we can anticipate some of the countermeasures that may be needed in the future. We know, for example, that terrorists have downlink satellite receivers, so that they can monitor cable news and network reports about their operation and potential countermeasures. We know too that they have experimented with portable uplink satellite transmitters to broadcast internationally—in effect, creating their own terrorism show. Any government wishing to avert humiliation and defeat ought to be preparing now to have the capability to selectively block transmissions in or out of a hijacked plane, train, or ship.

In many other areas, contingencies can be studied and responses prepared to turn the tables on terrorist operations and retain the offensive.

Ultimately, technology can offer no long-term solution to the problem of terrorism. What it can provide, however, is a new roster of capabilities to help prevent the terrorists from achieving their goals: new ways to assess our internal vulnerability; new physical safeguards against attack; and a more effective real-time response. Perhaps more importantly, a flexible and cutting edge technological advantage may create a truly credible deterrent against many attacks—especially state-sponsored.

The Military Option

The trend in the 1980s toward a more forceful response to terrorism stemmed in part from President Ronald Reagan's belief that there had been too many funerals of Americans and too few of terrorists. Reagan was determined that terrorists and their state sponsors would pay a price for attacking the United States. As his Secretary of State George Shultz put it: the issue was no longer whether we would retaliate, but when and how and under what circumstances.

Bold rhetoric aside, deciding when and how to deploy military force is itself a difficult question. The use of force is clearly not applicable in every terrorist incident nor would the American public likely accept the engagement of U.S. forces abroad on a routine basis.

Questions of distance and national sovereignty also complicate military operations. Projecting power quickly over thousands of miles is an arduous logistical and operational task. Moreover, there are no precrisis agreements to permit U.S. forces to operate on foreign soil, nor are such agreements feasible. We would not permit West Germany, for example, to send its rapid deployment force into Miami to rescue its own citizens from a hijacked Lufthansa jet. In the midst of a terrorist crisis, the United States is generally forced either to wait for an invitation to intervene, hope for a weak central government (such as the Germans enjoyed in Somalia and the Israelis in Uganda), or rely on the good offices and counterterrorism capabilities—competent or not—of the government in power.[27]

Military force is clearly not the answer to every terrorist incident, but the capability to use force ultimately lends credibility to a whole host of other potential options. A backpocket military option keeps the terrorists off balance, forcing them to devote far more attention and resources to protecting themselves than to planning new attacks.[28]

Too, it can provide sorely needed counterterrorism theater, if only to heighten the perceived prowess of the victim governments. The Israelis were lionized in the West for their dramatic rescue of hostages from Entebbe. The Germans basked in the same limelight following the rescue of hostages from Somalia. The Israelis even sent the Germans a telegram which declared, "Well done."

Because counterterrorism forces require specialized doctrine, training, and equipment, many governments have formed special forces to handle counterterrorism contingencies. The Special Air Service (SAS) in Britain, perhaps the oldest such unit, achieved recognition in 1980 when it successfully stormed the Iranian embassy at Princes' Gate in London to rescue twenty-six hostages. The massacre of Israeli

Olympic athletes at Munich sparked the creation of the West German Grenzschutzgruppe-9 (GSG-9), which carried out the Mogadishu rescue operation in Somalia. In France, the Gendarmerie Nationale (GIGN) have seen action more than sixty times inside and outside France and trained the Saudi National Guard prior to its operation to retake the Grand Mosque at Mecca from Iranian pilgrim-terrorists in 1985. In Holland in 1977, a unit of the Royal Dutch Marines, known as "Whiskey Company," stormed a hijacked train and schoolhouse where South Moluccan terrorists held some fifty hostages for twenty days. The Italian "Squadro Anti-Commando" or "Leatherheads" was instrumental in the rescue of General James Dozier in 1981.[29]

The United States, however, has lagged behind its allies in establishing antiterrorism capabilities. The Delta Force was the centerpiece of U.S. special operations until the disaster at Desert One in Iran. Out of that failure, detailed by a Presidential Commission chaired by Admiral James Holloway in 1979, was born the notion of a new Special Operations Command in the Pentagon, with dedicated forces and equipment and institutionalized command and control.[30] The Joint Special Operations Agency of the Joint Chiefs of Staff was activated in 1984. Legislation in 1986 institutionalized an umbrella command-structure for SOF forces and created a new assistant secretary of defense position for special operations.

Although still in the early phases, the new command structure remains beset by turf rivalries and budget, intelligence, and readiness problems. The U.S. Special Operations Command (USSOC) today remains an orphan child of the services; the Department of Defense delayed for over a year in even designating a commander and an assistant secretary of defense for the USSOC.

Foul-ups in its performance in the Grenada operation offer little cause for optimism. There, helicopters carrying the Delta Force took off late—time conversions having been miscalculated in the operations plan—which made Delta an easy target for the postdawn fire from scattered defenders. The Navy Seals, assigned to assist in setting up a drop zone for airborne paratroopers, met higher-than-expected seas and wind; four members of the team drowned.[31]

In general, displays of American muscle against terrorism have largely reflected our lack of readiness and adequate contingency planning. Desert One became an international symbol of U.S. military incompetence, organizational bungling, and failure of the highest command authority to overrule competing egos. Following the Marine barracks bombing in 1983, an offshore bombardment by the battleship USS *New Jersey*'s sixteen-inch gun firing eleven-hundred-pound shells not only failed to dislodge the PLO and Syrian positions but produced hundreds of "collateral" casualties among Druze villagers, and helped recruit new converts to terrorist organizations devoted to driving out America.

Similarly, the raid on Libya, while gratifying to many Americans, had limited success. There was no question at the time that Libya's Muammar al-Qaddafi was out to get America and was succeeding with virtual impunity. In one month of 1986 alone, he sponsored a successful attack on the La Belle disco in West Berlin and several other attempts against the American visa office in Paris, the American embassy in Beirut, and the U.S. ambassador to Rwanda. It was even rumored that Libya was trying to buy kidnapped Americans in Lebanon from their Shiite captors.[32]

The Reagan administration's answer was an extraordinary air strike designed to topple Qaddafi's government and kill him, but the mission was fraught with glitches from the outset. Several of the bombing sites, selected for political reasons, were last on the military's list of accessible targets. The F-111 bombers, based in England, were denied overflight rights by France and forced to fly an exhausting six and a half hours in lock formation over international waters. Although the United States achieved near complete surprise, most of the attack jets and bombers missed their designated targets, but nearly five tons of explosives landed on residential neighborhoods, killing or wounding a hundred and thirty people.[33]

Ironically, the Libyan operation, while a military fiasco, had an unanticipated positive twist. Although the effects on Qaddafi were marginal, the raid clearly terrified our European *allies*. Having dragged their feet for years on joint measures against Libya, they literally jumped at the prospect of nonmilitary cooperation to prevent the United States from launching any more rogue operations.

Within days of the operation, EEC ministers agreed to expand intelligence sharing with the United States; to reduce the size of Libya's diplomatic missions in Europe, which had served as command posts for its terrorist operations; to limit the number of Libyans domiciled in Europe; and to ensure that Libyans expelled from one member country could not seek haven in another. Within the weeks that followed, Europe expelled more than a hundred Libyan diplomats.[34]

In general, there is always an element of unpredictability in the use of force against terrorism. Even when the military operation is flawless, not every incident ends fortuitously. The 1986 midair interception of an Egyptair jet carrying the hijackers of the *Achille Lauro* was a superb demonstration of America's technical prowess. Once on the ground, however, the mission rapidly unraveled. U.S. special operations forces—deployed to take the hijackers into custody—were pinned between armed terrorists in the jet and armed Italian troops on their rear, who had orders to block unilateral American action. Outnumbered five to one by the Italians, the American troops were ordered to withdraw. By the following day, the Italian government had arranged for safe passage out of Italy for the mastermind of the atrocity at sea. In the aftermath of the incident, relations with Egypt were strained over the interception of its commercial airliner, while the government of Italy fell in the weeks that followed. The incident highlights the fact that macho plus technical prowess yields little when the other elements of counterterrorism policy are lacking.

The need for a backpocket military option against terrorists is not in dispute. What the United States has yet to prove is its ability to organize its forces for low-intensity warfare, or to think through the consequences of military invention, most particularly in the event of failure. What is in question is the ability of the United States to integrate a military approach into a larger counterterrorism strategy, involving overseas diplomacy as well as domestic politics aimed at uniting the nation for action but also lowering expectations for simplistic Hollywood solutions.

Covert Options

One of the dilemmas in coping with terror is that it falls into a gray area of threat in which neither the diplomats nor the generals always enjoy a high degree of success. It is part of the spectrum of international warfare, but without any of the rules of engagement that civilized nations have come to honor. Within that gray area, the

United States is all too often made to appear impotent—precisely the objective of the attacker.

One possible alternative is to explore the range of unconventional responses to meet the terrorist challenge. In practice, this generally means covert operations or the use of unconventional techniques by conventional military forces: subversion, political decapitation, assassination, or psychological warfare.

Americans tend to resist this alternative, viewing covert operations as ethically repugnant, inappropriate activities for democratic nations and a misuse of U.S. power. Success at any price is not a concept with which most of us in the West are comfortable. On the other hand, defeat at every turn is not a prospect we ought to accept with equanimity.

Unless we choose never to respond with force, it is clear that ethical decisions will be made, perhaps innocent lives taken, regardless of the tactics the United States opts to employ. Conventional operations, such as the shelling of Druze villages in Lebanon, have as unpalatable consequences as unconventional operations. If Colonel Qaddafi was the real target in the April raid on Libya, then it might have been preferable—at least for the bystanders who were killed or wounded—to attack him directly. Arguably, the ethical dilemmas involved in a lone gunman going in for a personal strike are at least as profound as the massacre by conventional forces of civilian populations. The point is that there are few "clean" options in the counterterrorism business.

Aside from the moral issues, it is not clear that the United States even has the ability to conduct such "surgical" operations with any efficiency. Certainly, the public track record is mixed. On the negative side, it includes the CIA sponsored "how-to" assassination manual prepared for the Nicaraguan Contras, the leaked report of a disinformation campaign conducted against Libya and the Iran-Contra debacle.

U.S. links to a rogue Lebanese force that killed scores of passersby in a botched car bombing in Beirut highlights some of the dangers in covert operations. The U.S. target was Shaykh Husayn Fadlallah, a radical cleric and spiritual leader of the thoroughly vicious Hizballah group. The Shiite Hizballah was involved in the American embassy and Marine compound bombings as well as kidnappings of dozens of Westerners in Lebanon. With its station chief, James Buckley, in captivity (later brutally tortured and killed), the CIA wanted to break Hizballah and eliminate Fadlallah.

CIA Director William Casey persuaded Ronald Reagan to approve a multimillion-dollar program to train Lebanese intelligence officers in counterterrorism techniques. In the past, similar proposals had been rejected out of hand, since no one could be sure that the training wouldn't ultimately be directed against Americans.

At Casey's insistence, however, the operation was approved. CIA agents and their "assets"—locals in their employ—located and surveyed all of Shaykh Fadlallah's residences in Beirut, and the agency provided communications and other specialized equipment to Lebanese intelligence officers. Just as the CIA officers were warning Casey that Lebanese action team members were becoming difficult to control, the proxy unit set off a bomb outside of one of Fadlallah's apartments near the Bir al Abed mosque in Beirut. Fadlallah escaped unscathed, but eighty bystanders were killed and many more maimed in the firestorm. Hizballah retaliated, killing eleven more and sending others fleeing for their lives. In a chilling reminder, three months later, one of the hijackers of TWA Flight 847 screamed as he dumped the body of Navy diver Robert Stethem on the airport tarmac, "Did you forget the Bir al Abed massacre?"[35]

Preemptive or retaliatory covert operations, if bungled, mistargeted, or leaked, pose disastrous risks for political overreaction at home and abroad. Either the action must be truly covert, and held at a distance sufficient to be plausibly deniable, or completely overt, with the concurrence of Congress and the American public. If the United States decides to use covert methods again, it must be able to carry them out better or simply abstain.

Even if the United States does it right, we must be prepared for worst-case contingencies and the possibility of escalation. Suppose, for example, that a SEAL team had been sent into Libya, fallen on bad luck and been seized, publicly tried, and sentenced to death. Would we have sent a larger force to attempt a rescue, possibly provoking a wider engagement, or decide to cut our losses, albeit ignominiously? The American President and public must understand in advance that no options are guaranteed of success and that no military ones are risk-free.

Successfully implemented, unconventional operations do offer a potential way out of the inaction-overreaction cycle. They provide far more precise and selective targeting options—for example, the executive committee of a terrorist group—with far less risk of collateral damage and international backlash. There should be no mistake; this business is not a pretty one. For the emerging spectrum of threats, however, it is not clear that more gentlemanly codes of conduct will suffice.

If one accepts the principle that covert force may occasionally be a necessary and legitimate tool in counterterrorism warfare, then the United States must begin to define, with considerable rigor and in open debate, the acceptable ground rules for its conduct. Turning a blind eye to an unpleasant set of problems tacitly encourages out-of-control, unconstitutional, and moronic operations such as the Iran-Contra affair.

There is little question but that the Iran-Contra scandal revealed an erosion of the accountability necessary to American democracy. Fears of congressional opposition prompted successive administrations to circumvent established procedures and entrust secret missions to the National Security Council, which has no reporting responsibilities outside the executive branch. Any covert operation will have that potential.

If there is to be secrecy, then there must be diligent oversight. If covert responses are mandated, then they must be carried out within agencies which fall under the constitutional system of checks and balances. Otherwise, we may lose far more than we gain in the struggle against terrorism.

When Deterrence Fails

Of all the potential tools in the counterterrorism arsenal, the ability to manage the aftermath of an incident has received the barest consideration. The last defense against terrorists is probably the most critical: to prevent them from achieving the depth of political, economic, or social disruption they seek.

Ironically, our greatest protection comes not through preemption or retaliation but through imaginative planning and a well-oiled crisis-management apparatus. What we seldom recognize is that the image of a forewarned nation (even if only partially true) is itself a powerful tool.

Target hardening, good intelligence, effective law enforcement, and multinational cooperation are key elements in deterring terrorist attacks. But, if deterrence fails, the United States must be able to limit the consequences of attack. If the lights go out along the Eastern Seaboard, putting handcuffs on the perpetrators is not the nation's most immediate concern. As the potential for terrorist incidents of mass disruption grows, even if only marginally, containment and restoration must become integral elements of the counterterrorism arsenal.

The unfortunate reality, however, is that the United States is not prepared to respond to most kinds of emergencies except on a make-it-up-as-we-go-along basis or, in polite terms: reactively, ad hoc, and ad interim. There are few contingency plans which would stand up to even casual scrutiny. We do not have an up-to-date inventory of medical or logistical needs, civil engineering, food, temporary shelter, or trained manpower.

Nor is there a nationally reliable means of command and control linking the myriad of federal, state, and local agencies charged with crisis management. The seriousness of the situation can be tracked by looking at the tangle of jurisdictional arrangements in a hypothetical example. Consider the case of a terrorist group that threatens to shoot down American airliners departing from a domestic airport, such as Denver's Stapleton Field, unless three members of their group, being held in the federal penitentiary, are released.

Immediately following the public release of this hypothetical demand, a myriad of government bureaucracies would leap into action, albeit not necessarily in the same direction. The FBI, state, and local law enforcement officials would be charged with determining whether the threat is real, as well as with apprehending the perpetrators. The U.S. and State Attorney Generals' offices would be involved in any decision to release (or not to release) the prisoners. The U.S. State Department would have primary responsibility for dealing with foreign terrorists in a manner that is consistent with U.S. antiterrorism policy, while Defense Department and CIA officials would be involved in threat assessment and potential military responses. The Airline Pilots Association and FAA would have concerns about the air safety considerations of not acceding to the terrorist demands. The Federal Emergency Management Agency and the state emergency apparatus would be charged with civil preparedness measures. Local and state politicians in Denver would be concerned with the local public relations crisis and with defusing potential public panic. The White House and Congress would have a vested interest (although from different perspectives) in demonstrating decisive leadership during the crisis.

It would be optimistic indeed to assume that the lines of responsibility and jurisdiction would remain untangled with so many actors involved in the incident management. Past experience reveals that these multiple actors typically have competing goals, a different sense of urgency, ambiguous lines of authority, different access to information, differences over turf, and personality conflicts, which all tend to impede any coherent or rapid resolution of the crisis.

As a result, most government planners hope either for a series of small disasters or one giant one. The effects of little crises, managed poorly or well, tend to fade quickly. A superdisaster, such as a thermonuclear explosion or a category five hurricane, is generally perceived to be beyond human managerial skills or credible planning.

The real dangers lie in the middle of the spectrum of man-made or natural calamities. For example, terrorist attacks against life-supporting physical networks or biological or chemical agent attacks do not simply fade away. Since they may well exceed the self-healing limits of the society, the American public has a right to demand responsible management.

What is clear is that the United States can no longer rely on the blind faith that such attacks could not happen here or on sheer luck that we will somehow muddle through. We need to begin to coordinate our visible and invisible resources—and then test them to prove that we are in fact a porcupine target, not a sitting duck.

The goal of such crisis planning is not the compilation of thick sets of plans to gather dust on a thousand shelves across America. Rather, it is a process of continually asking "What if?", "Who?", and "How?" Effective crisis management should teach us to muster the people, plans, and resources to prepare for the next set of crises, not the last.

Given the very real potential for awful damage, crisis management must become inseparable from crisis preparedness. What is needed is a professional cadre of crisis managers who do not change hats on nonemergency days. The typical crisis manager is just another kind of victim, pulled away from his normal duties after emergency conditions already exist, given few guidelines, limited resources, poor information, and a great deal of political pressure.

Ideally, when a crisis hits, there should be no difference between the current reality and previous planning simulations. The same people that planned for and managed the last crisis should be prepared to handle the new one, and they should have "gamed" one like it at least once.

Crisis games, or simulations, such as the one recorded in the Appendix, can be used as a training and sensitization device. Games can expose managers to the rigors of crisis, forcing them to identify the resources at their disposal and the limitations and consequences of alternative strategies. The most practical end of this kind of training is not the creation of a perfect crisis management mechanism, but rather an awareness of the problems that managers are likely to face without the pressure and panic of a crisis situation.

The only logical organizational placement for this group of professional crisis managers is the Executive Office of the President. Only from the White House can action authority, management responsibility, and embracing policy be readily and visibly delegated. Only to the White House would sufficient respect flow from state and local governments in times of terrorist attack.

One approach would be to provide the President with continuing and immediate situation-room access to a corps of professionals familiar with the planning and operational techniques of crisis management. A lean, elite crisis institution would provide an interface between the White House and the relevant state and local agencies— maintaining one hundred professionals at the command center and two hundred liaison and field agents. It would possess an up-to-date control center relying on the latest communications, display data, and information technologies.

More importantly, the group must plan to exercise the crisis management apparatus on a regular basis. All such sophisticated management and communications systems are for naught unless the decision makers, particularly senior government officials, are willing to familiarize themselves with the sorts of dilemmas they may have to face.

Other governments, such as Britain and Israel, routinely conduct crisis simulations, involving government leaders at the Cabinet level, as a way of sensitizing decision makers to the rigors of crisis management. In the United States, crisis decision-making is somehow viewed as a latent skill of America's leadership, akin to throwing a baseball or kissing a baby. In a series of crisis simulations run at the Center for Strategic and International Studies in Washington, however, we discovered that nothing could be further from the truth. Even experienced decision makers can waver in crisis; the ability to quickly focus and establish priorities is not an intuitive human talent, but must be learned.

The objective of simulations or gaming is not to prepare for every conceivable crisis event, but to anticipate new types of threat and to develop a range of options, modes of operations and an awareness of available resources. Provided that the simulation is challenging, stressful and realistic, the participants will be forced to consider multiple options (and the limitations of each), and experience firsthand the problems of decision making under time constraints and in a complex bureaucratic setting with penalties for failure.

Decision-makers ought to be confronted regularly with the most serious risks affecting the nation's security. How would we aid New York City in the event the electric power grid was disrupted for a month or more? How would we handle the emergency conditions following the threatened or actual detonation of a natural gas tanker in a major harbor or the insertion of a virus into a nationwide computer network? Responsible response to terror requires a public policy structure that is competent to react quickly and decisively.

The society attacked by terrorists must be able to react at three levels. First, there is the immediate problem of the attack. The specific incident must be dealt with and concluded on the most favorable terms we can achieve.

Second, there is the phase of domestic and international damage control—dealing with the derivative and delayed political, social, economic, security, and military implications of the terrorist event. This can range from reassuring international partners that basic commitments will be upheld (after, for example, a nuclear incident) to emergency economic recovery programs (after the breakdown of basic services).

Third, and rarely considered, is the phase of creating opportunity from adversity and consciously using the incident as an element to move forward basic national policy. The alternative, to try to encyst such events and then to rely on the passage of time to remove them from the public consciousness, has a grave disadvantage: it continues to encourage new incidents because the field is always fresh for public exploitation.

Exactly because the society itself is hostage in the largest-scale terrorist extortions, the leadership must embrace the quality of mature response that the threat warrants. A danger in the past has been a tendency to downplay the overall threat and to treat each conventional incident on its own theatrical merits. A graver danger of the future is the probability that unconventional incidents will have much greater impact than they perhaps warrant and will be allowed to resonate until they eventually fractionate some of this society's important stabilizing social and political structures.

If we think of these unconventional conflict problems as terrorist crime alone, it is all too likely that we will not develop the needed technologies and machinery—because we will continue to react convulsively as the occasional dramatic event occurs. If we think of terrorism as part of a larger form of low-intensity conflict, we will wisely come to view it as a symptom of a serious national security matter in need of coordinated efforts from the highest levels of government.

A Counterterrorism Campaign If coping with terror were easy, the problem would have been solved long ago. In the nether world of low-intensity conflict, there is no "light at the end of the tunnel"; the radicals, revolutionaries, and rogue states will keep coming after us. The tactic is simply too effective to fade away.

There is little purpose in continuing the search for simplistic solutions to terrorism. In the past, the United States has focused on the unimportant or the obvious, lacking the more subtle long-term strategies that might reverse the leverage in our direction.

Counterterrorism minitheater can be useful, offering up the superiority of a system of laws and due process. Thus, the arrest of Fawaz Younis represented merely a small battlefield ripple rather than a major triumph. The big fish have yet to be fried.

In the same way, the attack on Libya was fortuitous because, in combination with other factors, such as Assad's retreat from the terrorist scene, it produced a temporary lull in terrorist attacks in Europe. As Lieutenant General and *New York Times* staff writer Bernard Trainor pointed out: It's not a bad idea to strike a serious blow every now and again—if only to remind one's adversaries of the overwhelming military power of the United States.[36]

As a result of such actions, we may rhetorically claim a victory over terrorism. But the important point is that we not succeed in deluding ourselves into thinking that the rhetoric is reality. Any success in this area lasts only until the next spate of attacks.

United States anti-terrorism policy tends to alternate between piety and sometimes desperate overreaction. The fact is, however, that a truly effective counterterrorism apparatus is neither virtuous nor straightforward. Rather, it is a complex and torturous interweaving between all of the tools at our disposal, with few short-term guarantees of success.

Preventing terrorist attacks or containing their damage will require sophisticated planning, subtle tactics, and multilayered lines of offense and defense. The terrorists and their sponsors are in this game for the long haul. The United States must be prepared to be there too.

Coping with terrorism is a multifaceted problem. Passive measures intended to reduce the vulnerability of critical targets, such as better security of banking networks or having spare large electrical transformers, can make the difference. But such means alone may not save the lives of the passengers trapped aboard a hijacked airliner. For that, a highly disciplined rescue team is needed.

But what about deterring the next event? Does an aggressive military approach accomplish more than catharsis? By reacting violently following a terrible incident, such as the destruction of Pan Am Flight 103, are we playing into the hands of religious zealotry, reviving an already crumbling revolution, such as Iran's?

A great deal is at stake, for the next terrorist incident—wherever and whenever it may occur—is but a precursor of a further provocation. And every time unseemly means are used to combat terrorism at home, America's civil liberties are diminished. Yet there are compelling reasons to punish the culprits, especially if the underlying villain is a nation, such as Syria or Iran.

If military options and the more extreme covert options are excluded on pragmatic grounds, the alternative is to impose diplomatic and economic sanctions against the terrorist states. A massive effort would be required—more international cooperation than has been seen to date. Past attempts at embargoes and diplomatic isolation have failed, not because they were poorly conceived but because there was no political will to enforce them.

With or without the help of its allies, the United States will be forced by public pressure to investigate and respond to serious attacks against Americans here and abroad. In all likelihood, if the response is not weak-kneed, there will be counterattacks. A responsible President must tell the public the truth. He must not foster denial as a means of national escape.

Countering terrorism is a process of coping, not winning.

CHAPTER FIVE

NEWS MEDIA: MESSENGERS OF TERROR

Terrorist violence—from car bombings to airplane hijackings—is made-for-television drama. All other media are less important contributors to the terrorist goal of applying immediate and overwhelming pressure to the public consciousness, pressure designed to make the mass audience feel that the victim government is weak, inept, or out of control.

It is critical to understand that no group of terrorists really expects to bring a strong nation to its knees by brute force. The true goal is to exploit the power of the media—particularly the visual media—to horrify the viewing public and erode its confidence in government and democratic values.

The televised horror show shocks the viewer on several levels. First, the very randomness of the attack brings home the reality that anyone can be at risk. The victims, with whom we can easily identify, are all too often just unlucky people who chose the wrong airplane, the wrong cruise, or the wrong street corner. Second, the fact that the attack occurred at all implies that one or more governments failed to protect their citizens either by deterring the attack or by intercepting it. Although impossible to achieve in reality, citizens tend to expect that level of security from their elected government. Finally, during prolonged episodes, it rapidly becomes apparent that the government was not only powerless to prevent such an incident but is unable to force a resolution.

While all of this holds true for terrorist incidents reported in the

155

printed press or even over the radio, the written or spoken word lacks the emotional charge of the picture story. It is television coverage of terrorist incidents that almost always empowers the terrorists while damaging the interests of the victims and their governments.

Lights! Camera! Humiliation!

If you are an American who was old enough to stay up after eleven-thirty on weeknights in the winter of 1979, you probably remember the ABC half-hour special reports on "America Held Hostage." It made Ted Koppel a star and became "Nightline." It was a paragon of fine reporting on the seizure of the U.S. embassy in Tehran and the taking of fifty-two hostages at the embassy. Unfortunately, the show, along with other regularly scheduled newscasts, had an impact beyond informing the nation. The newscasts all played and replayed the most sensational, humiliating pictures of the hostages, the sacked embassy, and the furious and apparently powerful Iranian fanatics. That had the effect, at least in part, of making millions of viewers feel that they, too, were somehow being held hostage—at least emotionally. The name of the program, "America Held Hostage," presented that ill-defined feeling as though it were an unquestioned truth. It also offered up interviews with spokesmen for the Iranian government, who came off as reasonable people, essentially trivializing the monumental travesty of international law. But it did, as they say in the business, make for "great TV." Most terrorist incidents do.

President Jimmy Carter at first used the hostage crisis and the superheated political climate, which television news coverage had created, to his political advantage. But the embassy hostage debacle, including the courageous but poorly managed military rescue mission that ended in tragedy on a remote desert in Iran in 1980, stretched out endlessly. Ultimately, Mr. Carter and his advisors made the mistake of allowing the terrorists and their state sponsor—the Ayatollah Khomeini—to set the agenda for the rest of his presidency, keeping him a virtual prisoner in the White House, just by prolonging the nation's agony.

Carter became a caricature of weakness and indecision. It infected his re-election campaign and made many voters feel uncomfortable about identifying with him. He paid the price for surrendering his presidency to Iranian terrorists by losing the White House to tough-talking Ronald Reagan, who warned all terrorists on the day of his first inauguration that they better not mess with him. He vowed "swift and effective retribution" for any terrorist acts against the United States.

Less than three years into his presidency, Reagan, like Carter, suffered at the hands of Khomeini. Like Carter, he failed to take the kind of action the Ayatollah would respect—and indeed, feared, in the first two and a half years of the Reagan era. There was no "swift and effective retribution" after Iran's Lebanese action arm, the Hizballah, hit the U.S. embassy in the spring of 1983, nor when it obliterated the headquarters of the U.S. Marines in Beirut later that year. Less than two years later, in the spring of 1985, Iran, through Hizballah, did it to Reagan again. This time terrorists seized TWA Flight 847 and flew it to Beirut. Before that spectacle would end, the White House was forced to ask Moscow to use its influence with Syria to intervene on behalf of the American hostages.

Despite its declared policy of no concessions to terrorists, the Reagan administration agreed to a package deal—766 Shiite Lebanese captured by Israel during its invasion in 1982 would be released and sent home to Lebanon in exchange for the airline hostages. Driving the President and his advisors throughout was the virtually constant television coverage of the hijacking, including the outrageous interview with the plane's pilot, a pistol to his head, with reporters asking him questions as though it were a walk in the park:

REPORTER: Thank you, Captain. How do you feel?
CAPTAIN TESTRAKE: All right.

Freeze frame. Hold it right there. In that ABC interview with the captive pilot of Flight 847, the world saw a hostage with a gun to his head, two aggressive, gutsy reporters grabbing an exclusive, and an intrusion into a crisis of international proportions in which reporters simply have no business and stand only to be manipulated by the terrorists as they seek to exercise control over the decision making of a sovereign nation.

REPORTER: Captain, many people in America are call-
                             ing for some kind of rescue operation or
                             some kind of retaliation. Do you have any
                             thoughts on that?
CAPTAIN TESTRAKE: I think we'd all be dead men if they did
                             because we're constantly surrounded by
                             many, many guards.
REPORTER: Do you have any thoughts on whether or
                             not the United States should ask Israel to
                             release the people it's holding in Israel?

It was sensational stuff, the kind of material that brings triumph in
the headquarters of the news organization that scores this kind of
world exclusive. But those cheers were purely visceral. No one, it
seemed, had bothered to think through the effect of what was being
done. Was it right to handle this story as though it were just another
event? Were there no additional considerations beyond "getting *there
first*, getting the best, getting out with it, and making air"? The planeside interview with a hostage who obviously dared not say anything for
fear of his life was bizarre. But the news conference later, which
featured the hostages held under terrorists' guns, calling upon the
U.S. Government to make concessions to the terrorists in order to win
their freedom, attained a new low for the media.

"It was an obscene travesty of a news conference, serving no one's
interests but the hijackers," wrote *New York Times* critic John Corry.[1]
Peter Jennings, ABC News' anchor and mainstay during the coverage
of Flight 847, looks back on that episode as a time of pain and learning, "Watching ourselves in action at that horrendous news conference was a public embarrassment as it should have been. In the wake
of Flight 847, we had some very serious meetings around this place in
which a number of us, who were disturbed by our own performances
[over the seventeen days of the crisis], looked quite hard at what we
had done and vowed that we would not make the same mistakes
again. We are forever making vows in our lives and not living up to
them. But when the next incidents came along—granted, they were
different, in that there was much less access for the media than in
Flight 847—there was the feeling in everybody's mind that we
shouldn't rush as we had in the past. This competition either to get on
the air ahead of the other fellow or to knock down the other fellow's

story was unseemly at best. Because we [television news] play such a unique role in these circumstances, we have to be that much more restrained. I think 847 taught me how much more access we had to events on the ground than just about anybody."

That degree of access explains why the officials assigned by President Reagan to manage that crisis spent so much time glued to their television sets. Where American diplomats had little or no access, television news was there to fill the information gap. However, the networks were not in a position to detect easily the difference between news and propaganda. Their best people were—and still are—reporters and camera and sound technicians, not diplomats. They were—and largely still are—highly vulnerable to being used by the terrorists, who know that in the transaction of the news event, they trade access to themselves and their victims—the hostages—in exchange for air time. Of course it is rarely laid out in those businesslike terms, but that is the underlying reality.

Bigger by far than all of the above is the fact that even cool, nonhysterical television coverage of a hostage crisis invariably works against the government whose citizens are held hostage. Televised captives whose faces and words are broadcast not once but over and over again become familiar, valued—almost as friends. The lesson is simply that the longer hostages are held and the more access television cameras get to them, the more pressure will mount on the government to make concessions to buy their freedom.

The other lesson is that television coverage of hostage events can be orchestrated to make the terrorists look sympathetic, even statesmenlike. Television, by capturing only one slice of reality, changes that reality. Pictures of Yasir Arafat hugging babies or making pleas for moderation in Middle Eastern peace negotiations alters the perception that Arafat sits atop the largest and most brutal terrorist organization in the world. During the Iranian hostage case in 1979, Iranian spokesmen representing the radicals who tortured and illegally imprisoned Americans were treated by the media as ordinary newsmakers.

Perhaps the most egregious case of a misleading media was during the TWA hijacking. Nabih Berri, Justice Minister for the essentially nonexistent government of Lebanon, achieved unwarranted political stature when one network anchor asked him if he had any "final words" for President Reagan. Interviews with Mr. Berri—a fluent

English speaker—made him appear the very embodiment of moderation and restraint. This favorable portrayal was no doubt aided by his
cultivation of the network anchors and their producers, who daily
sought his help in arranging interviews with hostages. With the help
of the media, Berri was able to create the image of an opponent with a
human face, and at the same time find a forum from which to preach
the cause of the Arab movement in the cathedral of American public
opinion.

In retrospect, anchorman Tom Brokaw of NBC believes television
"can't get into a kind of hysterical competitive state, being manipulated by the terrorists to get on the air for whatever little contrived
development there may be in the story. I thought 847 did develop
into a feeding frenzy. I was over there. God, it was craziness! There
were negotiations going on in one corner of the Commodore [Hotel]
lobby for access to Nabih Berri . . . he was a dazzling guy. He
switched [so easily] from English to French. The first day I arrived in
Beirut, I was taken to his headquarters and, you know, was given a
kind of VIP escort because I was an anchorman . . . An awful lot of
manipulation was going on there. In a way, I think, that became part
of the story that did not get adequate attention from the networks
themselves."[2]

Television news organizations justify their participation in terrorist
events by cloaking themselves in a doctrine of moral superiority called
"the public's right to know," thus excusing themselves from charges
of irresponsible conduct in their coverage of terrorism. But the bright,
highly educated women and men who run the television companies
know full well that the media is not simply a neutral observer.

"I think," said NBC's Brokaw, "there is more than an element of
truth in [British Prime Minister] Margaret Thatcher's observation
that this kind of attention is the oxygen of terrorists. It is a real
dilemma for us."

"Everything a journalist does, in this context, interferes very directly in the government's management of a terrorist crisis," said *New
York Times* Deputy Managing Editor Leslie Gelb, a former senior
State Department official. "I think it calls for a hell of a lot of restraint
on the part of journalists as they handle these stories . . . A particular concern is stories that are broadcast or published right in the
middle of negotiations . . . While my disposition is that the press
ought to publish what it has, it's the obligation of editors to think hard

about the value of particular stories journalistically as against the possible damage to the situation."

In fact, the media no longer merely records the events. It has become part of them—an unwitting, yet hardly unwilling, participant in the terrorist act. Terrorism is unlike any other news story. Editors and writers, correspondents and producers must fully understand what they are dealing with and the implications of how they handle the story. Television hasn't yet figured out a way to cover terrorism that informs the viewers without making psychological victims of them.

NBC, like other major television news organizations, modified its coverage policies after TWA Flight 847 to make sure the network acts with greater responsibility next time around. But Brokaw admitted in an interview, "Some of this is situational ethics. Make no bones about it . . . we are constantly reevaluating what we do and how we do it. But it very often depends on the circumstances . . . One of the things we learned in 847 is that the discipline of [videotape] editing is important. There was, in that hijacking coverage, too much of the kind of raw, unexpurgated television transmission coming from Beirut. The people were getting a kind of voyeuristic experience. There was a real exploitation going on, which I don't think we should allow." But Brokaw made it clear, during the conversation in his office, that he could not be sure the same thing would not happen again.

Despite the best intentions, television news coverage of terrorist acts in most cases tends to do much more harm than good because of the *interactive* nature of the coverage, the emotional reaction to it, and the decision-making processes of governments and terrorists. News executives in general—but television programmers especially—need to review and drop their "Business as usual" approach to the highly visual, emotionally exploitive events *staged* by terrorists for their consumption. They should summon the kind of intellectual honesty and moral integrity that transcend the battle for ratings. Unfortunately, the deregulation of television by the Reagan administration and the gobbling up of the major American networks by retail organizations only intensified the race to the bottom line, distorting even further what was already a questionable set of values and operating assumptions.

With terrorism likely to persist and become even more dangerous, television's response to it will grow in importance. The contemporary economics of the television industry could easily come into play and twist the situational ethic completely out of shape. Television executives are confronted by their own special brand of terror—a steadily declining audience. What role might that play?

Plenty, according to Alan Beck, executive producer of the nationally televised newscast "USA Tonight." "They don't know where the viewers have gone. How far will they go to get them back? Will they be satisfied to stick with the entertainment lead-in their newscasts get? Or will they go supertabloid, playing up the most dramatic story they get in the least responsible way?"[3]

The search for viewer ratings has led some to extraordinary excesses. During the two and a half weeks of the 847 crisis, the three major networks devoted between 62 and 68 percent of their total evening news air time to the story. One reason that Beirut received so much air time was because it was a much more accessible story than, for example, the embassy seizure in Tehran, where reporters had no access to the hostages or the embassy for most of 444 days. By contrast, Beirut featured almost constant photo opportunities of the aircraft and a number of interviews with hostages, whose words were quite clearly influenced by their continued captivity. Despite the obvious coercion behind every word that flowed from a hostage's mouth, all the networks eagerly negotiated for those interviews with Amal militia boss Nabih Berri.

There was at least one other critical difference: the hostages in Tehran were U.S. Foreign Service officers and a handful of Marines—people who are trained to expect hard times, if not terrorism. But the forty Americans aboard Flight 847, except for six Navy divers (one of whom was murdered), were ordinary travelers. They were more like the viewers at home than were the hostages at the embassy. That meant they gave their captors even more leverage against the might of the United States of America than the Iranians had with their control of the embassy and its staff.

Displaying a high degree of media sophistication, the kidnappers of forty innocent Americans played American television news organizations as though they were captive stations. The networks even broadcast a videotaped interview with some of the captives—recorded and *edited* by the terrorists. Network executives excused their becoming propagandists for the hijackers by insisting that the tape proved the hostages were alive and reasonably well. In retrospect, that seems a hollow rationalization. The tape should not have been aired.

Terrorist control of the media coverage yielded an unexpected advantage. Like everyone else, the President watched television for his information, occasionally making major policy decisions, against the best advice of his most senior cabinet officers, on the basis of what he saw. In 1982 President Reagan had been appalled by a news report depicting the effect of Israel's bombing of Lebanon during the war against the PLO. Although General Alexander Haig, then Secretary of State, advised that it was in U.S. interests for the Israeli invasion to destroy the vast infrastructure of the PLO terror bases and to wipe out Arafat's army, the President brushed aside Haig's advice, got Israeli Prime Minister Menachem Begin on the phone, and personally told him to stop the bombing.

Three years later, Reagan had to be restrained by Secretary of State George Shultz from making concessions to the hijackers of TWA Flight 847. Reagan reacted just as millions of other viewers did —he identified with the plight of the hostages. But unlike the other viewers of this latest humiliation, he had the power to do something about it. He was ready to cave in. "It took more than an hour of strenuous argument, mainly by . . . Shultz, to persuade the President to suppress his feelings about the hostages and hang tough publicly against any concessions to the terrorists," a White House staffer confided later.[4]

It is possible that if Reagan had *not* seen the television reporting of the bombing of Lebanon and of the predicament of the passengers aboard Flight 847, the Israelis would have been left alone to finish off the PLO's military power, and the Reagan administration might have had more options to exercise against the terrorists who seized the TWA plane. Mr. Reagan's personal identification with the hostages must have made those planning a military rescue operation wonder if *any* losses would be acceptable to a Commander-in-Chief who took it all so personally.

At the headquarters of one of America's antiterrorist military units, a homemade sign hangs on a bulletin board. It reads: "By order of the President, there shall be no Special Operations undertaken which either threaten the lives of innocent bystanders or threaten the lives of American forces. Thank you."[5] The sign is a joke, but it is also a trenchant comment on the state of antiterrorism policy in the United States and of the frustration of the Delta Force and SEAL Team Six. They are ready, but there is no indication that President

Bush has the political will to use them. A key question is: would Bush be prepared to take the emotional and political pressures sure to be generated by televised images of innocent civilians killed and, worse, young American soldiers coming home in body bags from a failed or successful counterterrorist mission? President Reagan *did* send Delta towards Beirut in the TWA crisis, but they were never deployed for a variety of reasons, one perhaps being that their presence in the area had quickly become common knowledge.

The Flight 847 episode sent all the wrong messages to terrorists around the world. During the incident, however, the government did take a leaf out of Nabih Berri's book, in attempting to use media coverage. The Administration sent messages to the terrorists, with whom the government would not negotiate directly, that the heat was being turned up. Among its tactics was mentioning to reporters at the White House that "the President just met with his advisers and all options are being considered, including closing Beirut airport."[6]

Officials quietly let correspondents know that would entail dropping special bombs on the airport, cratering the runway, and making it physically impossible for the hijacked plane to take off. Then officials imposed a news blackout to let the people at the other end stew and worry about it. It's widely known that news blackouts traditionally precede any military strike; it was hoped this tactic would generate fear and uncertainty among the captors, and push them towards accommodation. Bud McFarlane, then the President's National Security Advisor (later to plead guilty in the Iran–Contra scandal), repeatedly tried to place the onus on people at the other end of the line, who may not have had the clout necessary to ending the crisis, but were portrayed by the White House as having the power to resolve the crisis. The administration publicly, through the media—mostly television—put the pressure on Nabih Berri, who proved more than a match for the U.S. Government.

As Richard Clutterbuck, a British authority on violence and subversion, points out: "A television camera is like a weapon lying in the street. Either side can pick it up and use it."[7] Nevertheless, the terrorists have proved to be far more adept than their victims at directing the power of the visual media.

The Uncapped Lens

Almost a quarter of a century after the first made-for-TV terror shocked civilization, the September 1970 Palestinian hijacking of a Royal Jordanian aircraft to Dawson Field in Jordan, the basic dilemma remains unchanged. Without the powerful amplification and instantaneous transmission of its images provided by television, terrorism simply would not wield the political power it still enjoys. As if nothing had been learned in all this time, television news is still the unwitting and seemingly helpless slave of the terrorists. The thinkers in the business are frustrated.

"World media coverage is crucial to terrorists who are taking people hostage," said CNN anchorman Bernard Shaw. "If all the television lenses were capped, I mean *capped,* and all the reporters went away, the situation would resolve itself in the fullness of time. We know that."

An increasingly important part of the problem is the trend of television news becoming entertainment. Viewing publics throughout the Western world have come to expect that they will be entertained at all times when sitting before the television set. To secure the loyalty of the millions to their channel, as opposed to competing programs, broadcast news executives have been seduced into keeping a constant eye on the entertainment value of the reports which they put on the air. Unfortunately, terrorism *plays* well on television. An airplane hijacking becomes blood theater with real live and dead and dying "actors." Unlike fictional films, terrorist incidents on the news require none of the willful suspension of disbelief necessary to making Hollywood movies gripping and entertaining. Viewers don't need to be convinced that what's on the screen is real. It *is* and they know it. When Americans are the victims, their countrymen stay glued to their screens.

Television news executives, hungry for successful ratings, get caught in a triple bind when it comes to terrorist events. If they don't broadcast the whole, manipulative episode, their competition almost certainly will. If they do not provide comprehensive coverage, their ratings could suffer as the public seeks out the channel with the "best" coverage. If they restrain the sensational aspects of their broadcasts, they may feel they have succumbed to government pressure, suffering a loss of self-esteem as well as power.

But the technology of television is changing so rapidly that news organizations may have no choice but to limit at least some live coverage or run the risk of being directly responsible for the failure of hostage rescue attempts and other counterterrorist operations.

Consider the following scenario: a jumbo jet, filled with holiday travelers, is hijacked to an airport in a Third World country. In short order, television news crews set up cameras at a great distance, offering 360-degree coverage of the jet and the surrounding area. Equipped with commercially available night vision devices, the cameras keep a constant vigil on the story, even through darkness. Portable broadcast satellite uplink packs (signal generators with small microwave antennas), which are already in the inventories of several news organizations, send the pictures back to the television companies' headquarters, thousands of miles from the action and any sense of reality. There, the executive producers can put it all on the air anytime they choose to say the words, "Take it live."

At some point in the hijacking, the negotiations go sour and one or more hostages are murdered. Counterterrorist units, like the U.S. Army's Delta Force or the British Special Air Service, are ordered to "take down" the aircraft and rescue the rest of the hostages. Seeing some signs of movement, or just sensing it, news producers issue their orders, and anyone watching sees exactly what the cameras covering the plane see. Live. What national security experts call "in real time." Unbeknown to the counterterrorist strike-force commander, the terrorists have aboard the plane a satellite television *down*link, a small dish or contour antenna, undetectable from outside the aircraft. It gives the terrorists the ability to see the same picture being viewed at home in the United States or Britain or Germany or wherever a producer has decided to "Take it live." Finally, when the troops move against them, the terrorists see them coming—live—on their own portable television, which they may even have plugged right into the jumbo jet's video movie system. Fully alerted, the hijackers slaughter more hostages, blow up the aircraft, or at least manage to wound or kill some of the assaulting troops, because television news coverage denied the rescuers the vital element of surprise.

Does this sound like mere hypothesis? It shouldn't. During the fall of 1985, Egyptian commandos were deployed into Malta to storm a hijacked Egyptair jet. Robert Oakley, former director of the State Department Office to Combat Terrorism, recalls seeing television pictures of the commandos approach, accompanied by a report explaining its supposedly secret mission.[8] While no one will ever know whether or not the hijackers were alerted by that story, fifty-seven people died in the battle that ensued.

Add to that volatile mix the vision of Chuck DeCaro, a writer for *Army Times* and former special assignments correspondent for Cable News Network. He owns and is preparing to operate *Aerobureau*, a plane equipped with standard television cameras, as well as extremely capable radar and infrared sensing devices for detecting movement and satellite transmission equipment. If it were flying near that airplane hijacking, it could offer not only an aerial look-down at the scene on the airport, but also a look-ahead at other planes arriving in the area—including any would-be rescuers. Mr. DeCaro's concept could revolutionize news coverage and indirectly provide governments with instantaneous intelligence on the location of terrorists and hostages if they should leave the plane; but it also would present yet another dilemma to antiterrorists, since any broadcaster subscribing to the *Aerobureau* service could go live with its pictures at any moment.[9] A former U.S. Army Green Beret, DeCaro says he would make sure *Aerobureau*'s transmissions would not endanger hostages or their would-be rescuers. But in the heat of a breaking story of the drama of a hijacking, DeCaro's best intentions could become moot if a news producer back in New York or Washington decides to put the *Aerobureau* video on television.

A much less dramatic and even more accessible medium hammered home the need for new thinking on all this. Following the 1988 hijacking of a Kuwaiti airliner by Hizballah, it became clear that the terrorists aboard the plane had been in radio contact with their own people somewhere on the ground. From now on, authorities would have to go on the assumption that whatever the news media broadcast about the hijacking, the terrorists would also know, immediately or within minutes. During the incident at the airport in Algiers, terrorists shot a hostage to death and threw his body onto the tarmac after they either heard directly or heard about a BBC news report. The broadcast quoted a wire service that said Britain had dispatched to the scene its hostage rescue military unit, the Special Air Service. After the hijackers murdered the hostage, they told the Algiers air traffic control tower to tell Prime Minister Thatcher to keep her elite SAS troops at home. The SAS didn't come. In fact, British security sources insist, they never were en route to begin with, and the report they were on their way was, quite simply, false. The lesson was clear: reporting of troop movements, true or false, can be heard by terrorists holding hostages and may trigger the killing of innocents.[10]

On several previous occasions, network television news correspondents in the United States had reported that American commando forces were either in the air, bound for the hostage situation, or were about to leave their bases and head in the direction of the action. Jack McWethy, national security correspondent of ABC News, insists his broadcasts are not provocative. "When I report the movement of Delta, it is a general kind of statement that traditionally, in situations like these, the United States will move its counterterrorist troops into position. I generally keep it pretty vague, but it's part of the story, and everyone who knows anything about how the government works knows it does certain things. So I'm just running down a checklist. It is no more provocative than speculating about anything else."[11]

But that may be wishful thinking. With the knowledge that the terrorists can be in radio communications with their comrades in the United States who are watching American television, it makes little sense to risk provoking them to violence by even hinting at a Delta Force strike against them.

Although it is contrary to the whole tradition of American journalism, the most responsible thing a television news organization can do during one of these incidents is to offer the basic facts but present no interviews, no emotional pictures of any kind. This is not a drill. This is the real thing. It requires respect, not exploitation under the cover of informing the public. The moment that the incident is over is the time to demonstrate the brilliance of the competing news organizations that should have been covering it from every angle—but for *delayed* broadcast, *not* during the incident. Television has got to stop getting in the middle of these things.

Ideally, the next time an airliner is seized by terrorists, what you'll get from your favorite anchor will be no more than: "Flight 747 with three hundred and seventy-five passengers on board is still sitting on the ground, surrounded by troops at the airport in Amman, Jordan. We're covering it all and when it's over, we'll tell you all about it. In other news . . ."

ABC's McWethy, who has made his reputation, in part, by learning about and reporting what government officials prefer to conceal, agrees that "probably the best way [in terms of a positive outcome] of dealing with a terrorist incident is to say nothing, but we live in a country in which freedom of speech is both a joy and a burden of our society, so when something like that happens, we report it. It's not just the way we do things in our business, it's the way we do things in our country; we have a very free press. But those of us who are engaged in this kind of journalism have to be careful, which is why I don't report, 'Fifty-five Delta men have moved to the Sigonella base in Sicily and are ready to jump off.' I simply say, 'As standard procedure, the United States has moved its Delta group to be ready to move if necessary.' "

David Martin, defense correspondent for CBS, once went beyond standard restraint in broadcasting the movement of the Delta Force. It was in the competitive journalistic heat of the 1985 crisis surrounding the hijacking of TWA Flight 847 that Martin went on the air with an exclusive report, including videotape, showing very muscular men with short haircuts carrying gym bags at an airport on an island in the Mediterranean. Martin knew that these tough-looking men were, in fact, members of Delta and he described them as such *on television.* That was a solid bit of intelligence that might have influenced the terrorists, if they had heard it, or seen it, or been informed of it.

In retrospect, McWethy said of Martin's decision to go with the story identifying the Delta team and placing them close to the scene, "I don't know if I would have done it." Martin himself now feels differently: "I don't think these days I'd do that. I mean, the terrorists know Delta moves during these incidents, so I don't think you reveal any great tactical secrets by saying so, but you do run the risk of inciting these guys."[12] Terrorists may "know that Delta moves during these incidents," but former Assistant Secretary of Defense Bob Sims, who was involved in the White House response to that hijacking, believes, "When the networks reported that Delta Force was on the way and the [hijacked] plane was moved from the place where we wanted it to be, back to Beirut, it appeared there was a cause and effect there. Others say, 'Oh no. There's no way they could have known on that plane what was being reported worldwide.' I'd say we can't be sure."[13]

Secretary of State George Shultz was clearly infuriated by the media intrusion into the dynamics of the incident. He regarded Algiers as a stable, somewhat friendly environment, in which the odds favored a quick resolution of the crisis. The terrorists' sudden decision to fly to Beirut, Shultz believes, was set off by the media reports of Delta on the move and "probably caused" the collapse of the Algiers negotiations and the relocation of the crisis to the hostile, utterly unpredictable, and violent surroundings of Beirut.

NBC's Brokaw revealed that in 1986 his news organization had prior knowledge of the U.S. bombing raid on Libya and censored itself in the interest of protecting the lives of the American servicemen heading into combat.

"We knew there was going to be an air strike on Libya. This network did. This news division knew that. We had not just circumstantial evidence but we had hard knowledge that the strike was going down that night. We knew where the ships were headed; we knew that the planes had taken off. We were able to develop, through our own sources, the fact that the strike was on, that the raid was on. We sat on that all day long. What we did was prepare for the moment of the strike, which we covered pretty well. I have been in media seminars in which people felt we had an obligation, a purely journalistic obligation, to broadcast what we knew *when* we knew it. There are others who believe, from a philosophical point of view, that we had a moral obligation to the people of Libya to tell them that they were about to be hit by a bombing raid. The fact of the matter is that I think, by and large, that military troop movement is something that we have an obligation to hold as best we can . . . I will be quite honest about this. We have to draw distinctions when there are American lives involved, you know, when there are American troops involved. The classic question is, 'What would happen if you got to the other side and had a camera crew and a reporter with, say, a Khmer or Viet Cong patrol of some kind and an ambush [of Americans] was being set up?' That would push your obligation."

In the environment of a terrorist incident, it is simply wrong—and dangerous—to broadcast leaked information about a troop deployment. Although responsible broadcasters genuinely hope their reporting will never figure in an innocent person's suffering, let alone murder, there is no escaping the hard fact that some terrorists do have access to what is being reported about them, and increasingly, because of technology, these killers will hear and even see the news *in real time,* as it is being broadcast.

News organizations must not disregard this development. If they do, it will truly be at their peril. To broadcast information that runs the risk of stimulating a single or multiple murder is to skate far over the edge of corporate responsibility. Those who play this potentially lethal game will run the risk of becoming accomplices to the terrorists and may have to look into the faces of widows, orphans, and a furious audience and be forced to say, "We're sorry" for very direct reasons.

What about the scenario we described earlier, in which the terrorists holding an airliner have the capacity to watch television's coverage of the incident? McWethy said the name of the game for governments in such circumstances is to interfere with the broadcasters' ability to do their job—deny them the crucial camera positions— keeping them out of range of the story. "If I were the authorities on the ground, I would make sure we [television] did not have a line-of-sight picture capability. Of course the advancing technology will create problems. No doubt about it. What should we in the news business do? I don't know. [The terrorists] can already tune in shortwave radio [as in the Kuwaiti hijacking]. That sort of possibility presents itself on the battlefield [of the future] as well. Live from the front lines, the enemy tunes in CNN and sees the Americans moving and says to his men, 'Hey! The Americans are moving out. Open fire!' "

Martin of CBS is clear on the military's options: "If the cameras are already in place when your Delta team arrives, the first thing it will have to do is cut the [camera] cables. Pull the plug! It's part of your overall military operation—as in the Grenada invasion, where the first thing U.S. forces did was seize the radio station [to make sure no tactical orders were given to enemy forces]. Of course if you *do* cut the cables, think of the heat you as a government will have to take afterwards, and you'll probably wonder if it's worth it." McWethy pondered the problems attendant to the availability of live coverage of the hijacking and came up with a mixed assessment of how network television might respond if the cables were not cut and coverage could proceed:

"I'd want to see these camera shots, but would I put them on the air live? If I were the executive producer [at ABC News], I would have to think long and hard about that. Would I withhold it? If I saw an attack [hostage rescue attempt] go down, I would wait until the attack was over. But if I were executive producer at CNN [twenty-four-hour-a-day news, with as much major news live as possible], I would probably show continuous pictures. You *would* see the troops move."

At CNN in Washington, Bernard Shaw, the worldwide television news organization's senior anchor and the one who would most likely be on the air throughout such a hostage crisis, discussed the scenario with a heightened sense of reality. That was imposed by his acute awareness of the spread of his own company's satellite-carried television signal. Officially down-linked in fifty-four countries, including the Soviet Union and Cuba (where only government officials have access to it), CNN is also "stolen" off the satellite by governments and private individuals in other nations around the globe. CNN is often the primary source of information for U.S. Government intelligence services at the outset of a crisis. At the headquarters of the FBI, at the White House and at the CIA, as well as in the Pentagon, CNN is monitored closely. Lieutenant Colonel Oliver North, of Iran–Contra fame, once said, "CNN runs ten minutes ahead of NSA [National Security Agency, the government's supersecret communications intelligence agency]."

Shaw was hopeful that good judgment would prevail, but apprehensive about how much self-restraint the network would impose. "No matter what we profess, journalists—print or broadcast—are still driven by competitive juices, and those competitive juices tend to override restraint . . . You don't want to be the person who invokes self-censorship while the rest of the pack is out there 'getting the story.' "[14]

He believes that the media will police themselves only after a catastrophic error in judgment. "It's going to take a crisis, with lives lost, before the media addresses that question [of restraint]. The terrorists make every effort to ensure that we have access to them. They understand how the Western media compete, and seek to exploit that. So I don't hold out much hope that we in the news media are going to sit down and have international or domestic councils about this situation."

Shaw acknowledges that media restraint—formal or informal—is necessary, precisely because the terrorists or their colleagues have ac-

cess to broadcast transmissions. A network, like CNN, has an obligation, he maintains, to screen *everything* it does or says, and to inform
its viewers that its coverage is being screened in the interests of security or individual safety. The final decision as to what to air would be
made by the network, although Shaw's input, as a respected member
of the team, would carry some weight.

As he notes, however, such a stance might require real professional
and personal courage. "If I were in a situation in which I felt we were
making the wrong decision, I hope I would have the courage of my
convictions to stand up and say: 'This is wrong and I won't be a party
to it!' If they make the decision to go ahead, then my stance would be
irrelevant. There would just be another person sitting in the [anchor]
chair, and I would have to deal with the politics of having lost one."

Unlike CNN anchorman Shaw, CBS Pentagon correspondent
Martin is not consulted by his management on whether it's a good
idea to go live with a story. He is simply given orders, which, he is
quick to point out, have never pushed him to do anything he found
objectionable. But if his bosses or anyone else in the business smart
enough to respect his views should ask, they will find that Martin
believes it is dead wrong to go live with what may be a hostage rescue
attempt: "You don't go live if Delta is creeping out on the airport
tarmac. You just don't. Anyone who does is irresponsible. The second
the shooting starts, the element of surprise is lost and *then* you go, but
certainly not until."

NBC anchor Brokaw also opposes any live broadcasting of a hostage rescue—by U.S. forces, at least. However, Brokaw said that, if
asked by the U.S. Government to cool down coverage of an ongoing
hostage crisis, NBC's response "would depend on the circumstances
. . . In the hypothetical, we would listen to the government officials,
we'd measure their request against what our own judgment is in terms
of what we think is the greater danger—broadcasting it or not broadcasting it. My own inclination is always to say, 'Listen, if media attention is oxygen for terrorists, information is oxygen for people who pay
attention to what we do. You have to make a rational judgment about
it. I always worry about what happens if we begin, if somebody knows
that something has happened and suddenly they can't find anything
about it. I worry about irrational acts [by the terrorists]. I think [all]
people are better off when they know about it."

Media people, in general, tend to be ambivalent about the dilemmas between national security and the all-encompassing "right to know." Television executives chafe at any suggestion of outside control. The problem is that if they refuse to exercise responsible restraint on terrorism coverage until the incident is over—at which point they will be as sensationalist as they like—then it will fall to the government to take the necessary steps to stop media meddling in a national security crisis. That alternative is likely to be even more unpalatable.

A Matter of Integrity

The best of the television reporters covering terrorism, including McWethy and Martin, are quick to rise to the defense of their colleagues' response to the government's specific requests for secrecy during terrorist incidents. They point with pride to the press silence on the whereabouts of three State Department officials who lived for more than a year in the Canadian Embassy in Iran while terrorists held the U.S. embassy and abused its hapless occupants. The fact that Beirut hostage William Buckley was the CIA's station chief was widely known among correspondents, who kept the secret until his body was dumped into a Beirut alley.

But the good track record of keeping silent to save lives crumbled, according to former Assistant Secretary of Defense Bob Sims, after the kidnapping in South Lebanon of Colonel William "Rich" Higgins, who was serving with the United Nations peacekeeping force in that hot spot. "Reporters were asked . . . to withhold information about his having worked very closely with Defense Secretary [Caspar] Weinberger and personal things about him, which would have told his captors more than would have been good for him. So, for about twenty-four hours we were able to say we were proud of news organizations, but then they began to crack and crumble and one network reporter, as well as some of those in print, went with enough information that it was very disturbing to those who were close to him [Colonel Higgins]. For the first time [in all these cases], I was able to look at it from the point of view of the family because I know the wife and the daughter. I felt close, as a personal friend, so to me it was so irresponsible to publish and provide information and, yes, you could assume that they pulled his fingernails and he told them everything, but how do you know that? So why provide them with information that he had access to all kinds of valuable knowledge about the Defense Department because of his previous job, or to suggest that he somehow had an intelligence background, or that he had a personal relationship [his wife is Jewish] that might have made him antagonistic to parties in the region? But the fact is, it didn't take long for most of that to get broadcast. This is not a problem government should solve; it's something news organizations should find a way to solve. They blanch at the suggestion of collective responsibility procedures that everyone will agree upon in a crisis. But it's not impossible. We've done it in the past. We did it in World War II when everyone agreed on the country's foreign policy. Even in Vietnam [where differences over policy were sharp], we had a press corps who could be trusted when told to 'Show up tomorrow at such and such a time, we're going somewhere' and it didn't break [as news] until it was cleared."[15]

Trouble is, since the Vietnam War, the number of news outlets around the world that are plugged into one another directly or indirectly has grown dramatically. Even if the four major networks—ABC, CBS, CNN, and NBC—agreed to abide by certain constraints around terrorist events, said Pentagon correspondent Martin, "It will be [broken somewhere else by] Reuters, Agence France Press [the British and French overseas wire services], or Al Shirra [the Arab news weekly that broke the story of the Reagan administration swap of weapons for hostages]. What are you going to do? It [the news media] is so widespread now, you could never come up with a regimen to do anything about it. You have to rely on good judgment."

Martin worries about being clear and cool amid the confusion and the life-and-death nature of the breaking story. "The damnedest things come out of your mouth when you're live on the air, and later you wonder where they came from. Of course, while you're talking, you've got people speaking into your earpiece [updating] you with what AP is reporting, what Reuters is saying. You're going along with what you hope is a careful explanation and then someone says in your ear, 'Wrap it up.'" As for the implications of the logical linkage of new television satellite technology and terrorism, Martin worries that there may be no definable solution: "This ungodly mix [of terrorists interacting with live television] is just going to require better judgment."

The bottom line is that, in the midst of terrorist crises, the capability for live broadcasts gives the media the extraordinary power to make life-and-death judgments. Live television has far more impact than a newspaper or wire-service report. It even has more impact than a videotaped piece about the same situation.

But the media remains largely reluctant to accept either responsibility or restraint—through unofficial industry agreement or government controls. McWethy of ABC News puts the onus on the government to make the story unattractive. "What the administration in power has to decide is 'How are we going to handle this?' It is largely up to the administration to make sure it's not very good theater. If we are able to get our cameras out on the tarmac, we will cover that side of the story. If the U.S. Government is basically mute, it is difficult to sustain the coverage. It takes a lot of fire out of the incident. We in the press are frequently blamed for these things, but government is an equal or greater partner in distorting these incidents and making them difficult to handle."

CNN's Shaw insists the networks are too fiercely independent to surrender any of their autonomy in covering such events—even to a supra-authority of the media's own making. Martin of CBS agrees and discounts any hope of the kind of crisis-management relationship Sims would like to see develop between television and the government. "That idea is a loser from the start. What we're supposed to have is an adversarial relationship. Anyway, once you start in on those things [crisis-management relationships], you just lose. Ultimately, the government will make demands the press won't go along with, and if it did go along with them, that would really be bad."

But what is the responsibility of broadcasters, particularly when their live coverage functions as the terrorists' intelligence agency, providing real-time look-down on the scene and potentially adding to risks faced by rescuers and hostages? Continued insensitivity to national security and individual safety may one day force the imposition of censorship guidelines, like the kind imposed on British reports on terrorism, which often create a virtual news blackout.

One way to keep that from happening here is for news organizations to develop the means to exercise collective responsibility and to work together with the government to exchange information on a private basis as circumstances necessitate. Many in the media say this can't be done, or that it shouldn't be done. But it *has* been done in a limited fashion with the Pentagon media pools, in which designated news people are on standby each month. In the event of a crisis, only those designated individuals are summoned to the Pentagon and flown to the area of conflict, where their reports are shared among the networks. This type of pooling arrangement was established to respond to a Grenada-type situation or a Persian Gulf tanker escort patrol. But it offers an interesting model of how the government and news media ought to be cooperating to handle coverage of terrorist incidents as well.

There is no question but that trying to organize the news business, especially the television side, would be extremely difficult. Nevertheless, it is time for the institutions of press, broadcasting, and government to come together on behalf of the national interest.

Could the White House help by convening a conference of network presidents and anchors? Shaw says he would be leery of any controls imposed by such a gathering falling unfairly on his twenty-four-hour news machine. CNN's top gun adds that if a president ever decides to hold such a television news summit, "It had better be done in secret . . . I am worried about terrorists getting the idea that we are other than neutral, that we are, instead, agents of our government. That could expose our people to being taken captive . . . all around the world and . . . very definitely even here in the United States."

The irony here is that the terrorists recognize that the media plays a far from neutral role. As David Broder of the *Washington Post* explains: "The ultimate objective of terrorists is to capture not individual hostages but the instruments of public opinion, of which television is by far the most powerful . . . The essential ingredient of any effective antiterrorist policy must be the denial to the terrorists of mass-media outlets, whatever the means of that denial may be chosen."

Increasingly, governments are aware that allowing terrorists access to television news cameras flies in the face of their own interests. At the next international aircraft hijacking, it may come to pass that cameras will be forced completely away from the scene or smashed by airport police. That will satisfy no one in television, and should satisfy the American people even less. When censorship of the media begins to occur on a routine basis, the society—and the values it holds most dear—stands to lose a great deal.

Terror Tech

Inexpensive video camcorders are becoming almost as common as point-and-shoot film cameras. Some amateur video cameramen and women have sold their pictures of fires and even plane crashes to the networks. Terrorists made early use of home video, taking pictures of their hostages and delivering the electronic proof of their captivity to news bureaus in the Middle East. In the very near future, terrorists may expand their use of this simple technology. Imagine the airplane hijacking scenario again. But this time, within minutes after landing at the airport, the terrorists ask for a representative of the news media. A scared reporter with her hands held high walks up to the aircraft. As she approaches, a masked hijacker calls to her and lowers a basket from the pilot's window. In it, she discovers a little Sony color television set connected to a black cable. "Turn it on!" shouts the gunman. The reporter switches on the power and on the screen there appears a clear, color picture of the inside of the jumbo jet. Someone is walking down the aisle, pointing the camera left and then right and then straight ahead. Passengers, blindfolded and handcuffed, are visible in their seats. "Take it back with you!" the terrorist shouts to the reporter. "There is plenty of wire. Pull it back with you. Do it now!" She looks up at the cockpit to see the terrorist with a machine pistol in his hands. Quickly she runs back into the airport, pulling two hundred feet of cable behind her. Once inside the building, other journalists and police rush to her side. Inside the basket with the Sony is a typed note. It reads, "This wire is connected to a live camera inside the liberated aircraft. We shall continue our broadcast from time to time to prove that we are keeping our promise to harm no one. You will also see that we have placed large explosive charges throughout the fuselage. In one hour's time we shall interview each passenger, allowing him or her to state name and place of residence and a brief greeting to loved ones. We expect that by one hour, the television media will have followed the attached instructions for taking this picture from us and placing it on your own broadcasts." Stapled neatly to the note are simple instructions in French, Arabic, and English that describe a procedure for taking the terrorists' video "feed" and distributing it to any camera crew that wants to plug in.

Would the networks plug in? Would they turn down the opportunity to see what is going on inside the hostage aircraft? Based on past performance, it is hard to imagine their turning down the "feed," but they should have the fortitude to turn down something that could inflame and send a situation like that out of control. There is, of course, the other side of the coin. Maybe the terrorists' running up and down the aisles with the television camera would unwittingly show how best to mount a military rescue of the plane, reveal who is alive and who is dead, provide clues as to the identity of the terrorists. In that best-case scenario, the CIA might even learn enough to have its agents snatch some of the relatives of the terrorists and offer a swap.

Unfortunately, the chances are very small that the President would allow the CIA to kidnap relatives of the terrorists, even if their identities could be determined quickly. The far greater likelihood is that the terrorist television feed would only serve as powerful leverage against the government.

The government would not necessarily be helpless in the face of such an incident; there appear to be possible high-tech solutions to the problem of unwanted video transmissions. On the short list of available tactics is jamming the actual transmission of the video signal with equipment currently aboard the special electronic countermeasures EC-130 aircraft of the United States and Israel. Flying well out of sight of the hostage plane, the extremely powerful transmitters aboard the EC-130 would fire bursts of radio frequency energy into the air around the plane. As a result, the video coming from the terrorists could be transformed into an unusable jumble. The disruptive electronic beam would be so wide that it might also disable the satellite uplink transmissions of the news organizations at the scene. Another approach to fouling the signal from the plane could involve aiming a microwave antenna, like a radar dish, at the plane and zapping it with rapid short bursts of energy.

Winning against increasingly sophisticated terrorists will demand more brains and creativity than muscle. Understanding the role of the television in terrorism and how it is almost certain to evolve tomorrow is one of the key challenges facing the government, the television industry, and the public.

The citizenry of democratic states is the ultimate terrorist target; the media merely serves as an all-too-willing conduit. If the media has an obligation to screen its reports or to limit live coverage, the public has an obligation to respond to what it sees with greater caution. By now, we should know that there are no easy answers or quick fixes to terrorist-induced crises. To respond with panic and a sense of anger at our own government is to fall into a trap of the terrorists' making.

There is no question that concerned viewers could motivate television bosses to act with greater care in their companies' coverage of terror. In early 1989, a lone housewife's persistent letter-writing campaign drove several major corporations to drop their sponsorship of a popular television entertainment show because of its coarse portrayal of American family life. Similarly, broadly based appeals to sponsors, as well as to network and local television station executives, could result in more responsible approaches to covering terrorism. The time to start is now.

CHAPTER SIX

TERRORISM AND BEYOND

The established bipolar order of East vs. West is weakening. A more fluid system, based on alliances of convenience, is arising in its place, one that fosters U.S.–Soviet cooperation on matters of joint concern. Terrorism is one of the most important of these matters.

International terrorism—political, media-driven events with lethal consequences—is dealt with by many as a law enforcement matter, falling into the same category as crime in the streets. If the tactics of terrorists advance ominously, the West can no longer continue making the fundamental error of treating terrorism as criminality. Even in the unlikely event of the incidence of terrorism remaining at the same level, it must be considered a major national security problem, a symptom of an increasingly chaotic and dangerous international environment. Therefore, effective means of deterrence, and failing that, containment, must be found.

During the 1960s and 1970s, many experts argued that international terror was simply a part of the East–West conflict, with the terrorists serving as proxies of the Soviet Union or its allies. In the waning 1980s, however, these perceptions seem less credible. Fueled by a multitude of political, economic, and religious forces, regional turbulence continues despite returned East-West detente. The U.S.S.R., once a principal backer and beneficiary of terrorism, now risks becoming the biggest terrorism victim of the future.

To appreciate why this is the case, stand back a bit from the grisly details of individual incidents and look at terrorism in its larger strategic setting, as one form of an ongoing conflict waged by state and nonstate adversaries around the globe.

Terrorism as Low-Intensity Conflict

In the West, experts are coming to understand terrorism as one manifestation of "low-intensity conflict" (LIC). This term embraces a broad set of military and covert activities that fall short of outright major war—terrorism, drug trafficking (to the extent that it deliberately erodes the social order and corrupts the government of involved states), political subversion, insurgency and crisis intervention, and even conventional warfare (short of a ground war among the major powers).[1]

To some extent "low-intensity" is a misnomer: Iraq's use of poison gas to decimate Iran's legions in 1987–88 was hardly low in intensity. Yet the phrase is useful, since it helps us separate terrorism from its usually distorted, exaggerated position as media event and places it in the context of true warfare, which the East and the West wage all the time.

Low-intensity conflict is a transnational problem, meaning that not all the adversaries are states, nor is the conflict confined necessarily to one region. For example, well-armed narcotics traffickers in Colombia use all the methods of LIC to eliminate political controls within their own country through corruption and assassination and to wage war against U.S. law enforcement agencies. They may increasingly align themselves with left-wing insurgent armies, such as Peru's Shining Path, who utilize drug revenues to wage guerrilla war against Latin America's fragile governments.

Bloody terrorist acts by nonstate elements have already become a way of life in Latin America. For example, in recent years, the Colombian drug cartels of Medellin and Cali used M-19 guerrillas to end extradition to the United States by a wave of assassination against Colombia's judiciary, culminating in the liquidation of Colombia's Supreme Court. These acts by the *narcotraficantes* blend in with a strife-torn region that is still in the throes of revolution, counterrevolution, debt-related economic chaos, and social instability.

Free-wheeling terrorism knows no state boundaries. Narco-terrorists may readily hide in Latin American immigrant populations in the United States. The agents of Libyan, Syrian, or Iranian terrorism are equally embedded in expatriate Middle Eastern populations throughout Europe and the United States. Thus, terrorism and low-intensity conflict thrive in a politically and economically interdependent world, where national borders are porous and security resources are already stressed to inefficiency.

Global LIC involves adversaries who are increasingly sophisticated politically, tactically, and technologically. The technological thrust is becoming the most worrisome. The tools of the trade are rapidly going high-tech. Terrorists and their political masters now use sophisticated, commercially available, encrypted communications systems, once only in the arsenals of the superpowers, and a range of high-powered weapons and explosives that are the norm of a modern army.

Far more alarming, however, is the proliferation of chemical and biological weapons. These weapons are being stockpiled by countries that sponsor terrorism, states that are capable of deploying aircraft and, in the near term, intermediate-range missiles to deliver these deadly munitions against military targets and population centers.

Nerve agents, capable of killing with just milligram doses, may soon find their way into the hands of terrorists. The discovery of a massive chemical weapons plant under construction by the government of Libya in early 1988 was a chilling preview. The parts engineering and ingredients were provided by greedy entrepreneurs from Japan, the United States, and Western European countries.

Libya is not alone in its creation and stockpiling of chemical weapons. Iran, Syria, and Iraq are equipped with them, and Iraq actually used these chemicals as a means of devastating attack during its war against Iran. More frightening, it appears that Iraq and Syria have built biological weapons and can deliver them at long ranges. In the near future, these weapons could be targeted on most of the major population centers in the Middle East and the southern U.S.S.R. and soon much of Western Europe.

Despite the history of Soviet involvement in international terrorism, such acts are no longer necessarily of Soviet origin. This is partly due to Gorbachev's political retreat from Third World revolution making and to the growing Soviet concern for domestic terrorism breaking out in the Baltic states, Armenia, and, of course, Moslem Central Asia.

In a looser and more chaotic world, the stage is set for consortia of regional states, and independent actors with their own agendas, to challenge indirectly both the United States and the U.S.S.R.[2]

Terrorism is but one of the tools of hostile statecraft. Low-intensity conflict is not exclusively a U.S. problem, nor a regional problem. It is increasingly part of an evolving global crisis, which may, ironically, find the United States and the U.S.S.R. sometimes harnessed together.

The Middle East and Moscow's New Thinking

Championed behind the scenes for thirty years by the Kremlin, terrorism has been redefined by Mikhail Gorbachev from a useful tool of secret statecraft to a potential danger to the Soviet Union's interests. He and his close associates seem to perceive *domestic*, possibly foreign-inspired, terrorism as a major future threat to their mission of *perestroika*—bringing the Soviet Union into the modern age. That would be a daunting enough task without the additional worry of terrorist attacks by opponents of the regime.

One apparent concern is that along the southwestern rim of Russia, predominantly Moslem Soviet republics may soon be seized with the fervor of Islamic renewal inspired by the Iranian revolution. Mixed with long-suppressed dreams of their own independence and national identity, the stuff of Moslem fundamentalism is emotional *plastique*, waiting for a fuse.

Soviet leaders are aware of the underlying lesson of defeat in Afghanistan: Islamic fundamentalism can be a devastating enemy, especially when it is married to high technology. Kremlin strategists know that those American-supplied Stinger antiaircraft missiles could not have turned the tide of the Afghanistan war if they had not been carried over hazardous mountain passes and fired at close range by hard-eyed men determined to drive out the unbelievers from their homeland.

Reagan and Bush administration spokesmen called them "freedom fighters," a label handy for winning public and therefore Congressional support. While the people of Afghanistan have always fought to be free of foreign control, it is not Western-style freedom they seek. They are almost certain to build a fundamentalist Moslem theocracy.

It was, in part, fear of Moslem irredentism, sparked by unrest in the Gulf region, which motivated the Soviet invasion of Afghanistan after the Ayatollah Khomeini's Iranian revolution in 1979. With the retreat from Afghanistan, Moscow's policymakers and their Central Asian deputies are certain to be watching closely for any possible spillover of religious and national frenzy in the years ahead.

This does not exhaust the range of possible terrorist threats to the U.S.S.R. spawned by nationalistic tensions. In the restive non-Slavic populations of the Baltic states, organized political violence to break away from the U.S.S.R. is a very real possibility. In Christian Armenia, as well as Moslem Azerbaijan, large stockpiles of weapons were seized during the riots of 1988. Had it not been for the disastrous Armenian earthquake that year, it would have taken occupying Red Army forces to quell the emerging unrest.

In early 1989, worried Soviet officials convened Moscow's first conference on the prevention of international terrorism. Acting under the thin cover of an intellectual exercise hosted by the *Literary Gazette*, ten Western experts on terrorism were flown in from the United States and Britain, where they met for a week with ten Soviets in an open and free-wheeling environment. Senior members of the Communist Party, the Red Army, and the KGB flowed in and out of the conference center, taking notes.

Even before the extraordinary colloquium got under way, there was a clear indication of the new Soviet interest in antiterrorism around the world. The deputy chief of the secret police, General Vitaly Ponomarev of the KGB, declared, "We realize we have to coordinate efforts to prevent terrorist attacks." The KGB's Number Two said that cooperation would have to embrace long-standing opponents, "even with the CIA, the British Intelligence Service, and the Israeli Mossad and other services in the West."

It is important to avoid euphoria over the Soviet switch on terrorism; it must be remembered that its primary motivation is finding ways to reduce the impact of potential terrorism within its own borders. At the same time, it is also true that the Kremlin is anxious to become a completely accepted member of the international community, working in tandem with other states to prevent the disruption of normal commerce. The KGB's Ponomarev should know even better than outsiders that Soviet internal security—his area of responsibility—is already menaced by ethnic and religious conflicts.

The prospect that national and religious fervor, primarily from the Middle East, most powerfully affects Moscow does not obviate Washington's enduring problem in these areas. The truce in the Iran–Iraq war caused only a temporary lull in Tehran's manipulation of terrorism until the Rushdie affair. Moreover, Iran is only one exporter of such violence. Indeed, more serious attacks may yet occur, possibly using chemical and biological weaponry supplied by Libya, Iraq, and Syria, as well as Iran.

The main impetus for renewed terrorism against the West comes in two forms. First, the U.S. public is becoming inured to existing levels of terrorist violence. State sponsors and their clients must ultimately either escalate their actions or risk being rendered impotent by flagging media and political attention. Second, with the conclusion of the Persian Gulf War, radical Arab states are left to turn their attention on Israel, and by extension on U.S. support. Now that the Palestinian problem is reaching a new level of political evolution, the likelihood of selected, fragmented violence by terrorist groups sponsored by Libya, Syria, Iran, and Iraq will surely increase.

Over the longer term, it is doubtful that peace can be maintained in the Gulf. This means that Iranian intrusion into the political affairs of the United Arab Emirates and Oman will eventually reoccur with increased vigor (perhaps during the next five years), as will Iranian/Saudi/Iraqi friction. The U.S. political-military commitment to this region, established by the precedent of the last Persian Gulf escort operation, may lead again to the placing of U.S. naval forces in demonstrative maneuvers during periods of crisis.

The mutuality of concern of the United States and the U.S.S.R. means that—to borrow the language of the late Ayatollah Khomeini—there will not be one Great Satan, but two. America may well be joined by the Soviet Union in the gunfight of fundamentalist Islamic anger, despite the February 1989 meeting in Iran between Khomeini and Soviet Foreign Minister Eduard Shevardnadze. The emerging

U.S.–Soviet partnership will obviously give both parties more clout, more weight, in their dealings with outlaw nations.

Ultimately, Middle Eastern forces still emerge as one of the most likely vectors of the new terrorism. The recent global fury over the publication of Salman Rushdie's novel *The Satanic Verses* demonstrated the depth and popularity of fundamentalist feeling that can be manipulated by fanatical leaders such as the Ayatollah, who called for Rushdie's murder. In this case, much of the Moslem world responded sympathetically. The Rushdie affair is an example of political terrorism of an unusual nature. Even moderate Moslems were incensed by the novel's content and publication. The geopolitical implications of this lesson are vast. It demonstrates the speed with which terroristic messages can be spread throughout the Islamic world, not only in the Middle East, but to cells within minority populations in non-Moslem states, such as the United States and Great Britain. The Western world will continue to be vexed by the ability of terrorist states to project their influence far beyond their regional power bases. This is by all means exacerbated by the Western news media, particularly television.

Beyond Iran, no one in the Middle East will figure more prominently in the process of deliberate disruption through terror than the thoughtful and cold-blooded dictator of Syria, Hafez al-Assad. He is the leader of a minority within a minority that has managed to hijack a whole country. Assad is a member of the Alawite sect, an offshoot of Shiite Islam. But Syria is a Sunni Moslem nation. The huge Sunni majority, whose faith tends to be less radical than that of the Shiites of Iran, is under the control of Assad's Alawite clan because he has placed his people in key defense posts. He rules with a combination of fear of his cabal and by whipping up hatred of Israel and its American "masters."

The master of the second-largest army in the Middle East (Iraq is first), with the biggest inventory of first-quality Soviet weapons, Assad knows he cannot hope to use any of that power against Israel and survive a ferocious and probably all-out counterstrike. So, to maintain his bona fides as a slayer of infidels, he uses terror groups as his surrogates.

When Israeli intelligence pointed to the Palestinian radical Ahmad Jibril as the likely bomber of Pan Am Flight 103, many in the United States tended to discount that as just another instance of

Israel trying to paint the Palestinians as responsible for everything terrible that happens. But there was good reason to suspect Jibril; he is clearly one of Assad's action arms. In fact, the two men were classmates in the Syrian military academy.

At a press conference in Libya in February of 1986, Assad's pal Jibril warned, "There will be no safety for any traveler on an Israeli or U.S. airliner."

The CIA determined in May 1989 that Jibril's Popular Front for the Liberation of Palestine-General Command did destroy Pan Am Flight 103, but on orders from Iran. Unless he is eliminated, Jibril is certain to strike others at the bidding of his longtime sponsor, the president of Syria. A relative of one of Assad's ruling circle boasted to a shocked American recently, "Yes, I am part of a terrorist state and what will you Americans do about that? Absolutely nothing!"

Along with the stunning arrogance of the Syrian's remark came a stinging blast of *realpolitik:* the United States long held strong evidence that Assad is the primary backer of Palestinian terrorism around the world. Syria is so important a player in terrorism that even organizations that get money from Qaddafi are dependent on Syria for intelligence and logistical support beyond the limited capacity of Libya's espionage service. Despite this evidence, the Reagan administration staged no military action against Assad while plastering Libyan targets with bombs.

Behind this clear double standard of antiterrorism justice lies this notion: because Assad is the major Soviet client in the Middle East and has influence over terrorists holding Americans hostage in Lebanon, the United States should take no action against Assad which might precipitate a conflict with the Soviets or possibly jeopardize the ultimate release of American hostages. In addition, hitting Syria poses a much more difficult military challenge, thanks to high-tech Soviet air defenses, which may still be manned by Soviet crews or commanded by Soviet officers. Nevertheless, none of the above addresses possible economic and diplomatic pressures which theoretically were, and still are, available to the U.S. Government.

The toughest U.S. response against Syria was temporarily recalling its ambassador from Damascus. This followed Britain's formal severing of relations with Assad's terrorist regime after the Hindawi affair. That is the name given to the exposed attempt by Syrian Air Force

Intelligence to smuggle a powerful bomb aboard an El Al flight from Heathrow in London to Ben Gurion Airport in Tel Aviv.

The bomb was not unlike the one that detonated Pan Am Flight 103 four days before Christmas 1988, killing 270 people. Had it not been for sharp-eyed Israeli security people, Nezar Hindawi's pregnant girlfriend would have completed the mission she didn't even know she was on: being the ignorant dupe who would carry onto the plane a bomb that would kill her and everyone else aboard the jumbo jet.

As far as American response went, the Hindawi affair had several results, all of them bad: Prime Minister Thatcher, who put herself in political jeopardy to help her friend President Reagan stage his 1986 air strike on Libya, learned that he would not fully back *her* maneuvers against Syria. The Syrian dictator was reminded of how weak the U.S. policy really is. The long-term cost of that is evident: it encouraged the Syrians to feel reasonably comfortable about sponsoring third-party attacks on Americans and American interests everywhere. Assad has every reason to regard the United States as a soft-willed giant, afraid to take decisive action to protect its larger interests that go beyond the handful of hostages.

Some analysts who have devoted their professional lives to studying the Middle East say perceived U.S. weakness amounts to an invitation to Assad and the Iranians to step up their assaults on America and her allies. That conclusion is correct; it is in Assad's interest to order new attacks on Americans, and he will continue to do so until Washington surprises him with military, economic, or diplomatic blows that disregard the old thinking about offending the Soviets— they may not care much, since Assad has been getting in the way of the PLO peace offensive that Gorbachev encouraged.

Even if Moscow manifested concern, it probably would not translate into an East–West crisis. Gorbachev's long-term interests are with the United States, not with Syria. The Soviet Union need no longer make sure that it is seen as the unflinching champion of small, underdeveloped states, if the price of playing that part is to encourage the further growth of state-sponsored terrorism.

Latin America and the United States Under Siege

Just as the U.S.S.R. faces an incipient threat on its southern border which intersects an explosive domestic problem, so too does the
United States. Throughout the past decade the U.S. foreign policy has
been unsuccessful in stemming massive influxes of illegal immigration
and massive infusions of drugs and drug-financed armament into the
United States. This coincided with the erosion of political cohesion,
from the Mexican border to the Andes, including revolution, guerrilla
warfare, terrorism, and widespread corruption of public officials.

By the late 1980s, terroristic violence and the full range of low-
intensity warfare had become a virtual way of life in Central America
and much of the Andean region. That low-intensity conflict spilled
into the United States with assassinations of policemen, gang violence, and the random criminal activity that accompanies the organized sale of drugs.

This situation may soon change for the worse. The United States
may become prey to more organized acts of violence used for explicit
political purpose.

Oliver L. "Buck" Revell, the FBI's top counterterrorist specialist,
worries that drug traffickers may replicate the successful campaign of
violence that intimidated the Colombian Government with the
United States, perhaps by knocking down passenger airliners.

The motivations for such assaults on U.S. civilian aviation would
be to punish the United States for daring to oppose their operations,
arrest their distributors, wreck their enterprise. Revell considers the
Medellin and Cali cocaine cartels capable of mounting terrorist operations against airliners in an attempt to make the United States lay off
its drug prosecutions.

They could use FARC (Revolutionary Armed Forces of Colombia)
and another Marxist terror gang, M-19, as their surrogates in these
projected attacks. Revell remembers with clarity how the cocaine lords
used the M-19 guerrillas to stop extraditions to the United States by
simply wiping out the Supreme Court of Colombia. There have been

no extraditions since that bloodbath at the High Court in downtown Bogotá in November of 1985.

The same drug barons have also gotten away with assassinations in the United States. They ordered and obtained the murder of one of their former pilots, who had turned government informant. "They have the resources and the will to use violence to any degree they deem necessary," Revell warns, as he contemplates a future of potentially unrestrained terrorism.

Units under his command are keeping watch on a wide range of potential terrorists: relatively dormant white racist groups whose imprisoned leaders will soon be getting out after serving time, regional and national motorcycle gangs currently dominating part of the drug trade whose muscle would obviously be for sale to any person or group, foreign or domestic, who wanted high-risk jobs done at high rates of pay. These gangs could become the domestic terrorist mercenaries of tomorrow, available for hire—ready-made terror armies.

More appalling in its implications would be the further spread of drug-related violence and political instability from Central America into Mexico. A foretaste of this came in the torture-murders of U.S. DEA agents in Mexico, with the probable complicity of senior Mexican government and police officials.

If, over the next several years, increasing flows of refugees and drugs combine with the further radicalization of Mexico, U.S. leaders may yet confront widespread outbreaks of bombings, hostage seizures, and assassinations not only in Mexico but throughout the southwestern United States.

At the moment, U.S. border security is too porous, and the targets of opportunity too great, to forestall these developments. Consequently, the United States may be forced to redeploy its military away from its present overseas missions toward the closing and defense of U.S. southern borders. U.S. military history may come full circle, bringing the U.S. Army back to its original responsibility of frontier defense.

Other Emerging Threats: The Far East

Beyond the Latin American and Mideast problems, which represent an intensification of existing trends, some new terrorist threats are emerging with serious implications for U.S. security. By far the greatest new LIC threat, from the U.S. standpoint, remains the Philippines. The critical American military bases are jeopardized by the Aquino government's inability to check the growth of left-wing NPA insurgents. Besides the eroding political-military conditions in the countryside, a new "war in the cities," combining assassinations and bombings, can be expected as Aquino's term of office comes to a close. U.S. bases and personnel are NPA targets. Anti-Americanism, manifested in the form of populist propaganda, physical and psychological threats, intimidation and assassination of U.S. civilians and military personnel, will probably escalate.

The threat of international terrorism in other areas of the Far East, as well as the Philippines, including North Korean and Libyan sponsorship of attacks against American and allied targets, should not be ignored. Mercenary groups, such as the Japanese Red Army and Abu Nidal, can be expected to be active in the Far East and Australia, in addition to their traditional foci of activity in the Middle East and Europe. American businesses, and in Japan's case American military installations, could be targeted.

Whether such Far Eastern threats would find their way to the United States itself is an open question. The growth of strong organized-crime networks in the U.S. Asian community could presage similar trends for Far Eastern terrorists, although at the moment such suspicions are founded on speculation.

How the United States might respond to challenges in the Philippines is equally questionable. Given the large American military investment in the Philippines, it may require the use of U.S. Special Operations Forces, should the situation deteriorate further. Pressure for intervention will increase, particularly if additional members of the

U.S. diplomatic or military community become the target of assassination or kidnapping.

Terror vs. the Democratic State

It must never be forgotten that terrorism is, above all else, exploitation, creating fear to erode public confidence in constituted government. Most often, this fear is generated with some violence and enhanced by the "smoke and mirrors" of propaganda and media amplification. But with advances in counterterrorism, some terrorists must be expected to up the ante. Future terrorist attacks, which use innovative methods, inflict high numbers of casualties, or disrupt daily life by disabling elements of the infrastructure, will cause widespread fear and pressure elected leaders to end the attacks, either by neutralizing the terrorists or by making concessions to them.

Terrorists will not be without problems of their own making if they escalate their tactics and bring more torment to more people. There could come a time, depending on how the terrorists handle themselves and the manner in which government responds, that the terrified public could undergo a major transformation of attitude—from victim to fighter.

Palestinians failed utterly to comprehend the risk of pushing the Israelis too far in the late 1970s and early 1980s, and thus set the stage for their own nearly catastrophic defeat in 1982 when the Israel Defense Forces smashed through Lebanon, destroying the entire PLO military apparatus. That would not have been possible, politically, for the government of Menachem Begin to achieve, had terrorists not pushed the Israeli public over the edge of fear and into rage by committing a string of atrocities. They galvanized Israeli and vital American public opinion, painting the Palestinians as subhuman monsters—worthy only of elimination—certainly not the sort with whom decent people would even consider negotiating.

Six years later, Palestinian strategy had improved, but not in one crucial aspect. Whoever was in charge of the Intifada in the summer of 1988 badly misjudged the impact of their actions when they set fire to groves of trees. They had been planted not only by Israelis, but by and for overseas Jews commemorating births, bar mitzvahs, bat mitzvahs, weddings, and deaths. Before the burning began, there had been a groundswell of sympathy toward the uprising among hundreds of thousands of Jews, who sensed something noble and even heroic about the resistance to occupation of the West Bank and Gaza. But when the Palestinians set fire to the trees, the symbolism changed; they were perceived by many to have crossed the line from unarmed rebellion to active terrorism.

Burning the trees ignited acts of terror from some Israelis. A few West Bank settlers armed with Uzi machine pistols went out hunting for Palestinian stone throwers. That added to the heap of dead Palestinians and further poisoned the political environment. Palestinians in the Old City of Jerusalem stabbed to death an old Jewish man; others murdered a Jewish farmer on the West Bank. Jewish terrorists set fire to the apartments of two Jewish members of the Knesset (Israel's Parliament) who had dared to meet with PLO officials in search of a peaceful settlement. It was a grave mistake to burn the trees. The Palestinians thus crossed an emotional boundary, touching something very special to Israelis.

In a matter of weeks, tree-burning was abandoned, but not before the Intifada sewed fear and suspicion among many who had been compassionate. It was an object lesson in the transformation of an ennobling act into one of terrorism. The Intifada also demonstrated the inherent limits of terroristic conduct, where the initial goal is to pressure the authorities into making political concessions. The leaders of the uprising on the West Bank and in the Gaza Strip did not believe their tactics could vanquish the Israelis, but they did hope to create a new situation, favorable to their interests. After more than three hundred deaths, and a little more than a year, the revolt by Palestinians did mandate major changes. The political forces put in play forced PLO Chairman Yasir Arafat to strike a moderate pose, pushing him to recognize Israel and renounce terror, while driving Israeli Prime Minister Yitzhak Shamir into the untenable position of appearing as the roadblock to peace.

Within the Intifada affair lurks a tempting but unfortunately false conclusion that amounts to an emotional-intellectual trap for Western thinkers: since terrorists "really want to win change" and not just bloody victories, they can be counted on to attenuate their violence. Though comforting, that simply is not so.

For the terrorist who is riding an inner wind of messianic fury, who is fired by the conviction that any and all means are acceptable to accomplishing his or her sacred mission of cleansing the earth of the corruption of an oppressor, what Western minds would call rational, outcome-oriented constraints may *not* apply—thus the classic trap of ethnocentrism amid alien cultures.

Fanatical Iran is expected to continue the late Ayatollah Khomeini's terrorist policies. A former student of his, Ayatollah Jalal Ganjei'i, said in an interview shortly before Khomeini's death, that Iran's terrorism "will know no bounds, no limits other than that which is tactically possible for [Iran's] agents." Ganjei'i, now living in exile in Paris, supports the People's Mojahedin of Iran, the Iranian counter-revolutionary forces fighting to overthrow the Islamic Republic. He warned that chemical and biological weapons would be used by Khomeini in his terrorist war against the United States and the rest of the West. If Khomeini's heirs persist with terror, what can be done?

"You cannot control Khomeini by appeasing him . . . only shutting down his government's access to arms and money can help . . . If you examine his history during the conduct of the first decade of the Islamic revolution, during his war with Iraq, you will find that when the West was denying his regime money through boycotting his oil and when weapons were only trickling into Iran, his terrorism was at a low point. But once Western nations resumed trading with him, buying his oil, putting hard currency back in his hands, his terrorism once again had a budget."

Tighten security, advised Ganjei'i, boycott Iran, and tell your allies to do the same; otherwise, its terrorism will persist and intensify without restraints.

This proposal by a former student of Khomeini is clear-headed, solid good sense. In fact, it was the strategy of the Reagan administration until it undertook ill-advised and bizarre behavior, including the swap of American arms for hostages. Once that fiasco became public, the U.S. State Department lost the ethical foundation necessary for convincing allied governments to forsake profitable business deals with Tehran. Largely unconcerned about fighting terrorism on a strategic basis, as opposed to playing at tactical security, several allies greedily dove for the Iranian trough and resumed feeding.

That was not only destructive to counterterrorist efforts vis-à-vis Iran, but it also sent a clear signal that America was not serious about fighting terrorism in general. It took almost two years for the U.S. Government to convince all players that Washington was solidly back on the counterterrorist track. Still, there remains in the minds of some allied security officers the nagging doubt that the United States will stick to its stated policy of no deals with terrorists, if the going gets rough and American lives are at stake. *Consistency of behavior* by allied countries is absolutely essential; of similar importance are good intelligence, well-conceived, culturally unbiased analysis (as opposed to the trap of mirror-imaging), and the political will necessary for confronting terrorism. No waffling, no double standard, no surrender. If any of the above are absent, neither the United States nor its allies will be able to cope with terrorism. To function with power and credibility in the secret realm of counterterrorism, America and her friends must inform their populations that terrorism is here to stay, that there is no easy solution, that certain kinds of attacks may occur, that some or even many Americans may be killed before it's brought under a semblance of control, that there is no question that the United States, its allies, and the Soviet Union have the resources necessary to putting almost all of these terrorists so completely on the defensive that they will be able to do little damage. But it will take a tremendous amount of work to deter, preempt, and defend against most terrorists. Bureaucratic infighting, egomania, and traditional international political turf warring must not be allowed to get in the way of accomplishment.

One vital future step is the creation of a supranational antiterrorist police agency whose authority would empower its investigators to cross national boundaries, to obtain immediate assistance from local police, to make arrests on their own wherever necessary to stop terrorists before they strike, and to capture those who already have hit and are on the run. West German senior antiterrorism prosecutor and High Court spokesman Alexander Prechtel agrees that such a special force is necessary, but he does not believe it will come to pass, because of the history of wars among European powers. But it must. Until there is such a police agency, terrorists will probably continue to stay a jump ahead of governments most of the time. In a period of increasingly innovative, sophisticated, and violent terrorism, that is obviously unacceptable.

Finally, if counterterrorism is to prove effective and still obey the law, an international police agency with wide-ranging powers and resources must be created. Otherwise, the free-for-all tactics of covert warfare, under the guise of "national security," will take over. Then innocent lives will be taken by both sides. In that case, liberal democracy can easily become no better than the terrorism it is fighting.

So, there is even more at stake in this warning than lives—it is the character of governments and peoples. To prevent the triumph of terrorism, the antiterrorists must not become as evil as that which seeks to destroy them. Governments must end their pretense of being serious about antiterrorism and, with the informed cooperation of their peoples, take the steps necessary to be stronger, smarter, and as dedicated to preserving life and national institutions as terrorists are to destroying them.

Failure to meet the terrorist threat head-on is to invite disaster.

Tackling the Problem

It is by now a cliché to note that there is no panacea for terrorism. Indeed, as terror comes to blend ever more intimately with other intractable problems, such as drugs, illegal immigration, and sectarian strife, it is understandable if informed people become increasingly pessimistic that existing policies and programs can cope with the current threat, let alone tomorrow's even more lethal events. Bolder and perhaps more ruthless measures will necessarily be called for.

On a world-wide level, it will be necessary to galvanize international partners to help the U.S. cope with terrorism and the underlying causes of regional instability. This means not only the European allies or besieged clients in Latin America. It also means engaging the Soviet Union at a wide range of diplomatic levels, including cooperation between U.S. federal law enforcement agencies and their Soviet counterparts.

Some possibilities for partnership with the U.S.S.R. were advanced at the January 1989 conference in Moscow mentioned earlier. The group advanced the nine-point program presented below and urged its adoption by the two superpowers:

- creation of a standing bilateral group on terrorism for the exchange of information and crisis communications
- provision of mutual assistance (information, diplomatic assistance, technical assistance, etc.), when requested, in the investigation or resolution of terrorist incidents
- prohibitions on the sale or transfer of military explosives and certain classes of weapons to nongovernment organizations, restrictions on the sale or transfer of military explosives and the same classes of weapons between states
- the initiation of bilateral discussions to explore the utility of adding chemical or other types of "tags" to commercial and military explosives, to make them more easily detectable, and to aid in the investigation of terrorist bombings
- initiation of joint efforts to prevent terrorists from acquiring chemical, biological, nuclear, or other means of mass destruction
- exchanges of technology that may be useful in preventing or combating terrorism, consistent with the national security interests as defined by each nation
- conduct of joint exercises and simulations to develop further means of Soviet-American cooperation during terrorist threats or incidents

Representatives from the two nations also agreed to work together to strengthen existing antiterrorism agreements through the UN Security Council and to extend international law to cover threats or acts of violence that deliberately target civilian populations and that have an international dimension.

The future will also demand a greater willingness of the United States to threaten or actually to use force unilaterally. Past resistance to the use of force, sometimes preemptively, against terrorist training camps and leadership targets or attacking objects of value to state sponsors of terrorism indicates weakness on the part of the United States and has proven to invite further attacks.

At home, U.S. citizens will have to expect stricter immigration and law enforcement policies. This means more assertive border controls, more vigorous search-and-seizure measures, and also the willingness of U.S. law enforcement officials to capture terrorists outside of U.S. borders.

Such activities create apparent conflicts with America's most cherished civil libertarian values. Unfortunately, the more that the challenges we face become domestic, the more pressure there will be for individual rights to be ignored. The challenge for U.S. leaders in the coming years will be to strike a balance.

Beyond the law enforcement dimension, the government at the federal and state levels must become more proficient at dealing with disaster and crisis management.

The civil and military infrastructure on which this country depends for its survival is a highly visible and systematically vulnerable target for low-intensity warfare. As the increasingly fluid global environment multiplies opportunities for such warfare, that vulnerability is increasing. At the present time, the United States has few defenses against this kind of focused attack. U.S. strategic planners have tended to be shortsighted, measuring the strength of defense simply in terms of weapons systems and troops. The U.S. logistical base in fact, if not in prevailing policy, is only as strong as its domestic technological infrastructure.

Surviving Future Terror

Surviving major attacks of the infrastructure will require advanced civil defense response that does not presently exist. The Federal Emergency Management Agency (FEMA) lacks the authority to perform essential tasks of planning for and coping with the effects of natural disasters, industrial accidents, or highly disruptive acts of terrorism.

Therefore, FEMA must be relocated to the White House, reporting to either the Vice President or the National Security Advisor. The agency should be reorganized as an elite group, reducing its current staff to two hundred professionals drawn on a rotating basis from various agencies involved in responding to crises. Half of this reduced staff would remain in the White House to do planning and crisis management; the other half would operate in the field, working with industry and with local, state, and federal officials in the reconstructive phases of disaster.

This elite staff would perform only essential functions, operating under the imprimatur of the White House with bureaucratic authority to perform essential tasks. Among other responsibilities, this reconstituted FEMA should be intimately familiar with the set of contingency plans to cope with disaster, know what the nodes of greatest infrastructure vulnerability are, and understand the resources needed to manage crises and the logistical difficulties involved.

Information technology plays a particularly important role in improving both emergency preparedness and ability to cope effectively with crisis. The professional crisis manager must have a modernized "situation room" from which to handle the various problems of resource allocations and command, control, and communications during times of crisis. Modern digital equipment for more reliable communications, computer conferencing capabilities to allow multiple inputs without physical proximity, and interactive use of computers for problem analysis are largely underutilized tools in disaster management.

The federal, state, and local governments must develop a program of command post and field training exercises. An effective crisis management structure requires joint planning to iron out jurisdictional issues among the agencies involved. For crisis planning and management, these include most agencies in the government in various ways, from the Internal Revenue Service (for tax relief) to the Defense Department (for relief functions and maintenance of civil order). Joint "gaming" exercises and computer simulations, both at the FEMA command center and in the field, are essential to developing smooth working routines for crisis conditions. Simulations, such as the one in the Appendix, should provide training and testing opportunities at many levels of threat.

Government must rethink the implications of infrastructure vulnerability for national security. While the United States has made some provisions for redundancy, it tends to prepare for the wrong crises. The estimated fifteen billion dollars' worth of materials stored in the Critical Strategic Materials Stockpile would be useful to refight World War II, but it is not tailored to deal with the range of likely crises currently facing the United States.

FEMA should take immediate planning steps under the Defense Production Act to reconfigure the stockpile with a view toward protecting the nation from technological disruption. This should include stockpiling semifinished and finished goods instead of raw materials and critical components, such as very large custom-made electrical transformers—the procurement of which takes several years and without which widespread economic and social disruptions would occur if terrorists knocked out several and no replacement is at hand.

These are by no means new recommendations. Experts have been suggesting many of these reforms since the early 1970s. Yet, the perilous neglect of such measures at a time when the terrorism threat was relatively low means that new high-tech terrorism will find the United States completely unprotected. American leaders must find the resources to overcome the neglect of the past before disaster strikes.

Technology and Counterterrorism

Similarly, remedial steps must be taken in the area of R&D to develop the technological arsenal for the counterterrorism war. Our official declaration may solemnly proclaim that terrorism is one of the most troubling security threats to the nation; however, until the government chooses to fund the tools of counterterror, these pronouncements remain largely rhetorical.

The need to bolster U.S. technical response capabilities is profound. Although the capacity for massively destructive attacks is increasing—chemical, biological, radiological, infrastructural attacks—there is no long-range vision to anticipate and prepare for a continuously mutating challenge. Most of the research being done today is geared to meet yesterday's brand of terrorist attack.

The United States has no umbrella organization or technological blueprint to move forward reliably against future types of threats. On the technology side, a great deal of focused research is needed. In the nuclear arena, the NEST (Nuclear Emergency Search Teams) provide rapid response capability, scientific knowledge and experience, a logistics and communications base, and specialized equipment in the event of nuclear threats. Unfortunately, no similar capacity exists to respond to chemical, biological, or toxicological threats.

One of the primary needs is instrumentation to detect and identify such agents, particularly at long ranges. By the time we can discern an aerosol cloud approaching, it is far too late to prevent a crisis. Technologies for neutralization, immunization, and detoxification are either rudimentary or nonexistent.

Threats to the technological infrastructure will require a better understanding about where the key nodes of vulnerability lie and how to defend them. The technical characteristics and interconnections among the various systems are complex and require highly sophisticated computer modeling to design cost-effective defenses. Clearly, the federal government must take the lead.

Such technological requirements have not been addressed in any systematic way. Organizationally, it might be appropriate for DARPA to take the lead in prioritizing high-technology defenses. The national laboratories and others might develop and test new devices, thereby broadening their national security responsibilities to encompass emerging threats as well as time-worn problems.

Moreover, even for the spectrum of current threats, the United States lacks imagination in acquiring and implementing low-level technologies and user services. One of the primary obstacles here is attitudinal; we act as though there is little more we can do to prepare for routine terrorists' threats when, in fact, nothing could be further from the truth.

In airport security, for example, there is available an array of low-technology approaches that are not being applied systematically. These include simple changes in the way airports are run, such as restricting nonpassengers from almost all of the airport, widespread use of behavioral profiles, centralized intelligence and communications for all airlines, and meticulous screening and training of well-paid security personnel.

Akin to the adventuresome, creative can-do attitude of the scientific community in World War II, we must face new problems that await improvisation. To save lives, interim efforts should be the order of the day, not an interminable wait for complete solutions. While we await better technologies, such as thermal neutron activation to scan passenger baggage, we ought to be able to rapidly access the utility of hybrid, on-the-shelf options, such as the use of bomb-sniffing canines in conjunction with passing baggage through low-pressure chambers that increase the relative vapor pressure of the explosive. Another option is the use of microwave chambers for some substances or sonic devices for others, intended to resonate RDX, the basis for almost all plastic explosives, and other molecules. We might even use electromagnetic power generators in facilities located well away from the passengers to disarm or safely detonate bombs.

The underlying reason for this mediocre technological performance by this highly sophisticated nation is the lack of a management structure to provide policy and technological oversight across the spectrum of low-intensity warfare. Although there are a great many pockets of expertise on various aspects of low-intensity conflict problems—insurgency, drug trafficking, terrorism—there is no organizational mechanism to provide technological, much less strategic, guidance.

Effective leadership will require a more thoughtful approach to the challenges we are increasingly likely to confront—a leadership that is able to exploit the commonalities in applying useful technology to achieve economies of scale and to integrate national resources to meet a variety of threats. Such an approach can only be orchestrated at the highest levels of government, involving the President, the National Security Advisor, and the Secretary of Defense. Until now, the government's approach has been long on rhetoric and short on realism.

Into the Darkness

It may appear that the waning of the Cold War can only mean greater global harmony. The evidence, however, does not support this conclusion. Terror as it has been known will advance and the phenomenon will be enveloped in drug-inspired violence and religious fanaticism.

The problem is that political stability and random violence are now accompanied by widespread proliferation of advanced weapons.

These will be set against vulnerable infrastructure targets and population centers. Terrorist incidents could involve mass casualties, including chemical or biological incidents. They would almost certainly involve attacks on civil aviation, including the sabotage of aircraft and hijacking of aircraft; attacks on ships and platforms and the mining of sea lanes; and attacks on internationally recognized protected persons (e.g., diplomats, children).

At best, international terrorism can be contained; sometimes it can be deterred; but it cannot be eliminated. Major accomplishments in the fight against terrorism can be had if aggressive policy initiatives are taken. America's vulnerabilities must be assessed, crisis-management techniques developed, and imaginative R&D funded. Resources must be made available, and tough diplomatic and military sanctions applied to states that harbor terrorists. When these efforts are combined with relentless intelligence collection, covert operations, and serious law enforcement, terrorism can be reduced to an episodic annoyance. The key is to punish severely those states that provide safe haven and logistical support to terrorist groups. Without secure bases, arms, and money, terrorist groups are largely ineffective. The United States and its allies must move quickly. If not, terrorism will mestastasize beyond control.

Admittedly, there is a difficult trade-off between strongly held civil liberties, in favor of tougher protective measures and covert action against those who would destroy us. Without resolve, the United States will forever be the victim of barbarism, with few tools to defend itself.

If these hard choices are not faced head-on, we may wake up to find that terrorists are operating on our home ground against innocent Americans with the same impunity that they operate abroad.

THE TERROR GAME

The potential escalation of techno-terror and the role of the international media in heightening its drama vastly complicate the process of coping with contemporary terrorism. In a rare glimpse at these decision-making dilemmas, the deliberations of a seasoned team of experts were tracked through a simulated nuclear terrorism crisis, one which ultimately threatened nuclear confrontation.

Simulation or "gaming" is an unusual technique used to explore the opportunities and pitfalls of crisis resolution. When properly done, the players in the simulation feel all of the stress and near-term pressure of a real world crisis. Games, like the one recorded here, provide an opportunity to expose individuals to the rigors of crisis, forcing them to anticipate the unexpected and to identify the range of possible tools of response, as well as the limitations and consequences of their use.

The modern political-military game—whether a tactical counterterrorism game or global warfare exercise—is part of a long legacy dating back to the "Kriegsspiel" of the German General Staff. Military gaming was later modified in the 1950s at the Rand Corporation, at Harvard, and at MIT to accommodate the political dimension of contemporary conflict.

At the Center for Strategic and International Studies, the technique has been used repeatedly to explore a variety of crisis situations —from a coup in the Philippines to an invasion of South Korea by the North to a nuclear terrorism incident. Several of the games were televised to sensitize the American public to the harsh choices that crisis decision makers must confront.* What these broadcasts were intended to make clear is that there are no straightforward answers in a crisis situation, that each decision carries its own set of penalties.

All live-actor games are structurally similar. The organizers, commonly termed "control," break up the players into one or more teams. Each team simulates a specific decision-making or advisory group, such as the U.S. National Security Council, other governments, or the adversaries, such as the executive committee of a terrorist group.

The teams receive simulated inputs in the form of messages supplied by control. They then fashion their responses based on these messages and play against each other, as in the more traditional wargame, or against the control group.

Control simulates all elements of the real world not specifically represented by the playing team. For example, a team playing the National Security Council might request information or issue orders to a subordinate entity, which is "provided" or "carried out" by the control group. Control creates the environment surrounding the decision makers, a sometimes capricious environment in which orders go astray, bureaucracies miscommunicate, or nations miscalculate.

Some simulations are pencil-and-paper, in-basket-out-basket exercises. Others are million-dollar efforts, requiring vast resources, sophisticated communications lines, computer assistance, and a large staff. Simulations can last from a few days to a few months.

What you are about to experience is a careful compression of crucial moments from fourteen hours of deliberation of one of the simulated crisis exercises organized by CSIS. Including staff support, about a hundred and twenty participants were involved in the game. On the control side, the supporting groups included former CIA and State Department officials, European diplomats on sabbatical at Harvard (to simulate allied governments), visiting military officers from each service, and Soviet and Eastern bloc émigrés playing the Soviet Union team.

---

* These included: "If You Were President" (1980), an ABC "20/20" special dealing with the prospects of a terrorist attack in New York Harbor; "A War Game: The Nuclear Threat" a CNN broadcast in 1986 of an exercise involving complications from U.S. presence in Nicaragua; "Fighting Terrorism: A National Security View" a Public Broadcasting System program on a nuclear terrorism incident released in 1986.

The NSC team included some of the most experienced defense and policy experts in the United States, including: General Brent Scowcroft, currently National Security Advisor to President Bush; Representative Les Aspin, Chairman of the House Armed Services Committee; Admiral Thomas Moorer, former Chairman of the Joint Chiefs of Staff; Robert McFarlane, former National Security Advisor; Richard Helms, former Director of the CIA; and Eugene Rostow, former Undersecretary of State; and Daniel Schorr, a veteran correspondent.

The game began on May 29, 1986, six weeks after the U.S. raid on Libya. As the players assemble, they are told that a U.S. civilian aircraft en route from Munich to Rome has been hijacked to a NATO air base in Sigonella, Sicily. Four hijackers, of German and Palestinian origin, identify themselves as the "April 15 Commando" and announce that they are retaliating for the U.S. raid on Libya. They insist that the United States cease its ongoing exercises near the Gulf of Sidra and demand additional fuel to fly to an undisclosed location.

The hijackers claim that explosives have been concealed in the cargo area of the plane and that they possess an electronic detonating device. They warn that the plane will be destroyed in the event of a rescue attempt.

In the first move period, the President opens the dialogue:

PRESIDENT:	Well, our first concern has to be for the lives of those people on that plane, of course.
NATIONAL SECURITY ADVISOR:	Mr. President, I agree we have to be overwhelmingly concerned with the safety of the passengers, but, as you know, our general policy is that we do not negotiate, in the sense of giving concessions, even at the risk of the present passengers because of the worldwide precedent of encouraging more hijacking and ultimately putting more Americans in jeopardy.
PRESIDENT:	Well, well, I appreciate that.
CIA DIRECTOR:	I have some information now. A situation report. From the liaison with the Italians. There are four hijackers, two Germans and

PRESIDENT:
two Palestinians. That's all we have, Mr. President.

PRESIDENT:
Anything from Defense?

CHAIRMAN, JOINT CHIEFS OF STAFF:
We have two carriers at sea in the Mediterranean: one about fifty miles southwest of Sicily. I've alerted the Delta team and also the SEAL team. They are ready to go. The Italians, however, initially had said they wanted us to keep hands off. Consequently, I don't think we have clearance at the moment to go into Sigonella.

PRESIDENT:
I'm going to have to leave, and I would like for you all to constitute yourself as a team and share all information with each other. The Chief of Staff over here, as always, will speak for me. I want to make sure that you come up with the appropriate set of options of things to say and consultations and so on.

The roles of President and his Chief of Staff were played out of the control group, in order to have some leverage on the pace of NSC decision making. Both individuals would consult with control on overall game strategy and periodically reenter NSC deliberations.

CHIEF OF STAFF:
First, I think we have a very serious question here about what we're going to tell the public about this. Second, we need some options for working with the allies: to what extent other allies besides Italy are going to have to be involved in this; and to what extent we cooperate; and to what extent we conduct some kind of planning or options with them. Third, we have to try and rescue the people out of the plane. That is the purpose of the whole exercise. The question I want to ask is: Who do we talk to? Should we talk to anybody? I'll have to leave this up to you to decide, as I've got to go to another meeting myself. But I would like to emphasize the

importance of this issue, from the standpoint
of the American public, in the light of the
action that we took against Libya. This is
now the next test. The question has been
posed time and time again as to how we
would respond to the next terrorist event. Are
we going to conduct another military operation? I want you to keep that in mind against
the background in which we are operating
here.

The Chief of Staff also leaves the room to allow for NSC deliberation. In their absence, the control group heightens the pressure with a
simulated broadcast on the television monitors in the council room.
Control strategy is to create the specter of a nuclear device onboard
the plane. This is a media feint on the part of control. The actual
scenario is that, unbeknown to the hijackers, the explosives on board
have been seeded with cobalt 60—a lethal gamma radiation emitter—
and have been preset to detonate that afternoon. Both hostages and
hijackers are being irradiated while the plane sits on the tarmac. Although control provides these details to the NSC through briefings
from DOE nuclear energy officials, the public concern and confusion
continues to mount. NSC officials are caught between trying to defuse
a possible public crisis of confidence and accelerating the process of
rescuing the hostages off the plane.

JACK SMITH, SPECIAL TV REPORT:	We have a special report now from our corre- spondent Clive Syddall in Beirut with new information on the hijacking.
CLIVE SYDDALL:	Usually reliable sources here in Beirut have told us that the group involved in the Trans- Med hijacking that calls itself the "April 15 Commando" is believed to have close ties to Libya. The most frightening news is the re- port of a nuclear bomb aboard the plane in their luggage. Where such a device might have come from is not clear, but Libya's Muammar al-Qaddafi has been known to

	have offered large sums of money to buy a nuclear weapon.
NATIONAL SECURITY ADVISOR:	Did everybody hear that the terrorists said that they have put a nuclear device on the aircraft?
SECRETARY OF STATE:	It seems to me that the entire situation is transformed by the presence of these nuclear devices. I think that the first thing to do is to ask the Joint Chiefs and the Department of Defense for a feasible operation plan as to what on earth to do with that plane.
CIA DIRECTOR:	What they say specifically is that the American Delta Force will not be tolerated on Italian soil.
ATTORNEY GENERAL:	It seems to me we have to get on the direct line with the Italians to tell them that they must take immediate action: that we are going to announce very publicly, in a matter of hours, that we've asked them to do so; that there is a time limitation; and that we've moved all possible forces in that area. I think the American people want that.
SECRETARY OF STATE:	I don't think we should declare war on Italy. I don't think it's necessary. I think everybody's reacting to the situation in approximately the same way.
SECRETARY OF DEFENSE:	We ought to go ahead and move those forces to intervene if the Italians won't act. But the Italians are on the scene and we ought to encourage them to do it.

The U.S. Army special counterterrorist unit, the Delta Force, is ordered to begin preparing for an assault on the hijacked plane, with or without Italian assistance, but the Chief of Staff rejoins the group, worried that Congress must be consulted under the War Powers Act if American troops are deployed overseas for combat.

CHIEF OF STAFF:	We do not want people running off and do-

	ing things half-cocked around this adminis-tration.
NATIONAL SECURITY ADVISOR:	Nothing is being done half-cocked around this administration.
CHIEF OF STAFF:	I would like to explore two possibilities. First, we need to talk to Congress. We cannot conduct this operation without some kind of consultation, as required by the War Powers Act.
NATIONAL SECURITY ADVISOR:	With all respect, the War Powers Act, first of all, is a crock. Second, it doesn't apply in this situation. What we're doing is rescuing American citizens and the War Powers Act specifically permits military force to do that.
CHIEF OF STAFF:	We've got a lot of things that we've got to deal with. To unnecessarily antagonize those people, just because we want to stand on our own technical interpretation of the War Powers Act, is to wreak havoc with the whole domestic program. We've got another agenda out there.
SECRETARY OF STATE:	Well, I've instructed the State Department team to consult with them as regularly as they're consulting with foreign diplomats.
CHIEF OF STAFF:	That's not good enough. We need the major players in this operation.
NATIONAL SECURITY ADVISOR:	We're on the horns of a dilemma. On the one hand, you're absolutely right that we ought to get the Congress involved. On the other hand, to have them all out on the front lawn of the White House giving widely divergent ideas would be a recipe for disaster.

While the National Security Council continues its debate, a number of smaller teams swing into action in a nearby room. These teams of experts wear a number of hats; they might play, for example, both regional specialists within the federal bureaucracies, as well as the representatives of other key governments, both allies and adversaries. These teams provide background information or international communications to the National Security Council, messages that are reviewed and passed through the control group.

A critical turning point in the game comes at the end of move period one when the NSC receives information that Libya is implicated in the plot. Radio messages have been intercepted between the hijackers on the plane and the Libyan embassy in Rome.

CIA DIRECTOR: So the conclusion is that Libya's involvement appears certain. Syrian cooperation is possible but not clearly demonstrated.

NATIONAL SECURITY   Well, it seems to me that's why we need a
ADVISOR: quick hotline message to the Soviets right now, that the Libyans are officially behind it, that we expect that the Soviets in view of their statements about terrorism will take immediate steps to call off that hijacking because we cannot wait.

As the hotline message is transmitted to the Soviets and the defense staff is put to work on a plan to storm the plane by an allied rescue team, the NSC is interrupted by another news flash over the television monitors.

ROBERT BATES   It's incredible, Jack, I've never seen anything
REPORTING: like it. After hours of no movement, no change, a virtual stalemate between the hijackers and Italian authorities, the whole aircraft just blew up and exploded right in front of us. No one could possibly have survived the explosion. Again, I repeat, the TransMed airliner hijacked to Sigonella earlier today has blown up in a horrendous shower of smoke and flame. No survivors from that plane can be expected, and it happened just moments ago. We'll be standing by with more reports as we learn more.

NATIONAL SECURITY   Can we get a report from the base com-
ADVISOR: mander on the existence of radioactivity being spread?

PRESS SECRETARY:	Gentlemen, you'll have to now urgently address the question of what the public is going to be told. The last thing the public heard is that there may have been some radioactive materials on board, and that is all. It will be thought before long that the President has been dilly-dallying. There's been an explosion, but nothing has been done.
NATIONAL SECURITY ADVISOR:	Nobody is to know that the President has dilly-dallied. I will hold each and every one of you responsible to give a view of the President as a positive leader of this operation. What we need to do is formulate a statement, a general statement of the planning that was under way, the decisive way we were moving to defuse this situation.
PRESS SECRETARY:	That's correct, but something has to be said publicly very soon.

President reenters the NSC situation room.

NATIONAL SECURITY ADVISOR:	Well, Mr. President, we have a very new situation in front of us now, the dimensions of which are not clear. The critical question now is whether or not there has been a scattering of radioactive material. We have asked urgently for a report on that.
PRESIDENT:	As soon as you have that report, I think I have to speak to the public.
FBI DIRECTOR:	The public is going to want to know what you plan to do about it. I think that's what the question will be.
NATIONAL SECURITY ADVISOR:	You should never, Mr. President, say what you will or will not do. I think the vague references you've given in response to other terrorists acts are still the appropriate line.
PRESIDENT:	All right, this gets us to the point of what to say, assuming that we're going to make a statement.

PRESS SECRETARY: I have just been informed that a story's going to be run on the wires almost any minute now, perhaps on television, suggesting that this was the fault of the President, because of his indecisiveness. We really need to get some positive spin on this because this is going to be really terrible for you. I suggest the following, but it's only an idea. I propose immediately an international conference of nuclear powers to strengthen our nonproliferation machinery and to try to make sure that, in the future, nuclear materials are kept out of the hands of terrorists. I figure a proposal for something like that will at least give a positive spin on all of this.

NATIONAL SECURITY ADVISOR: We want to stress NATO cooperation in this thing. That this was a great example of the alliance working together with a common threat.

PRESS SECRETARY: It sounds a little sad after the explosion.

NATIONAL SECURITY ADVISOR: I know, but it seems to me that we've got to take advantage of this situation. The Soviet Union, as a known patron of terrorist states, bears a responsibility to explain, beyond its condemnation of this, how it tried to avert this outrage or what it will do to cooperate in the future.

The NSC now devotes time to preparing a national address for the President. They attempt to play on the public's outrage to build support for his policies, even though there has been little concrete discussion of what those policies will be. The need to say something to the American public becomes a dominant factor in the decision-making process. Following the President's address, the players reconvene to discuss both image control and immediate retaliatory measures. The second move period begins twenty-four hours later in the simulated reality of the game.

CHIEF OF STAFF:	Gentlemen, good morning. I'm here to report on some conversations that we've been having with the members of Congress. We're taking a little bit of a hit this morning. The President, on television yesterday, made some veiled threats about taking action when those who are responsible are identified. That's being played back at us. We need something pretty dramatic for domestic, if for no other reasons. The question is: If we decide to retaliate, who do we retaliate against and by what means?
NATIONAL SECURITY ADVISOR:	As a result of the previous Libyan operation, it seems to me, even aside from the President's wishes, that we have no choice but to do something. This is a much more serious act. Defense ought to be dusting off contingency plans and looking at the various possibilities we have. This action has to be dramatic.
CIA DIRECTOR:	May I intrude to say there's been one air strike at Libya and Qaddafi is still in office. Now we've had this disaster. It doesn't seem to me that the options being considered can be taken in any context except to get rid of Qaddafi. If we don't take that option, then we're going to keep doing this over and over again. The American public is going to become increasingly impatient with each one.
SECRETARY OF DEFENSE:	I think we need to determine what it is that we need to achieve. I assert our goal should be to alter Libyan policy. I assert again, and I invite criticism of it, that you've really got to change the government. However, you can't change the government overnight. That's going to take time. It's going to take a massive amount of resources. But, it won't solve the short-term political pressures for doing something. I don't think it's the kind of thing

where you can go on TV today and say we're going to overthrow the government next month.

CHAIRMAN, JOINT CHIEFS: The only thing we can do quickly is an air strike. There's a clamoring for action in the Congress and in the public, but that would contribute to the success of later action, which would take us a few weeks to put together.

SECRETARY OF DEFENSE: Do you want to do things like mining, which does hurt him badly on economic grounds, or the alternative spectrum of military options, such as bombing military targets? We'll be glad to give you a fuller spectrum of options if you want.

The Secretary of Defense, along with the Chairman of the Joint Chiefs and the Secretary of State, meets with strategic planners to discuss retaliation against Libya. Since broad economic and diplomatic sanctions are already in force, the full range of military options is considered.

SECRETARY OF DEFENSE: I think it's probably very useful to drop some bombs on some terrorist camps as long as the President doesn't tell the American people the problem is solved. He tells them: "Let's vent our frustrations and go beat the shit—excuse me, the daylights—out of somebody, but then let's work quietly to do something effective."

CONTROL STAFF, DOD AIDE: Do we want to hit not just the terrorist bases but the oil fields at the same time?

SECRETARY OF DEFENSE: Strategically, it's the right thing to do. But you may have such a high political cost, because you get the Congress up in arms, that it screws up your ability to overthrow the government. It's not worth that.

CONTROL STAFF, DOD AIDE: You're saying you want two stages. We want to do something immediately and find some-

thing longer-term that is going to ensure that
the government is overthrown.

SECRETARY OF DEFENSE: That's correct. It's not necessary to destroy
the oil wells. All you've got to do is destroy
the off-loading sites, since what Qaddafi
wants to do is export the oil and get the
money. So you can stop right at the ports and
knock out the pipelines and all the oil-loading
facilities.

SECRETARY OF STATE: We had a naval warning, a parade of ships in
the Gulf. We've had the bombing raid and
that has not cleared up the situation. The
next step is an invasion of Libya.

FBI DIRECTOR: The Soviets have already said that they would
stand by if we do act against Libya. With
that information, would an invasion of Libya
be out of the question?

NATIONAL SECURITY
ADVISOR: I think an invasion of Libya is not the right
way to go. I think there are ways to eliminate
Qaddafi without an overt invasion of Libya,
with all the preparation it would take and so
on. We'd soon find both the Soviets and our
NATO allies backing away from us.

SOVIET AFFAIRS NSC
STAFF: If we're determined to get rid of Qaddafi, I
think we ought to look at quick, rapid actions, whether called assassination, kidnapping, or the like, that are more direct and
more limited in scope, than something that
includes a massive invasion and occupation of
this country.

FBI DIRECTOR: Is there a way to assassinate Qaddafi?

NATIONAL SECURITY
ADVISOR: It's against the law. *(Laughing.)*

ATTORNEY GENERAL: If Qaddafi died tomorrow, we would still
have terrorism. We would still have the Mid-
dle East problems. Our overconcentration on
Qaddafi, I think, is misleading to the American public. I think it puts the President in an
impossible position. The time has gone when

we can recommend a Band-Aid to the President. My point is I want to bomb the hell out of them. That's my option.

SECRETARY OF STATE: Gentlemen, let me remind you of something very important. Bombing the hell out of the Libyans may satisfy our impulses, but our strategic goals and the goals of our foreign policy have to dominate the situation.

CIA DIRECTOR: I can't for the life of me see why a series of strikes at not only military but economic targets in Libya wouldn't suffice. Take out the oil jetties. You can actually bomb the oil refineries if you want. It would put a stopper for quite some time on oil exports. I mean that's exactly what we're trying to do—to put pressure on that leadership so that there would be a revolution and down it would tumble.

CHAIRMAN, JOINT CHIEFS: You've got to launch not only an air strike but an air campaign. You can never go in on one group of sorties in the middle of the night and accomplish your mission. If you're going to do this, you've got to set it up so they can go in several times and keep working on it awhile to achieve the objective.

NATIONAL SECURITY ADVISOR: I have some sympathy with those views, but it seems to me there's an alternative way. If one strikes at his oil field, that's an irrevocable action. I apparently am the only one supporting something like a blockade, which would shut off Qaddafi's income. His army would soon start starving and no Americans would be killed. The Europeans, if they want, can cooperate, but we can mount a blockade without European support.

It seems to me that a blockade hurts Qaddafi in the same way without the serious downside of a U.S. invasion, which I think would be very difficult for us to mount without European cooperation.

CHAIRMAN, JOINT CHIEFS: Are you talking about a total blockade?

NATIONAL SECURITY ADVISOR: I'm talking about a blockade as an act of war. Declare war on him and blockade him. Then if the Soviets want to try to penetrate the blockade, we have legal rights to keep them out.

SECRETARY OF STATE: It has never worked, even against Rhodesia. I don't know why it would work against Libya.

NATIONAL SECURITY ADVISOR: That was never a declared blockade. This is a blockade that we can make quite effective.

CHAIRMAN, JOINT CHIEFS: I think that the mining is better than the blockade. If you have a blockade, then you have U.S. ships confronting Soviet ships when they come and go, whereas with the mining you just have to make a notice to mariners to tell them where the mines are. They'd be entering at their own risk.

PRESIDENT: Let me ask the Chief of Staff what the reaction to that would be on the Hill.

CHIEF OF STAFF: Nothing worries the Hill more than the possibility of getting bogged down in a long drawn-out situation where American lives are in danger. In that light, I think that an air strike looks good, the mining also looks good, the blockade looks less good, an invasion looks least good.

SECRETARY OF STATE: Of course congressmen would prefer to have a quick surgical air strike without any loss of American lives, but you know and I know that is not possible. The escalation of the Cold War and the intensification of this terrorist attack to the nuclear level has serious implications.

The National Security Council rejects the more extreme options to punish Qaddafi by invasion or assassination. Here, perceptions about how the media and the American public will respond play a key role. Despite doubts about the effectiveness of air strikes, economic sanctions, and coastal mining, these are the options that meet a perceived requirement of low casualties, immediate action, and quick exit. At the end of move period two, the President approves mining and air strikes against Libya. Move period three opens twenty-four hours later with a news broadcast on the NSC television monitor.

TV NEWS REPORT: Good morning. This is Jack Smith. We now have reliable reports that the United States has begun its campaign of retaliation against Libya. First reports indicate that air strikes have been carried out against both military and economic targets in Libya. U.S. military personnel from aircraft carriers in the Mediterranean have mined two of Libya's ports. This, according to top NSC sources, is the opening shot in a campaign to unseat Libyan leader Muammar al-Qaddafi. Reaction in the United States to these first strikes against Libya has been overwhelmingly positive, but the news has provoked a storm of protest from European allies. A quote here: "We are aghast that the United States has chosen to live out its cowboy fantasies once more."

NATIONAL SECURITY ADVISOR: We have continuing reports of increasing Soviet activity in various areas around the Middle East. We need to monitor this very, very carefully. Do we have any sampling of U.S. opinion? We're getting a lot of flack from the Hill.

PRESS SECRETARY: The first telephone survey that was made after the announcement of the mining indicated the President's popularity has soared to an unprecedented 86 percent.

NATIONAL SECURITY ADVISOR: That's what I like to hear. Do we have any European reaction to the first strikes?

EUROPEAN ADVISOR, NSC STAFF: They are upset. They don't feel that they have been consulted. They're concerned that we're seeing this in East–West terms and that it is a mistake of analogies, and a mistake of policy.

NATIONAL SECURITY ADVISOR: The European situation's getting out of hand. We need to smooth them and stroke them. The Europeans, above all, ought to be scared to death of the idea of further nuclear terrorism.

EUROPEAN ADVISOR, NATIONAL SECURITY COUNCIL STAFF: We also have to give them a rationale. That's what they're lacking.

SECRETARY OF STATE: Well that's true, but I think it's also true that we have not failed to consult. The consultation processes have been going on continuously.

EUROPEAN ADVISOR, NSC STAFF: Consultation is one issue, but explaining it to them to make the policy appear both rational and optimal is what I think we've been failing to do.

NATIONAL SECURITY ADVISOR: We'll get European support.

SECRETARY OF STATE: I think we must follow Porter's famous rule: "When in doubt, do the right thing."

While the NSC discusses reactions to Libyan air strikes, the CIA Director meets with his top spy master, the Deputy Director of Operations, played by a former chief of the CIA office of terrorism. The CIA operatives have come up with a new assessment of responsibility for the bombing, based on reports of allied intelligence services and intercepted transmissions by the supersecret National Security Agency. They now believe that, although Libya provided the financial wherewithal for the operation, Syria was directly implicated in training the terrorists. The control group has introduced this intelligence to test how the NSC will respond when the risk of retaliatory options is greatly increased. As a major ally of the Soviet Union, the escalatory consequences of attacking Syria are potentially far graver.

NATIONAL SECURITY ADVISOR: The President is clearly on record as saying that we will strike at the source of state-sponsored terrorism where we can identify it. We certainly need to make all preparations to give him a reasonable course of action in the event that it is necessary for us to implement that policy.

This discussion is interrupted by a television broadcast making public the news of a Syrian involvement.

JACK SMITH REPORTING: With further U.S. strikes directed against Libya expected at any time, there are now strong indications that Libya's role in the Sigonella tragedy may have been exaggerated. High administration sources now say that they have positive evidence that the terrorists at Sigonella were trained and directed by Syria.

NATIONAL SECURITY ADVISOR: Has the FBI started an investigation on these leaks?

PRESS SECRETARY: You notice how Jack Smith keeps quoting NSC sources. By the way, I'm going to get out there one of these days and find the law that can put him in jail if he keeps saying he's using NSC sources. We can not find NSC sources who tell him these things. But you can assume that at the next briefing there are going to be a series of questions about the President's policy toward Syria in the event there is conclusive evidence.

CIA DIRECTOR: I understand, but I think the way for you to deal with that is to say that the evidence is not conclusive in any sense.

PRESS SECRETARY: You mean you want me to indicate that what he calls a leak from the CIA of an intercepted message shouldn't be taken seriously, that the CIA's not good at this sort of thing.

CIA DIRECTOR: That it admits of other interpretations.

NATIONAL SECURITY ADVISOR: It's important we let the President know of this latest turn of events. There is a possibility, you know, that we're looking at what could be the most serious confrontation since World War II. Gentlemen, the President. *(President enters.)* I gave you a quick briefing over the phone, Mr. President. We're confronted with an entirely new turn of events now which do raise the possibility of an extremely serious confrontation.

PRESIDENT: I guess we start with the problem that we've hit the wrong country.

CHAIRMAN, JOINT CHIEFS: The attacks on Libya are well justified, in my opinion, because Libya is involved in terrorism overall.

NATIONAL SECURITY ADVISOR: There is no question about Qaddafi's support for terrorism, both in the general and in the specific sense. Had we failed to act, you would now be the most unpopular President since Calvin Coolidge.

PRESIDENT: Well, I'm interested in my popularity, but I'm also interested in hitting the coach rather than the cheerleader. It looks to me like we've unloaded very effectively on the cheerleader. Now its pretty clear that the coach is Syria.

SECRETARY OF STATE: Well, the coach is the Soviet Union, Mr. President. We must never forget that.

CHIEF OF STAFF: What is the role of Libya in the Sigonella hijacking? I don't question General Scowcroft's comment that, of course, Libya is involved in terrorist activities, but of course our retaliation and our focus has been on the Sigonella incident. Are we saying now that Libya had nothing to do with the Sigonella incident?

CHAIRMAN, JOINT CHIEFS: You put in the word "finance." Libya financed it.

CIA DIRECTOR: There was a message yesterday that indicated clear Libyan involvement in the operation.

NATIONAL SECURITY ADVISOR:	No question about Libyan involvement as well.
PRESIDENT:	Let me turn the discussion around from a rationalization of what's been done up to this point toward what we need to do now.
CHIEF OF STAFF:	The question, it seems to me, Mr. President, is: What are we going to do about the planned strikes that we were going to launch on Libya? Is the evidence such that we want to cancel what we had planned to do?
PRESIDENT:	What's the group's recommendation with regard to the rest of these strikes on Libya?
NSC STAFF, SOVIET ADVISOR:	They can only be taken in the context, Mr. President, of the question of the options against Syria, I mean there are finite resources involved. We have only so many carriers and they will have to be repositioned.
PRESS SECRETARY:	Mr. President, let me say something about the Americans in this connection. It's going to sound cynical, and I hope it won't leave this room, but you cannot afford, by statement or by lack of statement, to indicate that you goofed on Libya. Therefore I would suggest that the situation is going to have to be that Libya bears a large part of the responsibility. We'll find the proper words to say that and then decide whether you identify another country responsible. But, you cannot go back on your Libyan plan without being made to look like a fool.
NSC STAFF, EUROPEAN ADVISOR:	Mr. President, people talk about your popularity in the United States. You have to be aware that the European alliance is now really deserting us in droves at every level. It doesn't make sense to them. What will make sense to them is absolutely critical from here on in.
PRESIDENT:	Well, I'm willing to put up with whatever one has to put up with the Europeans. I'm

resigned to the fact that either the Europeans or the Congress are going to be upset at one thing or another, probably with whatever we do. One simply has to consult the best he can.

FBI DIRECTOR: If we're going to make a move on Syria, we had better do it quickly because, if it isn't, the Soviets will have reinforced Syria to the point that there is going to be a head-on confrontation.

PRESIDENT: What, if anything, can we realistically do against Syria that will have a decisive military effect? Are there any real military options?

UNDERSECRETARY OF DEFENSE: You have to realize how constrained we are in applying immediate military force to Syria. You've got two aircraft carriers that are now involved in attacking Libya. The amount of actual power they can bring to bear against Syria is by no means going to be decisive. If you want to step up, on a timely basis, decisive military power, you're talking about B-52 raids.

CHIEF OF STAFF: It appalls me that our discussion seems to be lacking in options. What is going on here? Have we nothing in the State Department, nothing in the Pentagon?

PRESIDENT: I'm afraid I agree with the Chief of Staff entirely. It would be nice to come up with a range of options that have some kind of impact.

UNDERSECRETARY OF DOD: I'm afraid in this case the options are few, if any. The one area where military action can be taken to demonstrate your decisiveness is to continue against Libya.

NATIONAL SECURITY ADVISOR: There is one option which still makes you look decisive, but leaves open the opportunity for the Soviets to back away from this: that is a strike against the Bekaa Valley camps. It is not striking Syria; it is striking terrorism. It

offers a possibility of defusing what otherwise might be a confrontation that could easily get out of control for the United States.

SECRETARY OF STATE: But I think that type of situation has to be reconsidered because bombing in the Bekaa Valley is useless.

PRESIDENT: Bombing in the Bekaa Valley is useless?

SECRETARY OF STATE: Totally useless. The Israelis have done it over and over again.

NATIONAL SECURITY ADVISOR: Bombing Libya has been useless because we've done it before, but we're still doing it.

PRESIDENT: I'm not hearing much from the military side about what we can do with respect to Syria. Let's hear what the Secretary of State has to say.

SECRETARY OF STATE: They're not very attractive options. The first is to get the Iraqis to support terrorism in Syria, which would probably cost us a great deal of money and be a very unpleasant thing to do. The second option would be to suggest a European trade boycott of Syria because Syrian trade is very occupied with Europe.

PRESIDENT: The Europeans' history of supporting trade boycotts is not high.

SECRETARY OF STATE: It is zero.

CHIEF OF STAFF: I think we also need a series of diplomatic moves that perhaps don't do very much on the ground but send the right signal: expelling people, closing the embassy, cutting off diplomatic relations with Syria.

SOVIET ADVISOR, NSC STAFF: The one problem that might be noted on these lesser measures is that we are in train with a set of bombing operations in Libya. Now that it is being publicly known that Syria's involvement is at least as great, if not more so, the idea of war against Libya matched by expulsion of Syrian students has an assymmetry that I think would be very

	hard to support politically, both at home and abroad.
PRESIDENT:	Now, it's one thing to say it looks weak, not to move militarily against Syria when we're already doing it against Libya. But, it's another thing to actually attack Syria under circumstances in which we may well end up with Soviet casualties. I'm not inclined to do that.
UNDERSECRETARY OF DEFENSE:	I'm afraid that over the short term, and even over the medium- to long-term, there are very few pressure points that we can apply with any degree of decisiveness and effectiveness against Syria. They'll be largely symbolic politically and eventually empty. I think that the issue that we have to confront is the larger possibility of crisis with the Soviet Union and the fact is that we do have one villain now and that is Libya.
SECRETARY OF STATE:	Mr. President, may I interrupt, because I just had an important message from the Soviet Union. They've put their rocket forces on the alert with regard to the possibility of an American attack of Syria.
PRESIDENT:	They meant the strategic rocket forces in the Soviet Union.
SECRETARY OF STATE:	That's correct.
CHAIRMAN, JOINT CHIEFS:	I just had word that they also alerted all of their command posts worldwide.

The decisive test for the NSC is how to deal with an unprecedented nuclear alert by the Soviet Union. The United States had several times put its nuclear forces on alert—notably during the Cuban Missile Crisis and the Arab–Israeli War of 1973—to warn the Soviet Union to back away from endangering vital U.S. interests. Now, the Soviet Union, for the first time, has put the United States on notice that it will not stand aside if its ally Syria is attacked. While U.S. decision makers automatically tend to view nuclear alerts by the United States as an extremely strong diplomatic signal without great military consequences, the control group was interested in learning what their reaction would be when the tables were turned.

PRESIDENT:	The Soviet Union has gone to a full strategic alert. I can't afford to stand here with submarines in port and all the rest. This is extraordinarily provocative behavior on their part.
SECRETARY OF STATE:	Mr. President, I suggest that we go on alert and tell them meanwhile that we'll back down if they back down.
PRESS SECRETARY:	All these Soviet moves are in response to what they think you may decide to do about Syria.
PRESIDENT:	Another way to put that is all these Soviet moves are designed to force us to back down.
PRESS SECRETARY:	I'm not sure yet what you've decided to do about Syria, so I'm not sure what backing down is. All they're trying to do is make a big show of force to try to keep you from doing something about Syria. If you simply escalate your alert without a decision about Syria, you may be escalating for nothing. Were you to decide you're not going to do anything about Syria, they'll call off their alert.
PRESIDENT:	I think a sequence of events of that sort would indicate to the Soviet Union that, not in this case, but in all future cases, whenever they want to affect American behavior, they need only to call out a strategic alert and we will do what they say.
SECRETARY OF STATE:	The notion of us backing down before a strategic alert is fatal.
CHIEF OF STAFF:	It seems to me that we need to put a full-court press on the Soviet Union, so that they understand exactly the extent of our concern, so that they do not overreact to what we're doing in a way that is likely to result in an overall World War III confrontation between superpowers.

NATIONAL SECURITY ADVISOR: Mr. President, I think you ought to give the Soviets one more chance to resolve this with us. It seems to me it's time for some fairly direct communication between you and Mr. Gorbachev to demonstrate that we will not back down, that you in fact are on the verge of ordering an alert, that you are determined not to let terrorism escalate to the nuclear level and that you would like his, Mr. Gorbachev's, cooperation in doing that. But you think nuclear terrorism is a peril to mankind that is equal to the U.S.–Soviet confrontation and that you would like to have his support.

PRESIDENT: I think that is a reasonable communication and I believe it ought to be a hotline communication. I have tentatively decided to order our forces to Defcon Three worldwide before I communicate anything verbally to the Soviet Union. My communication to them will be that the United States, in response to this outrageous provocation by the Soviet Union, has alerted its forces worldwide, and then go on with further discussions about whether we'll stand down.

NATIONAL SECURITY ADVISOR: I think we have a serious time problem. We have a need to communicate with the Soviet Union and Syria right now. We have the need to communicate with the press, with the American people, and with the Congress. While we are sitting here talking, Mr. President, things are deteriorating rapidly.

PRESIDENT: All very true. I want an announcement shortly that we are severing diplomatic relations with Syria.

The President decides to call a halt on the bombing raids on Libya and limits action against Syria to the breaking of diplomatic relations. The final act of the exercise is a fireside chat with the American public announcing these moves with a message that the Americans will stand down from the nuclear alert if the Soviets do likewise.

One of the chief obstacles in the study of U.S. crisis behavior is the lack of raw material. Fortunately there have been few crises which have ricocheted into superpower confrontations. Such simulations allow researchers to create data about crisis management under simulated conditions. While no simulation could truly replicate the stress of a major terrorist attack or a nuclear confrontation, these exercises provide several thought-provoking insights about the nature and process of contemporary crisis management.

First, crises are becoming increasingly difficult to cubbyhole. They come in all flavors and sizes. Occasionally, as in this scenario, you get two for the price of one.

Some crises are genuine, in that governments may collapse, economies falter, or large nations go to war. Others are staged as calculated risks—like the U.S. raid on Libya—in which the escalatory dangers are believed to be predictable and controlled. The risk, of course, is that even a carefully structured crisis may at times go awry. There are no standard rules of the road that set the parameters of either a crisis or crisis management.

Today, the management of crises has an added dimension of complexity: the instantaneous and global communications networks by which both the prowess of the perpetrators and the plight of the victims reaches an international audience. Crisis management has become a vicariously shared spectator sport. Unfortunately, the cinematic miracles of a James Bond are seldom reproducible in real life.

Second, there is a hierarchy of objectives in crisis management that do not always conform to resolving the immediate situation. Because the organism called government is inherently self-protective, a first priority for the simulated NSCs was to attend to the domestic audience.

In the game record, recall the curious priorities on the Chief of Staff's agenda: "We need, first of all, a public statement strategy . . . Second, we need some options for working with the allies. Third, we need, of course, to try and rescue the people out of that plane." This was not a control strategy but the natural protective instinct of a well-seasoned decision maker.

Policymakers across all of the simulations seemed to have internal-ized one principle of crisis management: foreign policy crises become domestic leadership crises when decision makers are not seen to be in control of events. The constant media pressure was viewed by the players as a challenge to their competence. Recognizing that they could not limit the news hemorrhage, they feared, nonetheless, that it would trigger public perceptions that the government was not on top of a fast-breaking situation.

Ironically, none of the NSC teams ever considered telling the media that they needed time and space for careful deliberations. Because they did not have the luxury of that candor, they felt compelled to give frequent and comprehensive news releases—more as a response to the barrage of media inquiries than any readiness to articulate U.S. policy.

In the simulated world, as in the real policy arena, the media exerted a powerful, sometimes disruptive, influence on rational decision making. Far from a contemplative environment, the NSC was forced at every step to address the media implications of their action or inaction. As a result, continual dialogue within the council about who would say what to whom—and when—diverted time and attention away from central security issues.

Finally, the simulations helped to highlight the fact that even experienced decision makers can waver in a crisis, that the ability to focus and prioritize under great stress is not an innate human skill, but it can be learned. Simulations offer a powerful technique to accustom individuals to the fast pace and quirky nature of a crisis situation. The pressure of a simulation forces participants to question strongly held assumptions, consider multiple options and their consequences, and engage in creative problem solving in a way that roundtable seminars rarely achieve.

This type of leadership training is routinely performed at the highest levels in allied governments such as Britain or Israel. Unfortunately, in the United States, it is concentrated in just a few departments and bureaus, generally at the working, rather than the policy, level. Several biases may account for this lack. First, some analyses indicate that officials tend to think of themselves as better crisis managers than they actually are. Second, since simulations are designed to point up shortcomings in crisis response, most decision makers prefer to avoid the possibility of embarrassment. Finally, many will argue that every crisis is unique and that no simulation can capture the essence of a real event.

Although there is no standard formula for crisis resolution, games do serve a valid role both in broadening the repertoire of policies and techniques of precrisis planning and in honing the skills of the individual decision makers. The most practical goal of crisis management training is not the elimination of crisis, but an understanding of the multifaceted crisis phenomena and the challenge humans face in coping with it.

Terrorism, as a potential tinderbox on the international landscape, promises to test the mettle of future decision makers. Gaming and other training tools offer introspective instruments to anticipate both these types of events and explore the human response to a variety of unpleasant stimuli.

ENDNOTES

Chapter One
Emerging Terrorism

1. David C. Martin and John Walcott, *Best Laid Plans,* (New York: Harper & Row, 1988), p. 105.

2. Ibid., p. 202.

3. Interview with Police Chief Richard Jewett, 1989.

4. U.S. and allied counterterrorism analysts who requested anonymity.

5. Interview with Hassan Rahman, 1989.

6. Interview with Sheila Hershow, former chief investigator, Transportation Sub-Committee, House Committee on Government Operations, 1989.

7. Letter to FAA from Representative Cardiss Collins of Illinois.

8. Interview with Noel Koch.

9. News conference by Secretary Samuel Skinner, U.S. Department of Transportation.

10. *Terrorism in the United States: 1987,* FBI public document, p. 5.

11. Interview with FBI Executive Assistant Director Oliver L. "Buck" Revell, 1989.

12. Interview with Dr. George Carver, former Deputy to the Director, CIA, 1989.

13. U.S. and allied intelligence officers.

14. Interview with Sheila Hershow, 1989.

15. Robert H. Kupperman and Jeff Kamen, "A New Outbreak of Terror Is Likely," *New York Times*, April 19, 1988.

Chapter Two
The Expanding Threat

(Please note: Biographical and statistical information on major terrorist groups was originally drawn from an array of scholarly texts. However, in January 1989, the U.S. Defense Intelligence Agency published an extraordinary volume, *Terrorist Group Profiles*, which contained considerable amounts of newly declassified force estimates, as well as updated notes on leaders and attacks perpetrated by these groups, essentially outdating previously available material. Since this compilation offered the very latest information, it has been cited under the abbreviation of "DIA.")

1. Daily press accounts, December 1988–April 1989.

2. Conversations with Soviet officials in Moscow and Washington, 1988 and 1989.

3. DIA, p. 114.

4. *Patterns of Global Terrorism: 1987*, State Department publication.

5. Colonel Stuart Perkins, CIA, speech to Dr. Yonah Alexander's conference on terrorism, the Eliot School, George Washington University, 1988.

6. Interview with Oliver L. "Buck" Revell, 1989.

7. DIA and Israeli government documents.

8. Interview with Dr. Marius Deeb, Senior Fellow, Center for International Development and Conflict Management of the University of Maryland, 1989.

9. DIA, pp. 5–6.

10. Ibid., p. 6.

11. DIA, pp. 7–8.

12. Interview with Dr. Deeb, 1989.

13. DIA, p. 8.

14. Daily press accounts and background conversation with Egyptian diplomat who asked to remain anonymous.

15. Interview with Revell, 1989.

16. Ibid.

17. Ibid.

18. Interviews with Islamic scholars who asked not to be identified.

19. *Terrorism in the United States: 1987,* FBI public document, p. 25.

20. Interview with Revell, 1989.

21. Ibid.

22. U.S. and Israeli intelligence officials who wish to remain anonymous.

23. Interview with Revell, 1989.

24. Dr. Deeb in "Militant Islamic Movements in Lebanon: Origins, Social Basis, and Ideology," paper published by the Center for Contemporary Arab Studies, Georgetown University, Washington, D.C., November 1986, pp. 13–15.

25. Interview with Ibrahim al-Amin, *Kayhan,* Tehran, October 19, 1985.

26. Interview with Fadlallah, *Middle East Insight,* Vol. 4, No. 2, Washington, D.C., 1985.

27. Fadlallah lecture published in pamphlet, July 18, 1984.

28. A confidential source and daily press accounts.

29. Interview with Fadlallah, *Monday Morning,* December 16, 1985.

30. In a sequence of actions, separated by several months, Hizballah sent suicide car and truck bombers against the U.S. embassy in Beirut, the Marines headquarters and the U.S. embassy in Kuwait, with virtually no change in tactics. But the government learned nothing from each preceding attack, leaving its installations open to identical assaults.

31. Daily press accounts.

32. Testimony in the Hamadei trial, 1988.

33. Kupperman and Kamen, "A New Outbreak of Terror Is Likely," *New York Times,* April 19, 1988.

34. Steve Emerson in *U.S. News and World Report.*

35. West German, British, and U.S. daily press accounts.

36. State Department document made available to reporters, 1988.

37. Documents released by Representative Cardiss Collins of Illinois, March 20, 1989.

38. Conversation with an Israeli security officer, 1988.

39. FBI, CIA, West German, British, and other allied intelligence services report many preempted terrorist attacks, including some that were clearly intended to have taken dozens, even hundreds, of lives.

40. Copies of the actual "murder manual," as it came to be known, were made available to the Washington press corps by members of Congress.

41. DIA, pp. 69–72.

42. Interview with a State Department official who requested anonymity.

43. DIA, pp. 69–72.

44. Statement by Minister Rotis and daily press accounts.

45. Ibid.

46. DIA, pp. 6–7.

47. Daily press accounts.

48. DIA, pp. 10–11.

49. For a brief but penetrating insight into this most violent of Sikh firebrands, see Mark Juergensmeyer, "The Logic of Religious Violence" in *Inside Terrorist Organizations,* David C. Rapoport, ed. (New York: Columbia University Press, 1988).

50. *Inside Terrorist Organizations,* p. 189.

51. *FBI Analysis of Terrorism in the United States in 1986,* p. 28.

52. Documents provided to the authors by the government of India.

53. Interview with Klaus Eberhard Thuessen at Hesse Police Academy, 1988.

54. Allied and U.S. intelligence sources.

55. Interview with Isaac Yeffet, former chief of security, El Al, 1989.

56. Interview with Noel Koch, chief of counterterrorism for Department of Defense during Reagan administration, 1989.

57. Interview with Revell, 1989.

58. Ibid.

59. DIA, p. 122.

60. *Patterns of Global Terrorism: 1988,* State Department publication, p. 23.

61. Interview with Alexander Prechtel, West German Federal Court spokesman, 1988.

62. British security sources who requested anonymity.

63. Interview with Revell, 1989.

64. DIA, pp. 35–37.

65. Ibid, p. 106. Reporting by the *Los Angeles Times, Washington Post,* and *New York Times.*

66. Speech by Colonel Perkins to the Alexander Conference on Terrorism, 1988.

67. DIA, p. 98.

68. Estimates range from $50–200 billion in annual U.S. illegal drug consumption, making narcotics the biggest single free enterprise in the world.

69. Interview with Professor Simon Dinitz, Ohio State University, in Columbus, Ohio.

Chapter Three
Techno-Terror

1. Kupperman and Kamen, "A New Outbreak of Terror Is Likely," *New York Times*, April 19, 1988.

2. W. E. Gutman, "Chemical and Biological Weapons: The Silent Killers," *NBC Defense and Technology International*, April 1986, p. 26.

3. Ibid.

4. Aaron Epstein, M.D., "U.S. Hid Japan's Experiments on POW's," *Miami Herald*, December 7, 1985, p. 1.

5. "Report of the International Task Force on Prevention of Nuclear Terrorism," in Paul Leventhal and Yonah Alexander, eds., *Preventing Nuclear Terrorism* (Lexington, Mass.: Lexington Books, 1987), p. 9.

6. Larry Collins, "Combating Nuclear Terrorism," *New York* magazine, December 14, 1980, p. 36.

7. Konrad Kellen, "The Potential for Nuclear Terrorism: A Discussion," in Leventhal and Alexander, op. cit., pp. 125–26.

8. Leonard Specter, "Clandestine Nuclear Trade and the Threat of Nuclear Terrorism" in Leventhal and Alexander, op. cit., pp. 82–83.

9. Kellen, op. cit., p. 112.

10. David Albright, "Civilian Inventories of Plutonium and Highly Enriched Uranium," in Leventhal and Alexander, op. cit., p. 287.

11. Leventhal and Alexander, op. cit., p. 20.

12. Specter, op. cit., p. 81.

13. Andrew Goldberg, Debra Van Opstal, Michael Brown, James Barkley, "Leaders & Crisis," CSIS, Vol. IX, No. 5, Washington, D.C., 1987.

14. Joseph D. Douglass, Jr., and Neil C. Livingstone, *America the Vulnerable* (Lexington, Mass.: Lexington Books, 1987), p. 146.

15. Ibid., p. 147.

16. Geoffrey Kemp, "Mideast Missile Madness: A Bazaar for Doomsday," *Washington Post*, March 27, 1988, p. C-1.

17. Douglass and Livingstone, op. cit., p. 12.

18. Ibid., p. 30.

19. Multinational Conference on Terrorism, Berlin, 1978.

20. B. J. Berkowitz, et al., *Superviolence: The Civil Threat of Mass Destruction Weapons*, Advanced Concepts Research, Santa Barbara, Cal., September 1972, pp. 7–9. Robert H. Kupperman and Darrell M. Trent, *Terrorism: Threat, Reality, Response* (Hoover Institution Press, 1979).

21. "New Exotic Germs on the Way," *Defense Week*, May 16, 1988, p. 15.

22. William Kucewicz, "Accident Prone and Asking for Calamity," *The Wall Street Journal*, May 3, 1984, p. 28.

23. Ibid.

24. Berkowitz, et al., op. cit., pp. 5–6.

25. Ibid.

26. Ibid.

27. "Designer Germs Crafted by Gene Engineers Increase Risk of Biowar, Says Defense Report," *New York City Tribune*, September 29, 1986, p. 4.

28. Douglas J. Feith, "Biological Weapons and the Limits of Arms Control," *The International Interest*, Winter 1986/87, p. 82.

29. Douglass and Livingstone, op. cit., pp. 25–26.

30. David Ottaway, "U.S. Gave Iraq Bacteria, Senator McCain Charges," *Washington Post*, January 26, 1989, p. A-16.

31. Richard H. Wilcox and Patrick Garrity, eds., *America's Hidden Vulnerabilities*, CSIS, Washington, D.C., October 1984.

32. For a more detailed analysis, see Robert H. Kupperman, *Technological Advances and Consequent Dangers: Growing Threats to Civilization*, CSIS, Washington, D.C., September 1983.

33. "Terrorists Knock Out Rail Bridge to Lima," *Washington Times*, June 26, 1984, p. 7.

34. John Burgess, "High-Tech Attacks Worry Japanese," *Washington Post*, December 25, 1985, p. F-1.

35. Leventhal and Alexander, op. cit., pp. 8–9.

36. Lewis Rothein, "Is Terrorism a Risk to Nuclear Plants?", *Des Moines Register*, July 16, 1986, p. 9. Kellen, op. cit., pp. 123–45.

37. Kellen, op. cit., pp. 111–12.

38. Kennedy Maize, "N-Plants as Terrorists Targets," *Defense Week*, May 13, 1985, p. 16.

39. Wilcox and Garrity, op. cit., p. 2.

40. Vin McLellan, "Computer Systems Under Siege," *New York Times*, January 31, 1988.

41. Ibid.

Chapter Four
Coping with Terror

1. See "Taking on Terrorists," *U.S. News & World Report*, September 12, 1988, pp. 26–34.

2. David C. Martin and John Walcott, *Best Laid Plans*, (New York: Harper & Row, 1988), p. 126.

3. Ibid., p. 368.

4. Oliver Revell, *Terrorism: A Law Enforcement Perspective*, U.S. Department of Justice, Federal Bureau of Investigation, January 1988, pp. 95–96.

5. Ibid., pp. 96–98.

6. E. Anthony Fessler, "Extraterritorial Apprehension as a Proactive Counterterrorism Measure" in Neil C. Livingstone and Terrell E. Arnold, *Beyond the Iran-Contra Crisis*, (Lexington, Mass.: Lexington Books, 1988), p. 234.

7. Terrell E. Arnold, "New Directions in Using the Law to Combat Terrorism," in Neil C. Livingstone and Terrell E. Arnold, *Beyond the Iran-Contra Crisis*, (Lexington, Mass.: Lexington Books, 1988), p. 220.

8. "TWA Hijacking Suspect Admits Sneaking Explosive into Frankfurt," *New York Times*, July 14, 1988, p. 2.

9. "Taking on Terrorists," op. cit., p. 28.

10. Ibid., p. 34.

11. "Taking on Terrorists," op. cit., pp. 32–33.

12. Geoffrey M. Levitt, *Democracies Against Terror*, (New York: Praeger, 1988), p. 19.

13. Parker, "The Evolution of U.S. Anti-Terrorism Policy" in Neil C. Livingstone and Terrell E. Arnold, *Beyond the Iran-Contra Crisis*, p. 12.

14. Levitt, op. cit., p. 94.

15. Borg, op. cit., p. 11.

16. Martin and Walcott, op. cit., p. 47.

17. Oliver L. Revell, Opening Statement before an Open Session of the Subcommittee on Technology and the Law, the Committee on the Judiciary, U.S. Senate, May 19, 1988, *Terrorism and Technology*, U.S. Department of Justice, FBI, May 19, 1988, p. 4.

18. Ibid., pp. 4–7.

19. Oliver L. Revell, *Terrorism: A Law Enforcement Perspective*, op. cit., p. 96.

20. Ibid., pp. 103–4.

21. Ibid., p. 99.

22. For a more in-depth review, see Robert Kupperman and Darrell Trent, *Terrorism: Threat, Reality and Response* (Hoover Institution Press: 1979), pp. 119–28.

23. *Washington Post*, August 28, 1988.

24. Ibid.

25. Peter J. Brown and Terrell E. Arnold, "Counterterrorism as Enterprise: The Iran-Contra Investigations Spotlight the Private Sector," in *Beyond the Iran-Contra Crisis*, op. cit., p. 193.

26. Chemical Biological Response Team, Final Report by EG&G Services for U.S. Army Chemical Research Development and Engineering Center, March 30, 1987, Contract No. BAA L03-86-D-0001, p. 6.

27. See Debra Van Opstal and Andrew Goldberg, "Meeting the Mavericks: Regional Challenges for the Next President," CSIS Significant Issues Series, Volume X, No. 7, Washington, D.C., 1988.

28. Neil C. Livingstone, "The Raid on Libya and the Use of Force in Combating Terrorism," in *Beyond the Iran-Contra Crisis*, op. cit., p. 81.

29. For a more in-depth discussion of antiterrorism forces, see LeRoy Thompson, *The Rescuers* (Boulder, Col.: Paladin Press, 1986), pp. 55–98.

30. Ross S. Kelley, "Special Operations Reform in the Reagan Administration," in *Beyond the Iran-Contra Crisis*, p. 87.

31. Martin and Walcott, op. cit., p. 134.

32. Ibid., p. 289.

33. Ibid., pp. 291–321.

34. Neil C. Livingstone, "The Raid on Libya and the Use of Force in Combating Terrorism," in *Beyond the Iran-Contra Crisis*, op. cit., p. 79.

35. Martin and Walcott, op. cit., pp. 219–21.

36. Bernard Trainor, *New York Times* staff writer, remarks to the Forum on Meeting Future Regional Challenges, March 28, 1988.

Chapter Five
News Media: Messengers of Terror

(Please note: The Twentieth Century Fund's study of the relationship between terrorism and television news, *Terrorist Spectaculars: Should TV Coverage Be Curbed?*, is a rich source in this field. Written by veteran journalist and news policy analyst Michael J. O'Neill, the 1986 document is cited several times in this chapter, referred to as "TV.")

1. John Corry, *New York Times*, June 26, 1985.

2. Interview with Tom Brokaw by Robert Kupperman, 1989.

3. Interview with Alan Beck by Jeff Kamen, 1988.

4. TV, p. 29.

5. Steve Emerson, *Secret Warriors* (New York: The Putnam Publishing Group, 1988).

6. Interview with former Assistant Secretary of Defense Bob Sims.

7. Richard Clutterbuck, *Living with Terrorism* (London: Faber and Faber, 1975), p. 147.

8. TV, p. 30.

9. Interview with Chuck DeCaro, 1989.

10. Interview with American and allied intelligence officers who requested anonymity.

11. Interview with Jack McWethy, 1988.

12. Interview with David Martin, 1988.

13. United Press International dispatch, June 23, 1985.

14. Interview with Bernard Shaw, 1988.

15. Interview with Bob Sims, 1988.

Chapter Six
Terrorism and Beyond

1. For more information, see Barry Crane, et. al., *Between Peace and War: Comprehending Low Intensity Conflict,* National Security Program Discussion Paper, Series 88–02, John F. Kennedy School of Government, Harvard University, 1988.

2. For a more in-depth discussion, see Debra van Opstal and Andrew Goldberg, *Meeting the Mavericks: Regional Challenges for the Next President,* Significant Issues Series, Volume X, No. 7, Center for Strategic and International Studies, 1988.

INDEX

243

BOOK MARK

The text of this book was set in the typeface Electra and the display in Helvetica by Berryville Graphics, Berryville, Virginia.

It was printed on 50 lb Glatfelter, an acid-free paper, and bound by Berryville Graphics, Berryville, Virginia.

Designed by Patrice Fodero